KANT'S THEORY OF KNOWLEDGE

KANT'S THEORY OF KNOWLEDGE

Selected Papers from the Third International Kant Congress

Edited by

LEWIS WHITE BECK

D. REIDEL PUBLISHING COMPANY

DORDRECHT-HOLLAND / BOSTON-U.S.A.

Library of Congress Catalog Card Number 74–83006

ISBN 90 277 0529 1

Published by D. Reidel Publishing Company,
P.O. Box 17, Dordrecht, Holland

Sold and distributed in the U.S.A., Canada, and Mexico
by D. Reidel Publishing Company, Inc.
306 Dartmouth Street, Boston,
Mass. 02116, U.S.A.

TABLE OF CONTENTS

PART V

Causality and the Laws of Nature

PART VI

The Thing in Itself

PART VII

Kant and Some Modern Critics

PREFACE

The Third International Kant Congress met in Rochester, New York, March 30 to April 4, 1970. The Proceedings, published by D. Reidel Publishing Company in 1972, contained 76 complete papers and 30 abstracts in three languages. Since this large volume covered many phases of Kant's philosophy from a wide variety of standpoints, it is unlikely that the entire contents of it will be of interest to any one philosopher. I have therefore selected from that volume the 20 papers that seem to me to be most likely to be of interest to English-speaking philosophers who are, to use a fairly vague description, in the 'analytical tradition'. The topics treated here are those which are most relevant to current philosophical debate in the theory of knowledge, philosophy of mind, and the philosophy of science. The division of papers under the seven principal topics, however, is in some respects a little arbitrary.

I hope this little volume, published 250 years after Kant's birth, will show philosophers who are not already convinced that Kant is one of the most contemporary of the great philosophers of the past. I believe that the efforts of the authors of the papers will show that there can be genuine Kantian contributions towards the solution of problems that have frequently been handled in opposition to, or obliviousness of, the eighteenth-century philosopher who did more than anyone else to formulate the problems which still worry philosophers in the analytic tradition.

LEWIS WHITE BECK

PART I

ASPECTS OF KANT'S METHOD
IN THE THEORY OF KNOWLEDGE

EVA SCHAPER

ARE TRANSCENDENTAL DEDUCTIONS IMPOSSIBLE?

Professor Körner[1] has recently argued very persuasively that transcendental deductions are logically impossible. If this were so, the detail of Kant's Deduction need no longer occupy us. Such optimism I believe to be misplaced.

Transcendental arguments exhibit the necessary presuppositions without which something we say, or want to be able to say, cannot be said at all. Such arguments include, but need not be restricted to, arguments eliciting the preconditions of conceptualizing experience in the way it is conceptualized by us, the necessary preconditions of empirical inquiry as we understand it. This formulation may not seem very close to Kant's definition of the term 'transcendental', but I am assuming what I cannot argue in detail now that Kant's central question "How are synthetic *a priori* propositions possible?" requires at least an answer to the question "What are the necessary conditions (if any) of our being able to speak intelligibly about the world of our experience?", and that it is this requirement which gives Kant's question its primary significance. When Kant insists, e.g., that the notion of describing experience presupposes distinctions which are prior to any specific descriptive statement, he is arguing transcendentally; in particular, when he distinguishes two basic kinds of prior conditions, space-time and the categories, he is claiming that a conceptual scheme adequate to the requirements of empirical knowledge must enable us to do at least two things: to individuate and to attribute.

If all transcendental arguments exhibited the conditions of conceptualizing experience as it is *in fact* conceptualized by us, they might be thought to be relatively unproblematic. Some of Kant's transcendental arguments, however, make much stronger claims than those just outlined. These arguments deal not merely with the conditions of making the empirical claims we do make, but rather with the conditions of making *any* intelligible claim at all about any conceivable kind of experience. Kant argued for this stronger claim in what he considered his most important transcendental argument, the Transcendental Deduction. A transcendental deduction, then, is an argument which shows, or purports to show, not only what the necessary features of a conceptual scheme are which underpin ('makes possible') a given structure of experience, but also that the conceptual scheme thus exhibited is based on specific principles without which we could not think coherently about experience at all. It is this larger claim which is problematic in a way the weaker transcendental arguments are not.

Körner expresses something like the distinction I have sketched in this way: a transcendental deduction is "a logically sound demonstration of the reasons why a particular categorial scheme is not only in fact, but also necessarily employed, in differentiating a region of experience" (318–319). A deduction must then satisfy two conditions. (1) It must show that a categorial scheme is "established," or can be established, i.e. that it has or can have application, and (2) that it is unique. According to Körner the first condition can be met, the second cannot logically be met. It follows that transcendental deductions, as Körner defines them, are impossible. Now though Körner's distinction between "establishing a scheme" and "proving its uniqueness" reflects the distinction I drew, it nevertheless leads to a misrepresentation of the relation between the two claims in Kant's case, and this gives a distorted view of what can be salvaged from the *Critique* if, according to Körner, we disallow transcendental deductions. But first I want to ask whether Körner, given his own definition, does in fact prove that transcendental deductions are impossible.

If we are to entertain the possibility of the uniqueness of a particular categorial scheme we must, of course, at least be able to ascertain that it has application, or, as Körner puts it, we must be able to establish the scheme. Statements about (a region of) experience presuppose that we have the means of differentiating within that experience between objects and their properties and relations. This is to have what Körner calls a "method of differentiation." Such a method belongs to a categorial scheme if and only if among the concepts exhibited by the scheme are, firstly, some which are constitutive of it, i.e. tell us what is to count as an object of experience. (This is Körner's condition of comprehensive applicability.) And, secondly, some which are individuating for those objects, i.e. tell us the criteria by which in general one object is to be distinguished from another. (This is Körner's condition of exhaustive individuation.) A scheme is then said to be established when it has been shown that a method of prior differentiation belongs to it.

In terms of these distinctions, in order to demonstrate the uniqueness of a categorial scheme, we would have to show that every way of differentiating experience belongs to the scheme for which we are claiming uniqueness. It is this which Körner says is impossible. His strategy is to show that all the abstractly possible methods of proving uniqueness must logically fail. In fact, and rightly ignoring any vague appeals to "other methods, e.g. some mystical insight or some special logic" (321), he thinks there can only be three such methods:

(1) A comparison of the scheme with undifferentiated experience.
(2) A comparison of the scheme with possible competitors.
(3) An examination of the internal constitution of the scheme.

The first method is, of course, not one which Kant would have thought possible, nor one which could in general plausibly suggest itself. For quite apart from the question of uniqueness, it requires that we should be able to think first of a pure experience untouched by any differentiation, and no sense can be attached to such a supposition. What I want to point out, however, is that it follows from Körner's *definition* of a categorial scheme and how it is *established* that this method is incoherent. For we cannot show uniqueness without establishing the scheme, and we cannot do that unless some method of prior differentiation belongs to it. Now this is a feature of Körner's discussion of the second method of proof also. It follows immediately from his *description* of the second method – comparing a scheme with possible competitors and finding the latter wanting – that this method is also bound to fail because it is self-contradictory. It requires anyone who uses it to admit before the argument begins that what he is trying to prove is false, otherwise he could not even try to prove it. The reason is simply that a possible competitor is a scheme which could be established by some method of differentiation and which is yet not identical with the scheme whose uniqueness is supposed to be demonstrable.

This argument prejudges the issue, however, and in a way which makes suspect *any* attempt to show uniqueness of something on grounds which involve the consideration of other claimants – a procedure which we do not normally regard as vicious. It is true that transcendental deductions claim to show that experience under such conditions as the scheme lays down is the only sort of experience we can coherently think of, and it is then difficult to see how we can talk about *other* conditions as possible alternatives. This does not mean, however, that we cannot think of schemes, so called, which masquerade, so to speak, as genuine schemes and need therefore to be investigated. The competitors we compare our scheme with seem to be competitors, but to see whether they really are is to consider the consequences, or lack of them, of their being applicable to experience. If our chosen scheme is indeed unique, these consequences should be uniformly damaging to the claims of competitors to be genuine. The trouble with Körner's description of the second method is that it precludes this element of uncertainty.

The reply to this will be that nothing has been gained by such a manoeuvre. Any method has to rule out not just this or that alternative, but *all* alternatives, and it has to show that any alternative must violate some necessary presupposition of experience. But then it seems to beg the question, for if the necessity violated belongs to the scheme whose uniqueness one is hoping to show, then the argument cannot begin. If it does *not* belong to the scheme, then either it ought to (i.e. we failed to see it as a consequence of the scheme), or the scheme is not unique. If this is so, we can go even further with this objection. For my modification of Körner's method two now seems to be a statement of his method three. In escaping the inconsistency of method two, it becomes the *petitio principii* of method three. By arguing in effect that the defence of uniqueness claims is *prima facie* plausible only in the sense of method three, I seem at the same time to have undermined this method as a possible proof.

Körner's objection to the third method seems to reinforce this. The third method, he says, proposes to examine the scheme in question and its application "entirely from within the scheme itself, i.e. by means of statements belonging to it." (321) We could not hope to show, therefore, in addition to *which* conceptual scheme we are employing, that we must employ *this* one and no other. If to determine the truth or falsity of judgements of experience presupposes the criteria and methods supplied by the scheme we are testing, then our conclusions are perfectly valid about judgements made in accordance with the scheme, but not as conclusions about the uniqueness of that scheme. We cannot, on such a basis, think outside the scheme in terms of which experience is organized. But this proves only that the scheme is the one we employ, not that it is the *only* one which could intelligibly fulfil the same function.

To loosen the hold which the picture suggested by these objections forces upon us, it is worth considering a very general point against it. This leads to what I believe is fundamentally unsound about Körner's way of approaching transcendental deductions. A defender of the third method might argue in this way. Given a scheme in use which qualifies as a categorial scheme, we cannot accept the possibility of alternatives because we have no means of stating what they are except in terms of that scheme. But equally, if Körner is right, we have no justification for rejecting them either. This must mean that 'alternatives to the present system' cannot be ruled out. But such a description would hardly be applicable to the kind of alternatives Körner has in mind. For once we have a scheme, alternatives to it are *specifiable* only if they do the same job which the present scheme does rather differently. And then, even if there are such schemes, they would not be real alternatives in the sense Körner demands, for questions about them which we could intelligibly raise would then be questions *within* the scheme in use. There is, therefore, a certain incoherence in Körner's rejection of the third method, which is perhaps of the kind Carnap had in mind when he said that the question of alternative schemes is a non-cognitive issue: that is to say, no *sense* could be attached to the question of whether the scheme in use is unique. To speak of falsifying and in that sense disproving a uniqueness claim must be as suspect as speaking of proving it: to argue about alternatives must be at least as 'non-cognitive' as to maintain the absence of them.

With this objection in mind, the point I wish to make can now be expressed like this. We are familiar in logical empiricism with the idea of alternative languages for describing phenomena in which one or other category presently occupying a central position in one language is replaced by others. This idea goes along with that of a translation of the one language into the other. Now, if nothing is lost in the translation, the result is an alternative only in the sense of reproducing in a different form those features in the original scheme which reflect those restrictions, if any, which impose limits on the form both may take, and on the form of any other variant we may still come to consider. For it might be argued that any translation, considered simply as such, presupposes what might be called 'general principles of significance' shared by both the original and the translation. If Körner means 'alternative' in this sense, therefore, the force of his attack on uniqueness is considerably reduced. If what is of moment in transcendental deductions is the establishing of those necessary features common to all variants, then Körner's arguments do not touch them. *They* are supposed to be indifferent to the existence of any restrictions which the shared principles of significance impose. On the other hand, if a categorial scheme is proposed which is incompatible with those principles, it presumably is not an alternative in the above sense, but unintelligible as an alternative. Either, then, alternatives are variants within a pattern of features necessary to all experience, which are the features transcendental deductions are essentially concerned with, or they must escape the restrictions on intelligibility which must be satisfied by any scheme. If categorial schemes depend upon, but do not include in their formulation what I have called, admittedly vaguely, principles of significance, the question of uniqueness becomes a question about the relation between these principles and the schemes which depend upon them. This *is* an internal question in the sense to be argued out in a manner analogous to method three.

As clarification of these points, remember Kant's *Refutation of Idealism*, which, though it does not figure in the text of the chapter Kant entitles 'Transcendental Deduction', is nevertheless intimately involved in it. This is an example of an argument against a particular scheme which has been claimed to be a possible alternative to the one Kant is defending. The supposition of the rival scheme is that idealism is true, i.e. that the notion of experiences as consisting solely of experiences which are not experiences of anything existing independent of mind or minds is an intelligible one which might satisfactorily offer a basis for the organization of experience. Since Kant argues that any experience which we can find intelligible must allow for the distinction between mind and what is not mind – a distinction which idealism denies – idealism is clearly a scheme claiming alternative status which Kant has to consider and, if possible, reject. Idealism either explicitly proposes or implies a categorial scheme which entails the denial of Kant's objectivity thesis. Now Kant argues that idealism assumes that all my experiences can in principle be known as mine. Idealism therefore has to assume that it can distinguish between the self and its experiences. But this distinction in turn requires the truth of the objectivity thesis as a necessary presupposition for even getting itself stated: experiences can only be counted as mine if at least some of them could in principle be experiences *of* something which is not myself. If this were not so, I would not be able to know experiences as mine at all: I could attach no meaning to calling them 'mine'.

The structure of Kant's argument is this. Idealism is said not merely to be false, but incoherent, because it requires the truth of the objectivity thesis which it explicitly denies, in order to formulate the position from which the denial is to proceed. This brings out what I consider to be an essential feature of the sort of transcendental argument which would qualify as a deduction. For idealism can succeed only by assuming that the distinction between experiences and what has them is one we must be able to make. The failure to recognize that what is explicitly denied is yet necessarily presupposed in the denial, undermines idealism as an alternative to the sort of scheme Kant argues for in the *Critique*. It is in this way that Kant defends his arguments about the necessary presuppositions of any experience we can coherently think of.

The kind of argument exemplified in the *Refutation of Idealism*, then, provides as much ground as we can ever hope to have for saying that a uniqueness claim *is* justified: when it can be shown that candidates for the title of competitors to the scheme in question must, if they are to be genuine alternatives, include or imply features inconsistent with other features of the same scheme. This is to show up such 'alternatives' as internally incoherent, not just logically incompatible with the scheme for which uniqueness is claimed. It is also, in a way, to argue by Körner's third method, because a rival scheme, in order to be *prima facie* intelligible, must adopt or be committed to, at least some of the shared presuppositions if only tacitly to reject them. Let me add that I am not now defending Kant's arguments in particular details. It may be that the most Kant could hope to show is that a world which we can find intelligible must have certain general features which, in the present scheme, are exhibited and designated as persistent objects independent of our experience of them. Whether these features are satisfied by material objects only or at all is a question I do not raise here. What remains is that the features have to be satisfied, and that any schemes which satisfy them are variants or alternatives to each other only in the sense which is irrelevant to the main purpose of a transcendental deduction, the establishing of necessary features. They are, moreover, alternatives in a sense different from Körner's. *His* arguments are conducted in terms of whether there could be a choice between categorial schemes without inquiring whether there might not be restrictions upon us in the way of what can be envisaged as alternatives. To bring out these limitations and restrictions on the choices open to us, is, it seems to me, what a 'proof of uniqueness' should be attempting.

If my arguments have any weight at all, it must be wrong to say that Kant in his Deduction is arguing from the application which a particular conceptual scheme has to its necessary presuppositions, and confusing this with an argument from the fact that a scheme has application to its uniqueness. Körner takes this view, and he therefore offers a defence of a modified Kantian claim, or so he thinks, to the effect that transcendental arguments show that a scheme applies *a priori*, though, of course, not uniquely so, but rather 'non-uniquely'. (I have considerable reservations which there is no time to go into as to whether Körner's arguments constitute even a partial defence of a Kantian claim.) It is certainly true that if Kant had simply argued from what is the case to what this necessarily presupposes, then the Deduction would have entirely failed in its intention. But this was not and could not have been his approach. Take the distinction mentioned just now between experiences and what these are experiences of. This distinction, which in fact we do make, presupposes, as Kant clearly saw, that we must at least occasionally be able to ascribe experiences to ourselves, and be able in principle to be conscious of them as ours. The temptation has to be resisted, however, to say now that if in fact we make this distinction, and this presupposes the possibility of self-ascription, then this must *therefore* be a necessary presupposition of all experience. The grounds on which we should be prepared to defend this cannot be that it is required by the way in which we fact do conceive of experience. This would involve us in having to produce arguments to satisfy Körner's objections. That is to say, even if we *think* that no other way of conceiving experience is possible, it still has to be shown that the necessities presupposed by this way are not *derived* from experience as we find it to be, though this is, of course, our only way of knowing that they do in fact operate. Kant tries to show exactly this in the case of his claim with respect to the unity of consciousness, without which the distinction between the subjective and the objective could not be made. His argument is complex, but it is certainly not an argument *from* our in fact making the objectivity distinction. Rather, it is an argument showing that something like this distinction must be drawn as a consequence of the unity of consciousness being necessary for any coherent question about experience ever arising.

It is significant that, on the one hand, nothing like the Unity of Consciousness thesis figures, or can figure, anywhere in Körner's account of what transcendental deductions are; and, on the other hand, that Körner's method of prior differentiation is itself very like Kant's objectivity thesis, namely that discriminating experience at all entails having at our disposal the means of individuation and attribution.

Kant's Deduction falls somewhere between the Unity of Consciousness thesis and the thesis that any experience we can find intelligible must provide for the distinction which the objectivity thesis articulates in his scheme. Without the former, no notion of experience can be entertained; or to use Körner's term, without it, a method of prior differentiation of experience cannot be formulated. The Unity of Consciousness thesis is a fundamental assumption, but only in the sense that we are here operating at the boundary of any conception of experience we can envisage; whereas in the case of the objectivity thesis, we seem to be working well within those limits and may therefore be prepared at least to entertain the possibility of a particular scheme associated with it not being indispensable. But we should not persist in this belief if it meant giving up Körner's method of differentiation. To show this in detail we should have to return to what is still the only full attempt at a deduction, namely Kant's. Körner's short-cut to settling the issue is, I have argued, premature. The skeleton is still in the cupboard.

University of Glasgow

NOTE

[1] Page references in brackets are to Stephan Körner, 'The Impossibility of Transcendental Deductions', *The Monist* **51** (1967), pp. 317–331.

MARTIN J. SCOTT-TAGGART

THE PTOLEMAIC COUNTER-REVOLUTION

To what extent is the first *Critique* continuous with the early writings? To what extent discontinuous? Neither question has, in my view, been adequately discussed. The impression derived from the manifold studies that have been published is that the *Critique* is, if at all related to the early work, related as supplementing, integrating, and, above all, finding the terminology in which to wrap up the themes that had been working themselves out independently of one another in the earlier essays. Attention to the history of each of Kant's many dichotomies and trichotomies, while valuable, has tended to obscure the over-all shape of his work. The brevity demanded of this paper makes it a good opportunity for sketching a line of approach to these questions which should show its fruitfulness for challenging dogmas of Kantian criticism.

In the *Critique* as a revolutionary project we get two major conceptual displacements. In place of talk about things represented we get talk about representings of things, and in place of talk about God we have an analogous role played by talk about man. The point is easily made. Take the following passage:

The transcendental unity of apperception forms out of all possible appearances, which can stand alongside one another in one experience, a connection of all these representations according to laws. (A 108).

Now make the following substitutions. For 'transcendental unity of apperception' read 'God'; for 'appearances' and 'representations' read 'substances'; and for 'experience' read 'world'. The result:

God forms out of all possible substances, which can stand alongside one another in one world, a connection of all these substances according to laws.

And this sentence could easily have occurred in the *Dissertation* or the *Habilitationschrift*; it could even have been an excerpt from Leibniz. Thus the world and substances become, respectively, our experience of the world and of substance, and God devolves into man.

When Kant is heralded as having made a Ptolemaic counter-revolution thought is obviously being directed towards the second conceptual displacement: towards the shift from talk about God to talk about man. This is the exoteric aspect of Kant's project. But nevertheless this is a relatively unimportant shift except in so far as it is connected with, through being dictated by, the first conceptual displacement. I do not want to deny that the move is important. In Kant's attempt to undermine the force of the displacement through his moral proof of the existence of God we have a decisive starting point for a new movement in theology, and in his attempt to find a new foundation for the belief that this world is, in the Leibnizian phrase, "simplest in hypotheses and the richest in phenomena" (*Discourse*, § 6), he discovered the creative nature of scientific activity. If attention is however given primarily to this conceptual shift we are very far from the real importance of Kant in the history of philosophy.

What, then, is the importance of the move from talk about things represented (substances) to talk about representings of things? It is that Kant wanted to establish certain propositions about things represented as true, and he came to see that the only way in which he could establish these propositions as true was by ceasing to talk about things represented and to start talking about representings of things. He came to see that a way – and perhaps the only way – of establishing ontological conclusions was by way of epistemological argument. Herein is involved the one-time titled 'epistemological twist' in the *Critique*.

Although often invoked, it is rarely stated in what this style of argument exactly consists. I proffer a suggestion more in the hope that it will encourage others to work on the problem rather than that it will edify them. Let us take the following proposition as the conclusion of an epistemological argument:

(1) If an item is to be knowable as an event, then it must be knowable that it is in causal relation to some other items. But because it cannot be knowable that p unless p, we may infer:

(2) If an item is an event, then it must be in causal relation to some other items.

And thus we would understand why, as Kant puts the argument in *Negative Magnitudes*, because something exists, something else also exists.[1]

But although it would not be knowable that p unless p, it is not the case that (in any straightforward way) p entails that it is knowable that p. We need some way of reminding ourselves of the restriction imposed over the range of the variables that would appear if we wrote (2) in the language of the predicate calculus, i.e. the legitimate substitutions on 'x' in the schema beginning 'For all x such that x is an event...' For we are not talking about all x's which are events, but about all x's which are knowable as events. We may mark this restriction by saying that the variables range over the domain of appearances. The term 'appearance' thus becomes synonymous with 'knowable object', and, as a result, the Kantian claim that we can have knowledge of, and of no more than, appearances, becomes analytically true.

I have said that Kant wished to establish conclusions to the effect that the world must have a certain structure. What is novel about the *Critique* is the discovery of a method whereby he can do this. The new style of proof has conclusions not of the form 'The world necessarily...' but rather of the form 'The knowable world necessarily...'. How should we understand the difference?

It would clearly be a mistake to view knowable objects as a sub-class of objects in the way that dolphins are a sub-class of mammals, for whereas we can know whether the class of mammalian non-dolphins is an empty class, we cannot know whether the class of non-knowable objects is an empty class. When Kant says that intuitions which we cannot bring to concepts are 'nothing to us' he is saying something which needs clarifying, for it is a claim about the important role which conceptualisation plays in our experience. But there is surely neither risk nor unclarity in saying that objects of which we can have no knowledge are "nothing to us." That whereof we cannot speak, therein we have no interest. There are no doubt those who believe that Kant was proving his lack of insularity when he held that 'our world' was not the only possible world, but at the same time that he made a distinction between 'our world' and 'the world' he eviscerated the distinction of content, for he showed that we could possess knowledge of no world but that world which is our world. Kant's 'lack of insularity' is rather nostalgia or an unjustified retention of old habits of thought which viewed human minds as non-spatial substances. For us today 'our world' and 'the world' coincide, so that the word 'appearance' ought to be stripped of misleading ontological associations. We ignore non-knowable objects as dreadfully boring objects and say: Kant established conclusions about the world. And if we retain the word 'appearance' it is solely to draw attention to the method by which Kant established conclusions about the world. It is for this reason that I have introduced the term in the above way.

We now come to something more substantive, in that I wish to look to the background of Kant's discovery of this novel style of proof, for this will enable us to get a clearer grasp of what is involved. We need to begin with the Leibnizian doctrine that "the slightest thought which we perceive enfolds a variety in its object" (*Monadology* § 16). Leibniz developed this to extremes, as, for example, in the claim that "I must have some perception of the motion of each individual wave on the shore, in order to perceive what results from the whole, namely, the great noise which is heard near the sea" (To Arnauld, 9 October, 1687). This led naturally to the view that each monad represents the entire universe from its own point of view, that is, that each monad is identical with every other monad except that, for any two, there will be at least one perception which is less obscure in the one monad than in the other. Kant adopted this thesis in large measure (although at one point he suggests that the monad only represents half a world): it helps to give the psychologistic twist to his writing (AK. VII, 135; cf. II, 199; XXVIII, 1.27). More important for our present purpose is that he adopted the basic related doctrine that every representing was of a complex of representeds. I shall refer to this as his complexity thesis. It was a thesis, leading to the doctrine of combination, which gave him a problem that he initially formulated by saying that "by taking several things together you achieve without difficulty a whole of representation, but not thereby the representation of a whole" (*Diss.*, § 2; cf. *Lebendige Kräfte* § 8).

Initially Kant's attention was focussed upon the question "Under what conditions is there a whole of things represented?" The answer to this question throughout his life was that the things represented should be substances standing in real causal connections with one another.[2] This led him into a quarrel with Leibniz. For according to Leibniz "the perceptions of external things occur in the soul at a fixed moment, by virtue of its own laws, as in a world apart, and as if there existed nothing except God and itself".[3] This had as a consequence that "modifications of monads are ideal causes of those in another."[4] Thus for Leibniz it would be possible, if it were possible for God to be perhaps a little more whimsical than he was thought to be, that God should annihilate all the monads in the world but one: and yet that this one should be unaware of the change. Kant wished to deny this possibility. He argued persistently from the datum that there are continual changes in my representings of the world to the fact that there are external things, for, he believed, these changes could not occur unless there actually existed substances distinct from myself whose changes were causally responsible for these changes in my soul.[5] Even in his first work Kant insisted that "only that which stands in an actual connection with the other things which are in the world can be reckoned as belonging to that world" (AK. I, 22). Yet the difference between the Kantian and the Leibnizian position rests on no more than a word, and this Kant came to see in the *Dissertation*, where, still insisting that there is a difference between the world's being a real or an ideal whole he confesses that the former alternative "has not been demonstrated" (*Diss.*, § 22). If he is going to defeat Leibniz on the objectivity of causal relationships it must be by the discovery of a new line of attack.

(An incidental remark: Hume is supposed to have given Kant a problem about the objectivity of causal relationships. But this particular battle Kant had been fighting, with Hume appearing under the guise of Leibniz, all his life. If this is correct what role *can* we assign Hume and *what* is to be made of Kant's awakening from his dogmatic slumber?)

If we add that it is possible for substances to be in real causal relationships with one another if – perhaps – and only if there is one God who is their creator,[6] we get the following picture of the early world:

> Given   : a whole of representings.
> To state when there will be : a representing of a whole.

The answer to the problem posed is that there will be representing of a whole only if

(1) There is a whole represented
which is a straightforward correspondence-theory-of-truth remark. (1) is true if and only if

(2) There are real causal connections between the items in this whole. This once more entails and is perhaps entailed by

(3) All the items in this whole are causally dependent on one God. Thus the answer to 'Under what ultimate condition do we have a re-

presenting of a whole?' is 'When the things represented are all causally dependent upon the one God'. It is in this way that the two terms which are "lost" in the Kantian conceptual displacements are related to one another.

Kant came to see that this basic structure was inadequate to support his dogmatic realism, and the important year was of course 1772. Here, in the famous February letter to Herz, he asked "What is the ground of the relation of that in us which we call representation to the object?" How is this question to be understood? How has it been understood?

It has been understood (rightly) as showing that Kant now sees that our knowledge of things represented must be obtained through our representings of them, and cannot be obtained by-passing these representings. It has been understood (wrongly) in a way which is difficult to pin down, but which I think runs in the following Rylean manner. The things represented exist 'in' our representings of them, and they exist 'in' them after the manner in which a portrait exists in a portrait gallery, with the proviso that the thing represented as it exists 'in' our representing can be seen by only one observer. At this point the beguiling nature of the word 'representation' appears: and let us give it a technical use corresponding to the way in which it has been understood by so many, and speak of the thing represented as it exists 'in' our representing of it as a 'representation'. What features does the representation possess?

Most importantly, it has been thought that just as we can give a description of a portrait independently of any description of the person of whom it is a portrait, so we can give a description of the representation which is independent of any description that we give of the thing represented. And this has apparently given Kant the problem of explaining how a representation can be *of* something (a problem some have taken to be solved by saying that a representation acquires intentionality by being rule-related to other representations!) This is of course absurd. And it is an absurdity into which we naturally run if we do not analyse out the ambiguity of 'representation' into the two terms 'representing' and 'represented'. Kant's question is not how non-intentional representations come to acquire intentionality. His question is rather 'How do I categorise the something of which my representing *is* a representing?'

Kant does not therefore give up his correspondence theory of truth, and thus he does not give up his claim that there is a representing of a whole only if there is a whole represented. But neither does he give up his claim that there is a whole represented if and only if there are real causal relations between the items in the whole. It is this that raises problems. For he can no longer suggest that we may establish structural truths about the world through an appeal to God. Epistemologically God is so to speak bracketed out.

The path to the new Critical solution lay in Kant's realisation that what he had previously accepted as given was not in fact unproblematic. The problem now appears: To state when there will be: a whole of representings.

That the problem has changed from 'Under what conditions will there be a representing of a whole?' to 'Under what conditions will there be a whole of representings?' is clear in the Deduction. And the move has been made because there being a whole of representings is a necessary condition of there being a representing of a whole. A representing of a whole involves – particularly in virtue of the temporal nature of our experience – representings of the parts of that whole, and these representings must themselves form a whole, i.e. be parts of the history of one consciousness, if there is to be knowledge.

As a consequence of this observation the whole investigation is turned upside down. But it would be a mistake to suppose that the investigation has turned into the investigation of something entirely new. In 1781 Kant is concerned with a whole of representings, where previously his attention had been upon a representing of a whole. But because there being a representing of a whole entails there being a whole of representings, any sufficient condition of the former is a sufficient condition of the latter: but where he was concerned with discovering the sufficient conditions of a representation of a whole, he is *still* concerned with discovering those conditions, although he is approaching them through a different route. He now claims that there can be a whole of representings only if the representings belong to one unitary consciousness, and to claim that they *can* belong to one unitary consciousness only if they at the same time form a representing of a whole. Thus in stating the conditions under which his new problematic premise is possible he lists: (1) There is a whole represented, and (2) There are real causal connections between the items in this whole.

These are purportedly deductions from his new premise, and, together with that premise, they form a set of not only necessary but also sufficient conditions for there being a representation of a whole, which is to say: true knowledge.

If this crude sketch of Kant's argument is in any way adequate it shows that it cannot be taken too strictly. Thus he was absolutely right when he said that not every whole of representings is the representing of a whole: there are distinctions to be drawn between true stories and false stories, between imaginary wholes and real wholes. Kant's conclusion in the Deduction must therefore be taken to be of the form: there can be a whole of representings only if *on some occasions* this whole of representings is the representing of a whole.

It has been my purpose not so much to assess the validity of Kant's arguments as to demonstrate their structure with a view to showing the essential continuity and yet the same time discontinuity in his writings. I have shown the essential *continuity* by showing that the problem which most concerned him since his student days was the same problem as that which critics who emphasise the Analogies rightly recognise as central to the *Critique*: The Humean causal problem was essentially the same problem that Kant had always had in relation to Leibniz. A further similarity has been roughly indicated in the parallelism of the refutations of idealism. I have at the same time spoken of the essential *discontinuity* as being involved in the two conceptual displacements. The first is from talk of things represented to talk of representings of things. This shift was designed to accommodate a new method of proof for his desired conclusions about the objective validity of the mathematical and metaphysical principles necessary to establish Newtonian science on a sound basis, where these conclusions were that the world must have a certain general structure. *Same* conclusions, *different* proof. I have also indicated how the second conceptual displacement, from talk about God to talk about man, is a straightforward consequence of the first conceptual displacement. We can establish that there is a whole of things represented only by appeal to man as that being to which our representings of things must necessarily relate, and through whom, therefore, they may be totalised. Yet it is doubtful if Kant could have achieved his ontological revolution if he had not for so many years relied upon God to provide a foundation for his Critical metaphysics. For, through inheriting the role of God, man, in the Kantian picture, acquired also properties analogous to those which had been traditionally ascribed to God. Thus man, in the Kantian picture, is imaginatively creative, and is not, as for Hume, a piece of Newtonian machinery.

University of East-Anglia

NOTES

[1] Why should it be easier to establish (2) via (1) rather than directly? Basically because statements about our experiences of things (e.g. that they are temporal) are that much more certain than statements about things that they may serve as premisses where statements about things may not.
[2] Connectedness in space and time was never sufficient, in that this sort of connection required a real ground even in the *Dissertation*, cf. Section 16.
[3] *New System of Nature*, § 14.
[4] *Philosophische Schriften* (ed. by Gebhardt), II, 747.
[5] Cf. Ak.I.415. Compare the conclusion of the early refutation of idealism ("There could not be a subjective series of representings unless...") with that of the strongest version in the *Critique* ("There could not be known to be a subjective series of representings unless...").
[6] *Dissertation*, Section 20. Thus in strictness only (1) and (2) are *necessary* conditions of there being a representing of a whole. And notice that if there is an imaginary whole, e.g. a man climbing a golden mountain, there is a whole of representings but not a representing of a whole.

PART II

LINGUISTIC AND TRANSCENDENTAL THEMES

K.-O. APEL

FROM KANT TO PEIRCE: THE SEMIOTICAL TRANSFORMATION OF TRANSCENDENTAL LOGIC

I. THE TRANSCENDENTAL DIMENSION OF MODERN 'LOGIC OF SCIENCE'

In comparing Kant's *Critique of Pure Reason* as a Logic of Science with the modern 'Logic of Science' one might find the profoundest point of difference between them in the fact that one is an analysis of 'consciousness', the other an analysis of 'language'.

Kant's concern is to make the *objective validity* of science understandable. For this purpose he indeed puts transcendental logic in the place of the psychology of knowledge as it was developed by Locke and Hume; but his method of inquiry is still related to the 'synthetic unity of *consciousness*' as its 'highest point'. And in accordance with this preconception he makes his synthetic *a priori rules*, which he puts in the place of Hume's psychological laws of association, rules of the function of psychic faculties such as intuition, imagination, understanding, reason.

It is quite different with the modern 'logic of science': There is not only no talk about psychic faculties, even the very problem of consciousness as a subject of scientific knowledge (in contradistinction to the objects of science) is nearly eliminated from the discussion. What has been put in the place of these requisites of Kant's transcendental logic is not, as many like to believe, *formal logic* in its renewed form as mathematical logic, but – for a closer consideration – the logical syntax and the logical semantics of scientific *languages*.

These languages as semantical frameworks provide the new subject for a priori rules which prescribe the possible form of description and explanation for 'things in as far as they form a context ruled by laws'. And the Kantian problem of the *objective validity* of scientific knowledge for every consciousness was to be resolved in the modern logic of science by logical syntax and logical semantics, which would guarantee the logical consistency and the verifiability (confirmability) of scientific hypotheses or theories.

The historical point of this syntactic-semantic reconstruction of epistemology becomes apparent if one puts the question of what has become of
the Kantian consciousness in the modern logic of science, i.e.: of the
transcendental subject of scientific knowledge. The official answer could
be: This supposition is no longer needed. In as far as the question refers
to man as a subject of science the subject may be reduced to an object
of science, that is, of human science as behavioral science; in as far, on
the other hand, as the question refers to a logical condition of the possibility and validity of science the transcendental function of the Kantian
subject may be substituted by the logic of scientific language: the logic
of language and the empirical confirmation of propositions or systems of
propositions together take the place of Kant's transcendental logic of
objective experience.

However, this official view of the modern logic of science, in my opinion,
has fallen short of the real problems with which it is confronted. It implies
an ideological moment which conceals the failure of the original programme of the modern logic of science, the programme of Logical Empiricism.
For the substitution of the transcendental function of the subject of
knowledge by 'the' logic of scientific language could be seriously propa-
gated just as long as one could hope to guarantee the *intersubjectivity*
of the possible validity of empirical science by the syntax and semantics
of *one* so-called *language of things or facts*. This was just the point by
which the young Wittgenstein in his *Tractatus* felt entitled to call the
'logic of language' 'transcendental', apparently with an allusion to Kant
(*Tractatus* 6.13), and to identify the *subject* of scientific knowledge as a
thing which does *not exist* in the world, with the function of language as
a limit of the world (*ib.*5.62; 5.631; 5.632; 5.64).

In the meantime, however, it became clear that neither the logical consistency nor, far less, the empirical testability of science can be warranted
by the logical syntax and semantics of *one language of things or facts*. It
proved necessary in two places to introduce the so called *pragmatical
dimension*, i.e., the dimension of the *interpretation of signs*, as a condition
of the possibility and validity of scientific propositions.

(1) One of the two aporetic situations was the famous problem of
verification, where it was necessary to connect the reconstructed language
of science with the observable facts. It became apparent here as a consequence of the very form of language-analysis that the modern logic of

science cannot confront the theories or hypotheses of science with bare facts but only with so called *basic statements*. But in order to provide validity for the basic statements themselves one requires an intersubjective agreement of the scientists as the pragmatic interpreters of scientific propositions, that is, as subjects of science in as far as they cannot in principle be reduced to objects of empirical science.

Moreover, the language of this intersubjective agreement cannot, in terms of logical semantics, be identical with the logically reconstructed language of science; it must rather coincide practically with the not yet formalised language needed for communication between empirical scientists and the designers of semantical frameworks about the pragmatic interpretation of a language of science.

(2) By this last observation we have also already indicated the second, still more fundamental, point, where the substitution of the transcendental function of the epistemological subject by the syntactic or semantical rules of a scientific language was doomed to failure. A formalised language of science just cannot make use of the *one* postulated logical form of language or of the world, which, according to the early Wittgenstein, is *transcendental*. A formalised language of science has to be introduced and legitimized as a conventional framework by scientists, who can and must provide the framework with a pragmatical interpretation in a *metalanguage*.

By this it has been shown, in my opinion, that the pragmatic dimension of the sign-function, which was introduced into the modern logic of science by Charles Morris, cannot, as Logical Empiricists would like, be reduced to a topic of empirical psychology. The pragmatic dimension may rather be considered as the semiotical analogue to the transcendental synthesis of apperception postulated by Kant. Just as Kant, as an analyst of consciousness, had to postulate as a presupposition of epistemology, that by cognition something like the *synthetic unity of consciousness* has to be reached, – in just the same way modern logicians of science, starting from a semiotic basis of analysis, could, or rather should, postulate, that it must be possible, for something like the *unity of intersubjective interpretation of the world* to be reached by the way of interpretation of signs.

(Advocates of modern, analytical philosophy might perhaps object that the difference between the modern logic of science and that of Kant consists in the very fact that one is not entitled to postulate a transcendental unity of interpretation of the world but has to be satisfied with a 'critical conventionalism' concerning the interpretation of scientific propositions by experts. I think that in this objection K. R. Popper, the later Wittgenstein, and the later Carnap would agree. One could, however, give the following answer to the objection from a quasi-Kantian point of view: *critical* conventionalism, in contradistinction to *dogmatical* (metaphysical) conventionalism, may not have the intention to reduce knowledge to *mere* convention; it may rather intend to make a difference, by the way of a *fallibilistic* reservation, between *ad hoc*-conventions of experts and the absolutely intersubjective consensus concerning the validity of scientific propositions. That means, however, that critical conventionalism, understood rightly, does not exclude but presupposes the postulate (the regulative idea) of an absolutely intersubjective *unity of interpretation*.)

Perhaps these critical remarks about the situation of the modern, analytical 'logic of science' are able to convince you that this discipline via *pragmatics* and especially by the problem of *intersubjective interpretation* implied in pragmatics is directed back to a Kantian type of 'transcendental philosophy'. If this should be the case you will not have overlooked that the way suggested by my remarks does not lead back to the historical Kant, not even to nineteenth-century type Neo-Kantianism but rather to a language-analytical or semiotical transformation of transcendental philosophy.

II. PEIRCE'S SEMIOTICAL TRANSFORMATION OF KANT'S TRANSCENDENTAL LOGIC

It is a remarkable fact that the very programme sketched out just now has in fact been developed in detail by an American contemporary of German Neo-Kantianism. It was Charles S. Peirce, the Kant of American Philosophy, as one may perhaps call him, who initiated the three-dimensional semiotic, which nowadays has been introduced into the modern 'logic of science' by Charles Morris, as the triadic foundation of his 'logic of inquiry'; and this logic of inquiry was intended from the beginning – that is: since the deduction of the 'New List of Categories' in 1867 – as a critical reconstruction (in the sense of setting up an equivalent) of Kant's *Critique of Pure Reason*.

I cannot – within the limits of this paper – develop *in extenso* my interpretation of Peirce's Philosophy.[1] But I will try to make clear my chief thesis, that Peirce's philosophical approach may be understood as a semiotical transformation of Kant's transcendental logic, in a discussion with some renowned investigators of the relationship between Kant and Peirce.[2]

Jürgen von Kempski is to be credited for having for the first time analysed in a serious way the close relationship between Peirce and Kant in his book *Ch. S. Peirce und der Pragmatismus* (1952). He has shown that Peirce in 1892 succeeded in deducing his three universal categories (Firstness, Secondness, Thirdness) from a classification of the propositional functions[3] into *singular, dual* and *plural* ones, and in this way has set up an analogy to Kant's metaphysical deduction of the categories from the table of judgments. Von Kempski holds, however, that this metaphysical deduction so to speak is hanging in the air, because there is no corresponding transcendental deduction of the categories from the 'highest point', that is: from the transcendental synthesis of apperception (von Kempski, *op. cit.*, pp. 57ff). Kant's highest point, so holds von Kempski, is for Peirce 'occult transcendentalism', and therefore he could not understand, much less resolve, the chief problem of Kant's: the problem of explaining the *necessity* of our ideas being determined by categories. Hence Peirce could not manage the transition from his 'logical forms' to the categories of experience, and finally had to give up the Kantian approach and to put in its place a phenomenological discovery of the categories and a pre-Kantian metaphysics for an inductive verification of the categories (*ib.*, 58ff). By this Peirce fell into line, as an original outsider, with Neo-Kantianism, or rather with its dissolution at the turn of the 19th century by the phenomenological turn.

It cannot be denied that von Kempski's analysis wins much plausibility not only by the suggested historical parallels but also by the development of Peirce's philosophy in its later period (especially by its establishing *phenomenology* or *phaneroscopy* as *prima philosophia* and the preceding conception of a metaphysical cosmology on the basis of 'objective idealism'.

Nevertheless, one may get quite another picture if one starts from Peirce's early writings of the '60's and '70's and analyses from this perspective Peirce's hierarchical classification of sciences of 1902/3. Even at this time phenomenology as *prima philosophia* has by no means taken the place of a logical deduction of the categories but only has to illustrate their virtual application after their formal deduction in the mathematical logic of relations (not belonging to philosophy!) and previous to their quasi-transcendental deduction in the normative, semiotical 'logic of inquiry'.

(It may be admitted in this context that Peirce did not succeed in setting up a consistent systematic representation of his philosophy, and that the fragments of his designed architecture leave a lot of free play to the interpreters).

But let us turn to the transformation of Kant by the early Peirce.

Von Kempski (p. 59) has realised that Peirce – in his opinion only in his later works – has found a kind of substitute for the 'highest point' of Kant: namely the category *thirdness*, which he conceives in 1903 as a 'synonym of representation' (Peirce, 5.105) and thus takes as the basis of his logic (of inquiry). Von Kempski is aware of the fact that *thirdness* as a *mediation* by signs or *representation* of something to an *interpretant* is in Peirce's language something like an analogue of Kant's objective unity of ideas in a selfconsciousness. But he holds that thirdness in Peirce's philosophy remains a conception of an abstract logical structure and insofar cannot take over the function of the 'highest point' in a transcendental deduction. Peirce did not realise – according to von Kempski – that "the necessity of the possibility of objective knowledge is identical with the (thinking) I", and he is said to have rejected Kant's doctrine that "the supreme legislation of nature" lies in our understanding (von Kempski, 60f., 63, 65f.).

It must however be stated that Peirce himself in plain contradiction to these theses has claimed for himself the 'Copernican step': so in 1871 he writes in his review of Berkeley, after having introduced his own theory of reality: "Indeed what Kant called his *Copernican step* was precisely the passage from the nominalistic to the realistic view of reality. It was the essence of his philosophy *to regard the real object as determined by the mind.* That was nothing else than to consider every conception and intuition which enters necessarily into the experience of an object, and which is not transitory and accidental, as having objective validity..." (Peirce, 8.15).

And in full accordance with this claim of the 'Copernican step' Peirce in 1868 and in 1878 appeals to Kant's supreme principle of synthetic

judgments, in order to answer with its help the question how synthetic
judgments are possible. He says in this context: "Whatever is universally
true of my experience... is involved in the condition of experience"
(*ib.* 2.691; cf. 5.332 M).

How can these transcendental arguments be reconciled with Peirce's
rejection of 'occult Transcendentalism', quoted by von Kempski?

The answer is that Peirce's rejection of 'Transcendentalism' does not
refer to the idea of the 'highest point' of a 'transcendental deduction' but
to those features of Kant's procedure which in Peirce's opinion are psychologistic and circular.[4]

The investigations of M. Murphey in particular have shown that
Peirce, in his long study and transformation of Kant, which resulted in
the 'New List of Categories' of 1868, had the transcendental deduction
of the categories just as much before his eyes as the metaphysical deduction.

As to von Kempski's criticism of Peirce's having neglected the transcendental synthesis of apperception one may find equivalent counter-
evidence in Peirce's reproaching Kant because his method 'does not
display that direct reference to the *unity of consistency* which alone gives
validity to the categories'.[5]

The phrase 'unity of consistency', used by Peirce in his criticism, shows
the direction in which Peirce himself is searching for the 'highest point'
of his 'transcendental deduction': His concern, it is true, is not with the
objective unity of ideas[6] in a *selfconsciousness* but rather with the semantical consistency of an intersubjectively valid *representation* of the objects
by signs, which consistency, according to Peirce, can only be decided about
in the dimension of sign-*interpretation* (afterwards called *pragmatic* by
Ch. Morris). The young Peirce characterizes the unity of consistency he
was searching for as follows in 1866: "We find that every judgement is
subject to a condition of consistency: its elements must be capable of
being brought to a unity. This consistent unity since it belongs to all our
judgements may be said to belong to us. Or rather since it belongs to the
judgements of all mankind, we may be said to belong to it".[7]

This early utterance shows that the 'unity of consistency' Peirce was
looking for lies beyond the personal unity of self-consciousness, which is
Kant's 'highest point'. Peirce confirms this in 1868 in his semiotical
Theory of Mind, where he says:

"... consciousness is a vague term... consciousness is sometimes used to signify the *I think*, or unity in thought; but the unity is nothing but consistency, or the recognition of it. Consistency belongs to every sign, so far as it is a sign... there is no element whatever of man's consciousness which has not something corresponding to it in the word... the word or sign which man uses *is* the man himself... the organism is only an instrument of thought. But the identity of a man consists in the *consistency* of what he does and thinks..."

From here Peirce comes immediately to the decisive conclusion which leads to the 'highest point' in the sense of a *semiotical unity of consistent interpretation*: He says: "... the existence of thought now depends on what is to be hereafter; so that it has only a potential existence, dependent on the future thought of the *community*" (5.313–316).

But how should it be possible to deduce from the 'highest point' which is suggested here the *categories* or even the *principles* of possible *experience*? Do not Peirce's formulations bear the appearance of being pre-possessed by a pre-Kantian rationalism which confuses the formal logic of language with the transcendental logic of the constitution of possible objects of experience?

This objection may be not without warrant if directed against the modern analytical 'logic of science', for example against modern deductive theory of explanation set up in the framework of a formalised language; but it does not hold for Peirce. He by no means considers the formal logic of conceptual – or propositional – symbols as a sufficient substitute for Kant's transcendental logic, but on the contrary he initiates for this purpose, with the help of Kant's Copernican turn, his new 'synthetic logic of inquiry'; and he postulates in his quasi-transcendental semiotic, besides conceptual *symbols*, two other types of signs which are thought to make the transition possible from the stimulation of sensation and the qualities of feeling to conceptions and judgments respectively. But the real basis of this transformation of transcendental logic is provided by the fact that Peirce in 1867 performed a 'transcendental deduction' of the *three types of signs* parallel with the *three kinds of inferences* as illustrations of the *three universal categories* which are implied, as he shows, in the *sign-relation* (*semiosis*) as provisionally 'the highest point' of his 'tran-scendental logic' (Cf. Murphy, ch. III).

The *sign-relation* or *representation* can be made explicit, according to Peirce, by the following scheme of definition: A sign is something that stands for something in some respect or quality to an interpretant (5.283;

2.228). This schema implies, according to Peirce, three categories:

(1) Simple *Quality* without relations, which makes up the respect or point of view, under which something is expressed *as* something in its *suchness* (category *the First*, later called *Firstness*). To this category corresponds the sign-type of 'Icons' which has to be implied – as Peirce later makes clear (8.41; 3.363; 5.119) – in every predicate of a perceptual judgment in order to integrate felt qualities of the real world into the synthesis of a hypothesis which makes up the argument of a perceptual judgement.

(2) The *dyadic relation* of the sign to its denoted object or rather objects (category *the Second*, later called *Secondness*). To this category corresponds the sign-type of 'Indices' which has to be found – as Peirce later makes clear (5.287, 296, 352; 8.41ff.) – in every perceptual judgement (for instance as a function of the *pronouns* and *adverbs*) in order to warrant the space-time-identification of the objects which are to be determined by predicates.

(3) The *triadic relation* of the sign-function as a 'mediation' or 'representation' of something as something to an interpretant (category *the Third*, later called *Thirdness*). To this category corresponds the sign-type of conventional 'Symbols', which is the subject or medium of the central function of synthesis qua the representation of something as something by concepts. But this *representation* by *symbols* would be 'void' without the integration of the function of *indices* and of *icons*, just as with Kant conceptions without intuitions are 'void'. On the other hand the function of *indices* and *icons* is blind if not integrated into the function of representation to an interpretant, just as with Kant intuition without conceptions is 'blind'. – Indeed: only *interpretation* fills the *index*-function with meaning, say of the pulse or of a sign-post as well as the *icon*-function of a model or a diagram or even of a picture. (The last point should be seriously regarded by the syntactic-semantic philosophy of formalised languages).

But in order to show how this semiotical deduction of three fundamental categories and of three types of signs may help to explain the possibility and validity of experience, it is necessary to coordinate with Peirce the three fundamental kinds of inference to the three kinds of categories and the three types of signs: that is to parallel *Thirdness* and conceptional *symbols* with *deduction* as a rationally necessary agent, *Secondness* and

indices with *induction* as the confirmation of the general by facts in space
and time, and finally *Firstness* with *abduction* as the synthetic cognition
of new qualities of suchness.

(This characteristic complementation of the analytic logic of deduction
by a synthetic logic of induction and abduction or hypothesis was also
in the sixties of the 19th century brought about by a criticism of Kant's
treatise *Die falsche Spitzfindigkeit der vier syllogistischen Figuren*. At this
time indeed Peirce was already convinced by Duns Scotus that the study
of the syllogism had to precede the study of the forms of judgment since
only in this way are the logically significant differences of the judgment
to be found (cf. Murphey, pp. 56ff.).

The discovery of *abduction* or *hypothesis*[8], which is an inference from
a given result of a possible deduction and a presupposed general premise
to the contingent (minor) premise of a syllogism, proved to be especially
important for Peirce's pragmatistic logic of inquiry: for *hypothesis* is
according to Peirce the single kind of inference by which our knowledge
is expanded in the sense of Kant's synthetic judgments of experience,
which therefore, according to Peirce, may be interpreted as unconscious
abductive inferences. But now, since every abduction or hypothesis
presupposes a general premise and therefore has to be tested by induction,
abduction and induction together provide the answer to the question
implicitly asked by Kant, according to Peirce; – to the question: how
synthetic judgements are *possible* and *valid* (5.348 and 2.690).

Abduction or *hypothesis* explains *possibility* of experience insofar as it
brings about the synthesis as a reduction of the manifold of sense-impressions and qualities of feeling to the unity of consistency in perceptual
judgments (and also in explanations by law). Here in the first place the
icon-function of predicates has to be mediated with the intensional
meaning of the predicates as symbols; as, for instance, in the statement
"This (which looks so and so) is likely to be a case of plague".

Induction, on the other hand, explains the empirical justification of the
general presuppositions of all experience, be they implicit in perceptual
judgments or explicit in lawlike statements. Here in the first place the
index-function of language as the identification of objects here and now
has to be mediated with the *extensional* meaning of the predicates as
symbols of classes; as, for instance, in the statement: "*This* (or *here*) *is* a
case of plague".

But now, according to Peirce, it is possible to examine in a procedure antecedent to the actual verification or falsification of a proposition whether or not a proposition is a genuine *hypothesis* implying a general element which *can* be confirmed by *induction*. For this purpose one has to *deduce* possible experimental consequences from the general (lawlike) meaning of the predicate by an experiment of thought with the form of an operationally conditioned prognosis. This very procedure which realizes the interdependence of analytical and synthetical phases within the logic of inquiry is explained by Peirce in his *Pragmatic Maxim* as a method of "How to make our ideas clear" (5.388–409).

Peirce now applies this method last but not least to the conception of 'reality' as it is used in propositions like "The object of my experience is *real*, it is not a mere *illusion*"; and by an explication of the meaning of reality in the light of possible experience as analysed in his 'synthetic logic' he reaches the final and characteristic conception of the 'highest point' of a possible *unity of consistency* of our knowledge. For the sake of conciseness I quote a summing up of this 'highest point', which precedes by years the explicit foundation of Pragmatism:

"The real... is that (more exactly: the object of the opinion[9]) which, sooner or later, information and reasoning would finally result in, and which is therefore independent of the vagaries of me and you. Thus, the very origin of the conception of reality shows that this conception essentially involves the notion of a *Community*, without definite limits, and capable of a definite increase of knowledge" (5, 311, from 1868!).

In other words: The 'highest point' of Peirce's transformation of Kant's transcendental logic is the 'ultimate opinion' of the 'indefinite community of investigators'. At this point one may find a convergence of the semiotical postulate of the transindividual *unity of interpretation* and of the postulate of the logic of inquiry concerning the *validation* of experience *in the long run*. The quasi-transcendental subject of this unity is the *indefinite community of experimentation* which is identical with the *indefinite community of interpretation*.

From this last presupposition of a quasi-transcendental logic Peirce cannot, it is true, deduce the 'principles' of science as synthetic judgements a priori in line with Kant's intentions. But from his highest point of view he can make plausible that those absolute *principles* a priori are not needed and that the maintenance of those principles amounts to preserving a remnant of metaphysical dogmatism. This he can show just by appealing

to Kant's supreme principle of synthetical judgements in connection with
his own logic of synthetic inferences, for from his postulate of the ultimate
opinion he can deduce as transcendentally necessary not any propositions
but the universal validity of synthetic inferences *in the long run*, that is:
of the *method* of induction and abduction.

This he did in 1869 and 1878 (5.341–52 and 2.690–93). In a way he has
put Kant's *regulative principles* of experience in the place of Kant's
constitutive principles of experience; on the assumption, that the regulative
principles in the long run turn out to be constitutive. – Thus by shifting
the necessary and universal validity of scientific propositions to the end
of the (indefinite) process of inquiry it is possible for Peirce to escape
Hume's scepticism without insisting with Kant on the necessity and
universality of propositions which for the moment are accepted by experts.
These propositions can, nay must, on Peirce's transcendental presuppositions, be conceived as fallible, that is corrigible, by hypotheses which come
nearer to the ultimate opinion. (There is no doubt that most of the modern
logicians of science prefer this fallibilistic and melioristic but not sceptic
conception to the Kantian doctrine, which clings to the Platonic idea of
science as *episteme*. Very similar to Peirce's conception is in this respect
for instance the position of K. R. Popper).

If one considers this position as a plausible and consistent transformation of Kant's transcendental logic of experience, then one will hardly be
satisfied by the criticism which Murphey brings forward against Peirce's
understanding of Kant in his great monograph on *The Development of
Peirce's Philosophy* (pp. 25ff.). Murphey's criticism is chiefly directed
against the fact that the young Peirce in his Kant-studies does not accept
Kant's 'critical' distinction between noumena and phenomena and in
consequence cannot justify synthetical judgments a priori as principles
of the possible experience of phenomena but takes his refuge with faith
as a foundation of the principles. – However, if one looks at this situation
in the light of Peirce's final achievement of the transformation of transcendental logic, the approach of the young Peirce seams to be consequent
and legitimate:

(1) From his semiotical conception of cognition Peirce could not accept
Kant's distinction between knowable objects of experience and things in
themselves which are supposed to be thinkable as existing (and even as
affecting the senses!) but basically unknowable. Our claim for cognition,

according to Peirce, reaches as far as the truth-claim of meaningful hypotheses, for, on the other hand, for Peirce, as we have seen, there is no cognition which would not, by its very essence, be a hypothesis, that is an abductive inference. Peirce's arguments against the very meaning of the conception of unknowable things in themselves – which I unfortunately cannot bring to the fore in this place – rank foremost among the strongest objections which have been directed against Kant since the days of Jacobi.[10] Still more convincing, in my opinion, is Peirce's positive transformation of the famous Kantian distinction, which takes into account Kant's legitimate motives without getting entangled in the nonsensicalities. Instead of laying the difference between unknowable and knowable objects Peirce distinguishes between the real as the knowable in the long run and whatever may be the result of an actual cognition basically underlying to the reservation of fallibility (5.257, 310). The problem of unknowable things-in-themselves by this turn is transformed into the problem of infinite approximation, which, indeed, is a paradoxical problem too.

(2) But now the distinction between unknowable things-in-themselves, which affect the senses, and phenomena which are predetermined as to their formal structure by the mind (that is, Kant's transcendental idealism) is the precondition for the Copernican turn. How can Peirce appeal to the latter and nevertheless reject the former? The answer is: Peirce does not, as we have seen, refer the Copernican turn to the mind as the *faculty of the principles* but to the mind as the *faculty of synthetic inferences*. He therefore is entitled, in my opinion, to cling to Kant's central doctrine, that a transcendental foundation of the objectivity of science is necessary and possible, and nevertheless postulate that all scientific propositions as hypotheses may be corrected by experience, that is: by confrontation with the real here and now as brute fact and by perception of its pre-conceptional qualities.[11]

(3) Finally, regarding the foundation of the principles of science in practical faith, which was critizised by M. Murphey, one has to state that this position of the young Peirce is consistent with his final pragmaticistic transformation of Kantianism. Also the later Peirce could not accept the Kantian distinction between theoretical and practical reason which he apparently rejected back in 1861.[12] For, together with the distinction between noumena and phenomena Peirce has also to nullify the Kantian distinction between regulative ideas and moral postulates: The indefinite

process of Inquiry as a real enterprise of human practice, the progress and outcome of which is in fact uncertain, is itself the object of logic and of a moral engagement.

At this point Peirce's semiotical transformation of the 'highest point' of the transcendental logic reaches its *highest point* in what later has been called Peirce's 'Logical Socialism'[13]: A man who wishes to proceed logically in the sense of Peirce's synthetic logic of inquiry has to surrender all the private interests of his finite life, also the private interest in *his* personal salvation (which is existential in Kierkegaard's sense) to the interest of the *indefinite community* since only the community has a chance to reach the ultimate truth: "He who would not sacrifice his own soul to save the whole world, is illogical in all his inferences, collectively. So the social principle is rooted intrinsically in logic (5.354ff., 2.654f.).

Unlike the pragmatism of James, who in his essay *The Will to Believe* of 1897 defends the subjective interest of the single man in a belief for his life just because he cannot wait for the ultimate opinion, the young Peirce considers his point of 'logical socialism' also as a practical postulate of ethics. For he expects – or hopes – that the social progress of science will bring about simultaneously a rationalization of human conduct[14], whose 'habits' may be conceived as being analogous to natural laws and therefore may establish in the long run the 'concrete reasonableness' of the universe.

This last thought of Peirce's too is a consequent transformation of Kantianism; for Kant's categorical imperative in its most speculative version reads: "Handle so, als ob die Maxime deiner Handlung durch deinen Willen zum allgemeinen Naturgesetz werden sollte".

University of Saarbrücken

REFERENCES

[1] Cp. K.-O. Apel: 'Der philosophische Hintergrund der Entstehung des Pragmatismus bei Ch.S. Peirce', in: Ch.S. Peirce: *Schriften I*, Frankf.a.M., 1967; und K.-O. Apel: 'Peirce's Denkweg vom Pragmatismus zum Pragmatizismus', in: Ch.S. Peirce: *Schriften II*, Frankf.a.M., 1970.

[2] Quotations of Peirce are, as usual, from *Collected Papers*, vol. I–VI (ed. by Ch. Hartshorne and P. Weiss), Harvard University Press, 1931–35, [2]1960, vol. VII–VIII, (ed. by A. W. Burks, 1958, [2]1960, as for example: CP, 5.263 =Collected Papers, vol. V, paragraph 263.

[3] Peirce had discovered the later so called *propositional functions* under the title *Rhemata*, cp. CP, 3.420. – Cp. J. v. Kempski: *Ch.S. Peirce und der Pragmatismus*, Stuttgart 1952, s. 55ff.

[4] Thus the young Peirce writes in 1861: "Psychological transcendentalism says that the results of metaphysics are worthless, unless the study of consciousness produces a warrant for the authority of consciousness. But the authority of consciousness must be valid within the consciousness or else no science, not even psychological transcendentalism, is valid; for every science supposes that and depends upon it for validity". (Quotation from Murphey, *The Development of Peirce's Philosophy*, p. 26.)

[5] Quoted from Murphey, p. 65.

[6] A decisive nuance of Peirce's interpretation of Kant is concealed by the fact that Kant's term *Vorstellung* is usually translated into English by 'representation'. With Peirce, however, such a translation already implies a semiotical transformation of the very conception.

[7] Quoted from Murphey, p. 89. Cf. Peirce, 5.289 n.: "... just as we say that a body is in motion, and not that motion is in a body, we ought to say that we are in thought and not that thoughts are in us".

[8] Peirce understood this discovery as an interpretation of Aristotle. Cp. his *Memoranda Concerning the Aristotelian Syllogism*, Nov. 1866 (CP, 2.792–807).

[9] Cp. the formulation in 5.407 (1878!).

[10] See for instance the following argumentation of 1905 (5.525): 'Kant (whom I *more* than admire) is nothing but a somewhat confused pragmatist... but in half a dozen ways the *Ding an sich* has been proved to be nonsensical; and here is another way. It has been shown (3.417) that in the formal analysis of a proposition, after all that words can convey has been thrown into the predicate, there remains a subject that is indescribable and that can only be pointed at or otherwise indicated, unless a way, of finding what is referred to, be prescribed. The Ding an sich, however, can neither be indicated nor found. Consequently, no proposition can refer to it, and nothing true or false can be predicated of it. Therefore, all references to it must be thrown out as meaningless surplusage. But when that is done, we see clearly that Kant regards Space, Time, and his Categories just as everybody else does, and never doubts or has doubted their objectivity. His limitation of them to possible experience is pragmatism in the general sense; and a pragmaticist, as fully as Kant, recognizes the mental ingredient in these concepts...". Cp. 5.452.

[11] Cp. above p. 97 ff. about the cognitive function of the 'indices' and 'icons'.

[12] Peirce writes in 1861: "... Faith is not peculiar to or more needed in one province of thought than another. For every premise we require faith and no where else is there any room for it. This is overlooked by Kant and others who drew a distinction between *knowledge* and *faith*". (Quotation from Murphey, loc. cit. p. 26f.).

[13] Cp. to this topic the Dissertation of G. Wartenberg: *Logischer Sozialismus. Die Transformation der Kantschen Transzendentalphilosophic durch Ch.S. Peirce*, Frankfurt a.M. 1970, (forthcoming).

[14] For a criticism in Peirce's 'Scientism' cp. G. Wartenberg, loc. cit.; furthermore K.-O. Apel: 'Szientismus oder transzendentale Hermeneutik?' in: *Hermeneutik und Dialektik*, Tübingen, 1970.

B 132 REVISITED

In B 132 Kant says:

It must be possible for the 'I think' to accompany all my presentations; for otherwise something would be represented in me which could not be thought at all, and that is equivalent to say that the representation would be impossible, or at least it would be nothing to me.

The philosophic insight of this for the transcendental deduction rather important point is obscured by the psychological, or semi-psychological, language in which it is expressed. The word 'representation' (*Vorstellung*) belongs to the psychologist's vocabulary rather than to the philosopher's. And how are we, in this context, to understand the crucial expression 'I think'? The fact that, in Kant's words, it must be possible to accompany all my representations implies that it is a psychological occurrence.

However, that a psychological interpretation is destructive to the epistemological character and nature of the *Critique* and is against Kant's declared intent is hardly disputed by anyone today. But if this is so how are we to interpret B 132?

The attempt to de-psychologize Kant has certainly not been easy, and it is probably correct to say that the de-psychologizing process has not yet been completed. And quite understandably so. Contradictory elements have tended to dominate any classical theory of knowledge. The concept of knowledge is conceived of partly as a psychological concept and partly as a logical concept. Knowledge has been regarded as the last point of a continuous scale beginning with such concepts as ignorance or doubt and – via the concepts of assumption, belief, and being convinced – leading up to the concept of knowledge. To conceive of knowledge this way is to conceive of knowledge as containing a psychological element. It is conceived of as a psychological concept only partly because it has almost always been realized that knowledge also is radically different from belief, assumption and supposition. It has, at least since Plato, been realized that knowledge belongs to a different category from that of such psychological concepts as belief and assumption. We may believe and assume wrongly but we cannot know wrongly. We ask *why* we believe that *p*; that is, we ask for the psychological causes; but we do not ask why we know; we ask *how* we know; that is, we do not ask about causes; we ask about evidence – we ask whether we have sufficient evidence to make a knowledge claim.

In spite of these opposing elements, it is difficult to free any theory of knowledge from being conceived of or expressed in psychological terms. And, as is well known, it has been particularly difficult, as it at the same time has been extremely important, to free Kant's theory of knowledge from psychological interpretations.

In what follows I shall investigate the possibility of giving a logical interpretation of B 132. I shall begin with the concept of representation.

Kant's use of the term 'representation' is admittedly rather liberal. However, the way Kant is using it in B 132 it surely means any kind of mental occurrence, happening, or activity of which I am conscious. It would have no meaning to maintain that the 'I think' should accompany something of which I had no consciousness. The term 'representation' must, at least in this context, refer to something of which I am conscious. However, to have a representation, to be conscious of something, implies that I must be able to ascertain something about it, must be able to assert something about it. If I am unable to say anything whatsoever, i.e. unable to say neither what kind of thing it is, what shape or extension it has, nor what color it has, etc., it is the same as to say that I am conscious of nothing. If no properties can be ascertained, no predicates be attributed, there is nothing I am conscious of. This is true even if the representation is nothing but a mental image, since a mental image, insofar as it is anything at all, must possess at least one property. And to have consciousness of such a mental image is to be able to ascertain the existence of this property; it is to assert that the image possesses this property. And as an assertion involves the employment of concepts it follows that I cannot have a representation unless it involves such an employment. Thus, to have a representation implies the assertion of a certain proposition *p*; it implies that the person who has the representation asserts that *p*.

In other words, what Kant is saying is this: "It must be possible for the 'I think' to accompany all my assertions for otherwise an assertion would be passed by me which could not be passed at all".

What does it mean to say that the 'I think' must accompany all my
assertions? Kant talks of the 'I think' as if it were a representation and
therefore involving an assertion. But this leads to difficulties.

Suppose that at a specific moment I have a special representation or,
to express it differently, that at a specific moment I assert that p. The
'I think' which should accompany this assertion would then have to be:
'I assert that p' and this is what leads us into the difficulties. Suppose
a person A is signing a letter. The statement 'A signs this letter' must
then be true. Likewise, if I sign a letter, the proposition 'I sign this letter'
must be true. And again, if a person A asserts that p the assertion: 'A
asserts that p' must be true. But if I assert that p, the proposition 'I assert
that p' is not true. That it is not true follows from the simple fact that the
expression 'I assert that p' is regarded either, although erroneously so, as
a report of what I am doing, namely, asserting that p, or regarded as a
performatory expression. As a report it is obviously quite different from
asserting that p – just as a report of signing a letter is different from signing
it. Furthermore, I cannot at one and the same time both be asserting that
p and be reporting that I am asserting that p. In fact, I can report only
that I *asserted* that p, not that I am asserting it; while I am asserting that
p I cannot also report that I am in the middle of asserting it. But if 'I
assert that p' cannot be regarded as a report it may be regarded as
performatory, i.e. as the act of asserting that p, but as a performatory it is
neither true nor false.

What the 'I think' must mean, however, is that whenever I have a
representation, i.e., whenever I am asserting that p, I know that I am
asserting that p. But also here we encounter difficulties. It is regarded as a
philosophic commonplace that whenever I claim to know that something
is the case I am committed to answer the question: 'How do you know?'
To claim to know is to be committed to give evidence.

Of course, if knowledge is conceived of as a psychological state, if in
other words to have knowledge involves having certain representations, or
certain experiences – if it is itself an assertion, it will be of no help. But
the point is that to say about somebody that he knows something is not
to say anything about his psychological state – as it would be if we said
that he was convinced or that he felt certain or that he doubted, etc. To
say about somebody that he knows is to say something about the evidence
he has for that which he claims to know. It is to say that his evidence is

conclusive; in other words, it is to say that he cannot be wrong. But such a conception of knowledge does not seem to apply in the present case. If I assert that *p* I know that I am asserting that *p* – if I did not I could not be said to have asserted that *p*. It belongs to the essence of assertions that the person who asserts something knows what he asserts. At the same time, however, it seems to have no meaning to ask questions about how he knows. A person may be asked how he knows that his assertion is true. But he cannot be asked how he knows that he is making an assertion. It seems, therefore, that we have to choose one of two alternatives. If a condition for using the concept of knowledge is that we can be asked how we know, how we found out, etc., it seems that we would have to give up saying that we know that we assert that *p* whenever in fact we do assert that *p*. Or we will have to say that as in fact it is the case that we know that we assert that *p* whenever we do assert that *p* it cannot be correct that a condition for applying the concept of knowledge is that we show our credentials. It cannot be a condition for the use of the concept of knowledge that we should be able to ask questions how we know, or how we found out. Not because we are in doubt about it, or have not been able to find enough evidence, but because it would make no sense to ask about evidence, etc.

It seems, however, that we have to distinguish between two different uses of the concept of knowledge. One use is contrasted to belief or to feeling more or less certain. It is the use where we may ask for evidence. I do not believe but know that Mr A is married. But I do not know but only believe that he is 57 years of age. Different from this use is the one where it has no meaning to contrast it with belief or feeling certain. I neither believe nor do I feel certain that I have a pain, am taking a walk, and am now asserting that knowledge is something not contrasted to belief. I do not know these things in the sense in which it meaningfully could be contrasted to such concepts as feeling certain or believing. I cannot meaningfully say that I feel certain that I am taking a walk, and am convinced that I am asserting whatever I at this moment am asserting. This use of knowledge has nothing to do with evidence. Rather, as Wittgenstein expresses it in *Philosophical Investigations*, knowledge is here used to emphasize "that the expression of uncertainty is senseless" (§ 242).

Now, I cannot be said to make an assertion unless I intend to do so.

An unintended assertion is simply not an assertion. And to say that I do something intentionally is, at least in part, to say that I know what I am doing and that it is knowledge which is non-inferential. I do not acquire my knowledge of what I am asserting by listening to my own speech-acts. I do not *discover* what I am doing, or, in other words, as Wittgenstein says, there can be no surprise. But the intention is not itself a certain act over and above the act performed by intention. It is not the cause of the intended act. If it were, we would of course be caught in an infinite regres: Is the act of intention itself performed intentionally? If it is, it must be caused by yet another act of intention, etc.

What we have arrived at so far is that what B 132 is saying is that the 'I think' which must be able to accompany all my representations is that it is part of the meaning of the concept 'representation' that it is intended – which in turn is the same as to say that an intention is a necessary condition for all assertions.

Now, Kant does not say that the 'I think' in fact accompanies all my representations; he only says that it is possible to do so. This should mean that whenever I assert something it must be possible to know it. But this is of course erroneous. It is to fall back on the assumption that to have knowledge of an assertion must be a psychological phenomenon. It is to talk as if it were something I sometimes do and sometimes do not do. But as we have seen it is not a psychological characteristic of consciousness but a necessary conceptual condition. In other words, if *p* is an assertion then it is a conceptual truth that the person asserting that *p* also knows that he is asserting that *p*.

Kant's statement that it must be possible for the 'I think' to accompany all my representations is thus analytic. It serves as an analysis of the concept of representation. The term 'I' in the two statements: 'I think' and 'I assert' has consequently the same meaning. What is the function of the term 'I' in such sentences?

In order to answer this question let us begin by directing our attention to the well-known conceptual fact that the use of cognitive verbs requires an accusative. I can neither see, hear, nor think, unless I see or hear something or think of something. The accusative is the object of consciousness. It is what has been called the content of consciousness. Whatever is known, whatever we are conscious of must function as an accusative for a cognitive verb. But neither can a cognitive verb be used unless it has a nominative. It must have a subject. The subject may be both a second and a third person pronoun; but whether it is one or the other it is necessary that for any use there must be a first person use. The first person use is the primary use for cognitive verbs. It is presupposed by all second and third person uses.

This use of the term 'I' does not imply any ontology. This can easily be seen. Suppose I say, like for example Descartes or Berkeley, that I am identical with my soul. If that were the case the proposition: 'I have a soul' should be the same proposition as 'my soul has a soul', which of course is not the case. The latter proposition is redundant while the former is not. And the same argument holds if I claim that I am identical with my body. The proposition: 'I have a body' should then be synonymous with the proposition 'My body has a body' which likewise is redundant.

It has been maintained that the word 'I' is an index word, i.e. a word which indicates that the person referred to is the speaker. No doubt, this is sometimes the case; but by no means always. If somebody asked the question: "Who put that book on the table" and I say: "I did", it may very well be argued that the 'I' in this situation is used as an index word. I want to inform the person who asked the question that it was I and not another person who put the book on the table. But suppose somebody asks me: "Where have you been?" and I answered: "I have been out for a walk" then I am not using 'I' as an index word. I am informing the person who asks the question that I have been for a walk and not for a drive, or in the garden, or any other place. It may be objected that in this latter use I might have answered the question without the use of the word 'I'; and this is probably correct. It surely would have been understood if my answer has been: "For a walk". The point is, however, that it is logically possible to apply the 'I' and that in such uses the 'I' is not used as an index word. In other words, it is always logically possible to use the first person pronoun whenever a cognitive word is used. In such cases the 'I' has neither an ontological nor an epistemological function. It is a necessary condition for the use of any cognitive verb. Or in epistemological terms: the 'I' is a necessary condition for all knowledge (and therefore cannot itself be an instance of knowledge). When Kant speaks about the pure apperception he wants to emphasize that the 'I' cannot have an empirical content. Within the problem about personal identity it is a meaningful but contingent question whether my body is identically the same body from one moment to another, and a meaningful but contingent question to ask whether my memory is the criterion or is what constitutes my personal identity. But the 'I' which is the presupposition for all questions about personal identity is neither an entity which is changing nor not changing; it is no entity at all but is a necessary condition for formulating any question about personal identity. In Kant's use, it is the transcendental unity of self-consciousness.

University of Aarhus and State University of New York at Brockport

JOSEF SIMON

PHENOMENA AND NOUMENA: ON THE USE AND MEANING OF THE CATEGORIES

According to Kant, all language is signification of thoughts (*Anthropology*, Part I, § 39). "Thought is the act which relates given intuition to an object" (B 304). Thus language as 'the faculty of signification' attaches to the 'objects' – which, according to Kant, constitute themselves only in the act of thinking – a specific sensuous intuition distinct from the intuition which immediately relates itself to objects. Accordingly, by the distinction of thoughts language also keeps the objects distinct. Thus 'the faculty of knowledge' and 'the faculty of signification', thought and language, co-operate. Transcendental philosophy claims to determine the constant activities of the understanding in the constitution of each specific empirical object. It claims to distinguish 'the pure concepts of the understanding' from the linguistic terms which signify the objects in their particularity. According to Kant, the relation between concepts of the understanding and the empirical concepts is the same as the relation between rules for the use of words and the words themselves.

Therefore Kant maintains that "to search in our common knowledge for the concepts which do not rest upon particular experience and yet occur in all knowledge from experience, of which they as it were constitute the mere form of connection, presupposes neither greater reflection nor deeper insight than to detect in a language the rules of the actual use of words generally and thus to collect elements for a grammar". But he pointed out that "we are not able to give a reason why each language has just this and no other formal constitution, and still less why any precise number of such formal determinations in general, neither more nor less, can be found in it" (*Proleg.* § 39).

The conception of such a transcendental grammar is still to be found in Kant's lectures on metaphysics: "If we analysed the transcendental concepts in that way, the result would be a *transcendental grammar* in which we would find the ground for human language: for instance, how the present tense, the perfect and the pluperfect are to be found in our understanding, what adverbs are, etc. These reflections would lead to a transcendental grammar. Logic would consist of the formal use of the understanding. Then transcendental philosophy, the doctrine of the general a priori concepts, could follow" (*Vorlesungen über die Metaphysik*, Darmstadt, 1964, p. 78). Kant seems to have no doubt that we have to proceed by using language as our guide, if we want to get at the concepts of the understanding, though we are not able to explain – as it is put in the *Critique of Pure Reason* – "why we have just these and no other functions of judgment" (B 146). Language and general grammar would thus precede the categories. It is language in which the categories are included in their 'entirety' and in which they can be "discovered in their completeness" (B 94). They are not to be found in logic. The system of formal logic is already a result of the fact that the categories have been discovered. Logic is a mere 'example' for the argument that "all the simple acts of reason can be enumerated completely and systematically" (A XIV).

We may discover the concepts of the understanding just as we find out 'rules of the actual use of words'. We may say that the concepts of the understanding may be discovered as semantic categories. Are they – to put it in terms of medieval philosophy of language – *general modi significandi*, differing from particular signifying elements of language? Does Kant, in his analysis, try to transcend language towards this conception? J. J. Katz explicitly refers to Kant and Aristotle in his treatment of 'semantic categories'. If we took up Kant's suggestion, we had to begin with the analysis of a certain language, trying to find out those characteristics of the words which can be isolated and generalized and which derive their determinative power not so much from the meaning of the words as from the manner in which these words are used in the synthesis of a sentence. After having analysed certain languages, we would have to point out those characteristics which are common to all of them, so that we might dispense with the grammatical peculiarities of individual languages and could arrive at a 'grammar of reason'.

There is a significant remark made by Katz in this context, saying that he would 'suppose', "that there are semantic categories of language" (J. J. Katz, *The Philosophy of Language*, New York and London, 1966, p. 230.) Unlike Kant, Katz does not enumerate these categories, but only points out the way to discover them.

However, Kant's transcendental deduction of the objective validity of the categories is, after all, also developed irrespective of any single category – which could serve the purpose only as an example – and solely rests on the assumption that there are categories at all.

Thus, the category of substance, for instance, regulates the use of words by systematizing those which have "always to be considered as subject and never as mere predicate" (B 129). Transcending the grammatical concept of subject, the category of substance makes clear how words, because of their meanings, and not only because of their grammatical form (for instance as a noun), will fit into syntactical structures or not. The category of substance allows the classification of meanings by those leading characteristics which are in their turn not determined by the content of the words, but by the mode of their syntactical usage. Thus a transition is gained from the level of 'empirical' meanings to the level of transcendental formal categories.

The essence of the category consists in a rule for joining together mere use and meaning, that is, possible reference to an object (A 244). – Kant defines the categories as having 'transcendental meaning', but serving an 'empirical use' (B 303, 305). Both sides belong to the category as its essential qualities, but the categories are transcendental only in so far as their meanings are concerned. Their transcendental meanings fulfil the function of rules for judging, these rules being realized only in the actual judgments on the empirical. The object to which the category may refer is the object characterized by a certain use and constituted as an object only by the fact that its characterization follows a rule, or, in other words, that its characterization includes a category.

From this point of view, the fact that each judgment includes a category means that a judgment is formed according to a rule of the actual use of the words, that is, according to a rule which comprises semantics and thus transcends grammar. Hence, the conception of the category is based upon the following suppositions: (1) that there is a fixed correspondence between words and their meanings by virtue of which these words refer to certain (empirical) objects; (2) that these meanings were transformed into categories by following the syntactical use, so that a consideration of content and semantics leads to a consideration of the syntactical form.

The second supposition depends on the first. The assumption that there is a fixed correspondence between meanings and words is characterized by Wittgenstein in the following passage from the *Philosophical Investigations* (§ 2):

That philosophical concept of meaning has its place in a primitive idea of the way language functions. But one can also say that it is the idea of a language more primitive than ours.

Following Wittgenstein, we may say that this is the conception of a language with a strictly regulated use. People speaking this language have been drilled in the implicit obedience to its rules and in clinging, in a 'one-dimensional' way, to the mode of life which this language belongs to. So far as such a rigorous drill in using language in only *one* manner represents a fictitious conception, this supposition is fictitious.

Since the second supposition is based on the first one, it has the same fictitious character as the first. Only on the assumption of a fixed correspondence between words and meanings may we suppose we could infer syntactical rules from 'these' meanings. Yet once we agree to the first supposition, we shall not find any particular difficulties in accepting the second. I should like to explain this by giving examples of the categories.

There are certain words which, by their meanings, need a specification (*consignificatio*) of *quantity* as an adjunct as soon as they occur in a sentence. Moreover, it is required that the connection of these words with the meaning of another word in the sentence expresses a compatibility or incompatibility of the meanings, that is, a *quality* of the judgment. – Especially by the example of quality is it made clear that syntactical consequences follow from the semantics of the concepts, namely those of the positive or negative formulation of a sentence. A sentence has possibly to be negated, because of the positive meaning of the subject or the predicate; or the sentence is affirmative, since the meaning is already negative as in the following proposition: 'Men are unfeathered'. – The categories of relation point out which of the meanings, in their relation to each other, may become either subject or predicate within a proposition; they explain which proposition is, by the meaning of another proposition, already implied in a proposition, *if* we state this other proposition (causality); and, finally, these categories point out the rules according to which propositions may implicate each other because of their meaning (reciprocity).

Consequently, the categories may be conceived as connecting links between syntax and semantics. According to Kant, they are therefore, contrary to empirical concepts, altogether lacking in empirical meaning; they are not significant, but only co-significant (classifying) by indicating aggregates of meanings with regard to their possible 'use' in the structure of a sentence.

Being only co-significant, the categories have no meaning at all when they are isolated. They serve an empirical use, that is, they possess meanings only when they are connected with empirical concepts. Yet they bring about the possibility of empirical concepts being connected in propositions. Since it is not words, but whole sentences, which can refer to reality, the employment of the categories implies the general (transcendental) pretension that empirical concepts could refer to *something* at all. Yet this possibility of reference to an object was explicitly defined by Kant as the meaning of a concept. Accordingly, the categories represent nothing less than the power of the empirical concepts to mean *something at all*. Slight modifications in the terminology will suffice to transform these 'linguistic' issues into the central topics of Kant's Critical Philosophy.

In the above mentioned definition of the categories there are already implied especially the distinction between phenomena and noumena as well as the function of this distinction drawn by Kant in his conception of knowledge. The categories cannot acquire meanings on their own; they are "empty concepts without objects" (B 348). Yet only by the co-operation of the categories do empirical concepts mean possibly *something*. Generally speaking, the categories point to an aspect of the empirical concepts, namely to the possibility of their being synthesized within judgments about *something*. It seems to be obvious that this reference to an 'object in general' which coincides with the transcendental meaning, conveys at the same time no meaning in itself, after having been isolated by reflection. We cannot have any knowledge of the 'thing in itself' because its concept 'in itself' has no meaning.

Thus Kant can no longer distinguish in an ontological manner between phenomena and noumena, but can only refer to "the *ground of the distinction* of all objects in general into phenomena and noumena" (B 294 ff., italics by the author). According to Kant, 'meaning' consisted of the possible reference of a concept to an object. This possibility proved to be identical with the possibility of being connected with other concepts, according to certain rules, as is the case in a judgment about *something*. The possibility of a reference to an object, thus regulated, lies therefore solely within the scope of concepts. It does not yet indicate that the rule will be employed, that is, that somebody will actually form a judgment according to these rules. The occasion for doing so would only lie in a given sensuous intuition that has to be judged.

The ground of the distinction between phenomena and noumena is this very reflection on a future 'empirical use' without which the categories "remained without sense, that is without meaning" (B 299). For, if we say that the categories were restricted to an empirical use, we are already conceiving the difference between this use and another non-empirical use. In this reflection on abstract syntactical rules for the use of empirical concepts, the understanding forms "a representation of an *object in itself*" (B 306). Hence, this representation results from realizing a distinction between a regulated use and the use in general.

Since Kant's conception of knowledge depends on the distinction between noumena and phenomena, it is instructive in respect of the philosophical analysis of this conception to continue in scrutinizing the *ground* of the distinction between phenomena and noumena.

In the light of our former considerations, the reflection on a regulated use proves to be determined, namely as a reflection on this linguistic distinction. It is thus distinct from a reflection in general, that is, from the mere potentiality of man's faculty of reflection. According to Kant, the mere faculty of reflection proves to be a fact belonging to the pure self-consciousness which cannot be explained any further, – of a self-consciousness which in itself distinguishes itself as a noumenon from itself as an appearance. It finds its unity in the original synthetic unity of the apperception, from which originates the possibility of a synthesis according to the categories as is performed in judgments.

By determining the supreme unity of the apperception, – that is, the utmost starting-point for deduction in Kant's philosophy, – in accordance with the linguistic distinction between rule and use, 'the conditions of the possibility' of knowledge which are deduced from this starting-point are themselves criticized and thoroughly determined by pointing out their own 'conditions of possibility'. The 'highest point' from which Kant's philosophy is deduced turns out to be of a peculiar quality: It is not language that can be transcended by Kant's transcendental philosophy;

on the contrary, Kant's starting-point is only comprehensible as more than an undeducible *factum*, if it is in its turn transcended by means of a philosophy of language. This starting-point depends on the *idea* of a language that is completely regulated in its use. In trying to point out the *possibility* of science by transcendental philosophy, a thoroughly regulated terminology of science is presupposed, *as if* it were actually used.

University of Frankfurt

PART III

ANALYTIC AND SYNTHETIC JUDGMENTS

RICHARD AQUILA

CONCEPTS, OBJECTS AND THE ANALYTIC IN KANT

Kant defines analytic truth in terms of 'conceptual containment'. He also claims that there are some necessary truths which do not depend upon conceptual containments. These are synthetic a priori. If 'true in virtue of conceptual containment' means 'true solely in virtue of the concepts involved' or 'true solely in virtue of the meaning of the terms involved', then many philosophers since Kant have argued that there can be no synthetic a priori. And there is some ground for concluding that this is what 'true in virtue of conceptual containment' did in fact mean for Kant, since Kant insisted that all synthetic judgments are validated only by reference to some 'third thing' over and above the concepts involved. The proper assessment of this issue requires a distinction between two theories of concepts, and two senses of conceptual containment. While in one sense there may be no truths which are necessary independently of conceptual containment, Kant has shown that in another sense there are such truths.

I. TWO THEORIES OF CONCEPTS

Crudely viewed, concepts may be considered a kind of entity, whether dwelling in some peculiar Platonic realm or, in the Cartesian tradition, as an 'idea' or 'representation' in the mind. Despite Kant's own revolutionary insight concerning the relation between concepts and rules, that Kant classifies concepts as a species of *Vorstellung* (B 377) reveals clearly enough the Cartesian element in his thought. Call this concept$_1$. Conceived as a kind of entity in the mind, concepts$_1$ have a special epistemological task to perform: they are to mirror (or 'represent') the properties of objects in a way which is itself representable by means of definitions.

Now Kant himself has shown that concepts$_1$ are empty apart from the system of rules for bringing objects (intuitions) under them. This insight leads to a more sophisticated view of concepts. Here, to speak of a concept is not to speak of a kind of entry at all, but simply of the fact that there are rules governing the application of terms (or, if we still want to speak of them, of our concepts$_1$) to objects. Call this concept$_2$. It is perfectly possible, then, to imagine the following situation. A given concept$_1$ A is not definable in terms of some other concept$_1$ B, yet the rules governing application of the word 'A' contain specifications relative to application of the word 'B'. In this case, though there is no containment relation between the concepts$_1$ A and B, there is a sense in which the concepts$_2$ do stand in a kind of containment relation. Hence while there is a sense in which the corresponding judgment is analytic, there is also a sense in which it is synthetic.

II. THE CONCEPT OF EMPIRICAL OBJECTIVITY IN KANT

Kant argued that 'E is an objective event in space-time' implies 'E stands in causal relations to other events both preceding and following it in time'. Kant's general argument for this claim is contained in the following passage:

> That which lies in the successive apprehension is here viewed as representation, while the appearance which is given to me, notwithstanding that it is nothing but the sum of these representations, is viewed as their object; and my concept, which I derive from the representations of apprehension, has to agree with it... It will be seen at once... that appearance, in contradistinction to the representations of apprehension, can be represented as an object distinct from them only if it stands under a rule which distinguishes it from every other apprehension and necessitates some one particular mode of connection of the manifold. The object is *that* in the appearance which contains the condition of this necessary rule of apprehension (A 191/B 236).

The argument appears to have the following structure:

(1)   What I mean by 'objective event' cannot be a succession of things in themselves, but only a succession of things in appearance.

(2)   A succession of things in appearance must be distinguished from the succession in our apprehension of such things.

(3)   The only way to distinguish a succession in objects as appearances from a succession in our apprehension of objects is to specify the succession in objects in terms of a particular mode of succession in our apprehension, i.e., in terms of some 'necessary rule of apprehension'.

The conclusion that Kant wants to draw from these three premises is then

(4)   "The object is that in the appearance which contains the conditions of this necessary rule of apprehension",

which seems tantamount to

(4′)   What one *means* by an 'objective event' is simply a 'succession according to a necessary rule'.

Kant's argument thus seems to establish that, once we see that we are talking not about succession in things in themselves, but only in appearance, then we will see that all that we *mean* by such succession is succession according to necessary rules. But then, it would appear, the proposition "Every objective event stands in causal relations to other events" must be an analytic proposition. For it simply unpacks part of what we mean by 'objective event'. Thus compare a slightly different formulation which Kant gives to the argument: "If, then, we experience that something happens, we in so doing always *presuppose* that something precedes it, on which it follows according to a rule. Otherwise I should not *say* of the object that it follows" (A 195/B 240). In other words, I would not say of any succession that it is a succession in an object unless I were also prepared to say that it is a succession according to a rule. What more do we need to conclude that the concept of an objective event contains that of succession according to necessary rules, and hence that the judgment in question is analytic, and not synthetic a priori?

This criticism has been applied not only to the Second Analogy, but to the First and Third Analogies too. All the propositions in question must be analytic, it is alleged, because all that they do, on Kant's own admission, is to state a part of our criteria for calling something objective in the first place. I want to argue that this sort of reply is based upon a misunderstanding of Kant's position. What does Kant mean by the 'object' in those contexts where he is talking not about things in themselves, but about empirical objects? One answer is suggested by Kant himself in the passage quoted earlier: "The object is that in the appearance which contains the condition of the necessary rule of apprehension". Or again: "The object is nothing but the *sum* of these representations" contained in the synthesis of apprehension. These passages suggest that

Kant is offering a phenomenalistic reduction of the concept of an empirical object: All propositions about empirical objects and events are to be analyzed as propositions about sequences and collections of representations and the rule-governed relations among them. Given such an analysis, it would follow immediately that all of the propositions Kant sought to establish as synthetic a priori must be obviously analytic. For the concept of a rule-governed relation among representations would be contained in the very notion of what an object as appearance is.

This interpretation of Kant cannot be sustained, however. First of all, Kant explicitly claims that empirical objects are necessarily represented 'in space'. And space, for Kant, is construed as a single, 'all-embracing' three-dimensional whole. But how could propositions about a three-dimensional whole, and hence about the three-dimensional objects represented in that whole, be analyzed in terms of propositions about our own representations? If they could be so analyzed, then it would follow that the predicate 'is represented in space' could be analyzed away in favor of some predicate which refers to no such objects a space at all. But Kant explicitly denied that propositions about space could be reduced to propositions none of which mentions space. This is just the point of Kant's view that space is an intuition, i.e., the referent of a singular referring expression. That space is an intuition for Kant is just another way of saying that the word 'space' in such locutions as 'object in space' really does refer to a singular object, and does not merely appear to do so. And this eliminates the possibility that propositions about objects in space might be analyzed into propositions none of which refers to space, and hence to objects *in* space.

There is another difficulty with the phenomenalistic interpretation of Kant. Kant tells us that all judgments about objects, whether about space itself or the objects in space, must have a certain form. They must, in Kant's terms, involve predicating a concept of some intuition (A 67/B 92). Thus the judgment that 'A is brown' must involve predicating the concept 'brown' of the particular referred to by the expression 'A'. But if all propositions containing the expression 'A' were analyzable in terms of propositions referring only to our own representations and the order among them, then it would follow that all judgments about empirical objects such as A merely *appear* to involve the predication of some concept of the object A. For they would really be judgments not about the

single object A, but about a whole collection of many different representations. Thus there are two reasons why Kant could not be intending to
offer a phenomenalistic reduction of physical objects. (1) Such a reduction
would imply that propositions about space were reducible, since propositions about objects *in* space would be reducible. And (2) it would imply
that propositions such as 'This horse is brown' were not really of the form
'A is f', but merely appear to be so.

What does Kant mean, then, by 'empirical object'? He simply means
an observable object in three-dimensional space and in time. And by
an objective event, he simply means a succession of properties in any such
object. And certainly Kant is right that this concept of an objective event
does not contain that of its being part of any causal order, in the sense
that being part of a causal order is not contained in the definition of an
objective event. There is no contradiction, therefore, in the concept of an
uncaused event in space-time.

Of course, this is hardly the whole story. There is a sense in which
'there is' no such entity as space for Kant and no such entity as an object
in space. This is the sense in which neither space nor spatial objects exist
as things in themselves. Call this exists$_1$. There is, however, another sense
in which spatial objects do exist for Kant, and he defines this in *The
Postulates of Empirical Thought*, under the category of 'actuality' (A 218/
B 266). Kant defines the actual as "That which is bound up in accordance
with the material conditions of experience, that is, with sensation", later
adding also "in accordance with the analogies of experience" (A 255/
B 272). Call this exists$_2$. It is then part of the very definition of 'exists$_2$'
that anything which exists in this sense must be subject to the Analogies
of Experience, and it is of course Kant's position that no other sense of
existence is legitimately applicable to spatial objects. Thus consider the
judgment 'E is an objective event'. Insofar as this is a judgment about a
particular event E, we may assume that in affirming it we are presupposing
the existence$_2$ of E. But it is part of the very concept of an event's existing$_2$
that it stands in causal relations. Therefore, the proposition 'E is an
objective event' analytically implies that 'E stands in causal relations'.

Consider, however, a judgment not about some particular event E, but
about objective events in general: "Every objective event stands in causal
relations". Since this is not a proposition about any particular event, it
does not presuppose the actuality of any particular event. Thus the con-

cept (schematized category) of actuality does not enter into the judgment, and all that we have to deal with are the two concepts 'is an objective event' and 'stands in causal relations'. But we have already seen that for Kant the concept of being an objective event does not contain that of standing in causal relations. To sum up this part of the argument, then:

(1)   Kant does not offer a phenomenalistic reduction of empirical objects and events; but

(2)   he does offer a phenomenalistic definition of the *existence* of empirical objects and events.

Accordingly,

(3)   It does not follow from Kant's conception of what an objective event *is* that all such events stand in causal relation; but

(4)   any judgment about a *particular* objective event logically implies (or at least presupposes) that the event stands in causal relations.

III. CONCEPTS AND CRITERIA

Now it might be objected that if any proposition about a particular objective event presupposes that it stands in causal relations, then this is to say that standing in causal relations is one of the criteria for something's being an objective event. And indeed, as we saw, Kant himself seems to grant as much: we would not *call* a particular occurrence an objective event unless we were prepared to assert that it stands in causal relations. But if standing in causal relations is one of the criteria for the concept of an objective event, then aren't we simply right back where we started? The judgment that every event must have a cause is analyticc because it simply presents one of the criteria for calling something an objective event.

Suppose, however, that we distinguish between concepts$_1$ and concepts$_2$. The concept$_2$ of an objective event is constituted by the rules for the use of the term 'objective event'. But our rules for the use of this term specify the conditions under which any particular phenomenon might be identified as an objective event. Hence the concept$_2$ of an objective event contains that of standing in causal relations. But consider instead the concept$_1$ of an objective event. Whatever is contained in the concept$_1$ of an objective event must be contained in a definition of the term 'objective event' together with a definition of all the terms occurring in it. But 'objective event' is just defined as a succession in the properties of an object observable in space. Hence the concept$_1$ of standing in causal relations is not contained in the concept$_1$ of being an objective event.

There is nothing mysterious about this. We are ordinarily inclined to insist that the criteria for identifying any particular thing as an f must be part of our very concept of an f. But this is because we tend toward a relatively sophisticated theory of concepts. Given a crude enough theory of concepts, of the sort which I have defined, there is no reason at all why the concept of an f should contain a determination which is nevertheless a necessary condition for our calling anything an f. Hence if conceptual containments are taken to define analytic truth, then those very judgments in Kant which on a sophisticated theory of concepts turn out to be analytic, will be synthetic a priori on the cruder theory. They will be synthetic because the concept$_1$ of the subject does not contain that of the predicate. But they will be a priori because the predicate specifies one of the criteria for identifying anything as the subject in the first place. Thus the criteria for the identification of intuitions as falling under concepts$_1$ provide Kant with the 'third thing' which he requires in the Transcendental Analytic.

Duke University

KONRAD CRAMER

NON-PURE SYNTHETIC A PRIORI JUDGMENTS IN THE 'CRITIQUE OF PURE REASON'

The arguments put forward in this paper attempt to show the relevance of a remark of Kant's on the propositional content of the principle of causality and the structure of the Analogies of Experience. This remark, though marking a decisive point in Kant's transcendental theory of experience, has not been dealt with adequately by Kantian scholars. Consequently, to some of them the very title of this paper may appear to contradict what they regard as basic Kantian doctrine. This paper attempts to prove that what may seem to contradict basic Kantian assertions is a basic, though problematic, Kantian assertion itself.

I

Section I of the introduction to the 2nd edition of the *Critique of Pure Reason* offers, under the heading 'On the Difference of Pure and Empirical Knowledge', a nominal and fairly negative definition of a priori knowledge. Knowledge is to be called a priori, if it is "independent of all experience and even of all impressions of the senses" (B 2). We will therefore be inclined to assume, that the concept 'pure' and the concept 'a priori' are equivalent, both designating that characteristic of knowledge which is its independence of experience. This very common assumption seems, however, to be falsified by Kant, when, in the same section, he goes on to say:

Among the cognitions a priori, those with which nothing empirical at all is mixed in, are named pure. Therefore, to give an example, the proposition: all change has its cause, is a proposition a priori, but it is not pure, because change is a concept which can only be drawn from experience (B 3).

Obviously, in this passage, Kant introduces a distinction *within* a priori knowledge, namely the distinction between pure and non-pure a priori knowledge. Consequently, the concepts 'pure' and 'a priori' as used by Kant have different meanings: 'pure' is a further qualification of knowledge claimed to be 'a priori'; 'a priori' knowledge need not be 'pure'. We should therefore be warned against the opinion that the concepts 'pure' and 'a priori' must be conceived of as equivalents. If knowledge exists which is both a priori and not pure, we should rather say that the very title of Section I is somewhat misleading, because it does not give an exhaustive disjunction of the class of all knowledge. A logically satisfying division of the class of all knowledge would then have to be made with regard to *either* the distinction between the a priori and the empirical *or* the pure and the non-pure. Pure knowledge will certainly have to be a priori, but not all a priori knowledge will have to be pure; non-pure knowledge might be either a priori or empirical. At least this is the conclusion, if we take the passage at B 3 seriously. To do so is, however, to state, and not to solve a problem.

II

Granted the nominal definition of the a priori, non-pure a priori knowledge will have to be independent of all experience and even of all sense-impressions. Were it not so, it would not be a priori knowledge at all. There will, on the other hand, have to be something 'empirical', 'mixed in with' such a knowledge. Were it not so, it would be pure, and not non-pure a priori knowledge. How can we, however, understand that both of these seemingly incompatible requirements are fulfilled?

Unfortunately, we are not entitled to dismiss this problem by referring to the class of analytic propositions in which empirically given concepts are analyzed. (Being analytic, such propositions would certainly be a priori, but not pure, as the conceptual content to be analyzed is drawn from experience itself). The reason why this is impossible lies in the very status of the proposition given as an example of non-pure a priori knowledge by Kant himself, namely the proposition: 'all change has its cause'. It goes without saying, that this proposition, being a somewhat reduced formula of the principle of causality, is a synthetic proposition. To deny this would amount to reducing both Hume's and Kant's problem to formal logic, and this certainly is absurd. Such a reduction would amount to a complete misunderstanding of the concept of 'change'. To take the principle of causality as analytic would mean to regard the concept of 'change' as equivalent to the concept of 'effect'. The principle would then read: all change, viz. every effect has its cause. The proposition 'every effect has its cause' certainly *is* analytic, but how can we give reasons for asserting that all change *is* an effect? Exactly this was Hume's question. Kant, in taking up this very question, agrees with Hume that the assertion that all change *is* an effect cannot be justified by an analysis of the concept of change itself. He disagrees with Hume as to the possibility of proving the principle of causality on rational grounds, contending that this principle must and can be proved to be both synthetic and a priori. He insists, however, that it serves as an example of a non-pure synthetic a priori proposition.

Are there other examples? The Kant scholar will remember that within Kant's critical system there exists a part entitled *Metaphysical Foundations of Science*. It is commonly acknowledged that the principles outlined there must be, and actually were considered by Kant himself, as propositions which are both synthetic a priori and not pure.[1] If we accept the program of the *Metaphysical Foundations*, we will also have to accept a system of synthetic and a priori propositions which are non-pure, because they concern movement of an object in space. If we reject such a program, we need not *ipso facto* reject the idea of the *Critique* itself. The *Critique* is not identical with, but rather serves as the premise of, such propositions. In neither of the two cases, however, will we have given an adequate account of the problem in question, for it goes without saying that the principle of causality is conceived of by Kant as one of the premises of the metaphysical principles of science, and not as itself one of these principles. It is an instance of that very class of synthetic and a priori propositions, whose validity is the main subject of the *Critique* itself. As one of the 'principles of pure understanding', viz. the second Analogy of Experience, it can be justified only in the transcendental part of the critical theory of knowledge which outlines the possibility of objects of experience in general, without presupposing any actual experience of objects. Should the principle of causality now be qualified as a non-pure synthetic a priori proposition, then the famous question of the *Critique* would necessarily imply the sub-question: "How are non-pure synthetic a priori judgments possible?" The *Critique* itself, and no other part of Kant's critical system, will have to answer this very question.

III

It might now be objected that the *Critique*, being the transcendental part of the critical theory of knowledge, is understood by Kant to be a *pure* science and therefore cannot possibly dwell on non-pure synthetic propositions a priori. Kant himself actually tires his readers somewhat with statements like that on B 28, where he says, that the most important point in transcendental philosophy is that no concepts are used which contain anything empirical; or that knowledge a priori which is treated in transcendental philosophy must be completely pure. According to this idea of the status of the *Critique*, we now are confronted with the following alternative: Either we shall have to dismiss Kant's suggestion in B 3 that the principle of causality is a non-pure synthetic a priori proposition, or give up the idea that the *Critique* deals only with pure propositions. I am, however, afraid that we shall have to dismiss the idea, commonly accepted by both disciples and critics of Kant, that transcendental philosophy cannot possibly contain non-pure a priori judgments. What I am suggesting, is exactly this: *If* the principle of causality is to be conceived of as a synthetic a priori proposition at all, then it must necessarily be taken as non-pure. Before giving a proof of this, a general outline of the problem as it now stands might be useful.

IV

Inasmuch as the proposition is claimed to be both synthetic a priori and non-pure, the synthesis of the subject-concept and the predicate-concept must take place independently of all experience. Were it not so, the proposition would not be synthetic and a priori at all. In order to be non-pure, either one or both of these concepts must be qualified as not being independent of all experience or sense-perceptions. One or both concepts will therefore have to be related to what Kant calls empirical intuition or sense-perception (*Wahrnehmung*). Were it not so, the proposition would not be a non-pure synthetic a priori proposition.

Kant himself, it will be remembered, seems to suggest an interpretation of this very relation, which only at first sight looks promising. In interpreting what makes the proposition in question non-pure, he says, that its subject-concept (change) is 'drawn from experience'. A concept 'drawn from experience' will be a *conceptus communis empiricus*, the content of which is 'abstracted' from specific sense-perceptions. It can now easily be shown that such a concept cannot possibly serve as a term in a synthetic

a priori proposition at all, be it pure or non-pure. Certainly it may serve
as a term in synthetic propositions which are empirical and therefore
imply a synthesis which is due to sense-perception itself. But we cannot
conceive of any other synthesis with regard to empirically given concepts
without running into a rationalism of the very worst sort. How can we
justify the idea of a synthesis a priori in non-pure synthetic a priori propositions? We will have to show that those concepts which are to serve as
terms in non-pure synthetic propositions a priori are opposed to empirically given concepts in that their *content* cannot be derived from
specific sense-perceptions. And yet these concepts still have to be *related*
to sense-perceptions in a way which allows for the proposition to be non-
pure.

V

Within Kant's theory of concepts the only group which might be claimed
to be qualified in this way is the group of the so-called 'predicables' of
pure understanding, the idea of which is given in A 81 = B 107 f. As to
their content, the predicables will be pure concepts, since they contain a
combination of primary pure concepts, the categories, and modes of pure
intuition respectively. What Kant now suggests, in his rather fragmentary
theory of the predicables, is that, although we can and must give an a
priori account of their conceptual content and thus are forbidden to
regard them as abstracted from experience, we cannot use them meaningfully in knowledge without perceiving something to which they apply. We
will therefore have to say in Kantian terms: the 'content' of the concept
which makes a proposition a non-pure synthetic a priori proposition will
have to be pure, but the 'objective reality' of such a concept will be
grounded in empirical intuition or sense-perception. In saying so, we will
have given an interpretation of the exact meaning of Kant's statement,
that something empirical is 'mixed in with' a non-pure synthetic a priori
proposition. If we can, with Kantian means, give any reasonable interpretation of such propositions, their crucial concepts must be predicables.
The very possibility of a synthesis a priori within such a proposition
would otherwise be altogether inconceivable. This is confirmed by Kant
himself, for among the predicables outlined in the *Critique* we find, as
indeed we now should expect, the very concept of change. 'Change' is
described as one of the predicables of the modal categories and defined in

the following way: "Change is the connection of contradictorially opposed determinations in the existence of one and the same thing" (B 291)[3].

VI

It would be a question all its own, by what argument all the elements of such a definition can be claimed to be 'pure'. Certainly the concept of time is involved in it, since time renders intelligible the very possibility of such a connection. Time, however, will here have to be time as one of the forms of pure intuition. The crucial point will be how to conceive of the concept of existence (*Dasein*) as a pure concept at all. To put this question is, however, only another way of coming back to the problem involved in Kant's contention, that predicables can be used meaningfully only when substantiated by the awareness of something to which they apply. What then is the relation to sense-perception which permits, according to Kant, the meaningful use of the concept of change? We will be inclined to answer that something which changes must be perceived. This idea, however, would be highly misleading. Again according to Kant, that which changes, is itself permanent. Change (*Veränderung*) is to be conceived of as alternation (*Wechsel*) or succession of states (*Zustände*) in 'a permanent' (*Beharrliches*). The concept of change therefore analytically implies the concept of substance which renders intelligible the very idea of something which changes while its states are exchanged. According to Kant's interpretation of the proof of the *first* Analogy of Experience, it is by means of *synthetically* referring the category of substance to the very concept of mere alternation (*Wechsel*) that we give this concept an *objective* meaning, the meaning of change itself (*Veränderung*). A reduced formula of the first Analogy would therefore be: "All alternation is change" (B 223). In order to make intelligible the very *meaning* of the *subject-concept* of the *second* Analogy (change), the *proof* of the *first* Analogy will there have to be presupposed. (Exactly this formal relation would be the systematic coherence of the first and the second Analogies. A similar relation accounts for the place of the third Analogy). We should therefore not say that in order to use the concept of change meaningfully, something which changes must be perceived. We should rather say, that something permitting the proof which gives the concept of alternation (*Wechsel*) an objective meaning, namely the meaning of change (*Verän-*

derung), must be perceived. This something to be perceived is not the proof. This proof (the proof of the first Analogy) will rationalize the concept of alternation (*Wechsel*) without referring to any sense-perceptions except those which must be assumed for any meaningful use of the concept of alternation itself. We will, however, now have to insist that the concept of alternation must have a meaning of its own, a meaning which is different from its objectivation or transformation into the concept of change. Were it not so, the concept of alternation would analytically contain the concept of change, *viz.* the concept of substance. The first Analogy would then be an analytic proposition, but this would amount to another complete misunderstanding, namely of Hume's and Kant's problem with substance.

Looking at the conceptual content of the concept of alternation, it will also have to be regarded as a predicable of modality, the definition of which would be: Existence (*Dasein*) of contradictorially opposed qualities as such. What then, we have now to ask, is the relation of the predicable 'alternation' to sense-perception which, according to Kant, is required to use this concept meaningfully at all? In answering this question, we will also answer the same question with regard to the concept of change, since what distinguishes change from alternation is *not* its relation to sense-perception in general nor to any specific class of sense-perceptions.

VII

There can be no other answer than that we can use the concept of alternation meaningfully only on the condition that we refer to the fact of being aware of a plurality of qualities. This does not mean that we must be aware of a specifically ordered group of qualities as opposed to other groups. Were it so, both the concept of alternation and the concept of change would be abstracted from this very group and hence be empirically given. To be aware of qualities as such does not, however, imply any further empirically given specification of the qualities in question, since to be aware of them means nothing other than to be aware of a mere manifold of qualities. Such an awareness is identical with the fact that more than one sense-impression is 'given', or that there are perceptions at all. It is on the basis of the plurality of sense-impressions that we conceive of qualities, and these will be contradictorially opposed to each other insofar as they follow each other in what Kant calls 'subjective apprehension'. It will therefore be the very fact of impressions following one another in 'inner sense' which *is* the relation to sense-perception of which we must be aware, if we are entitled to use the concept of alternation, and hence of change, meaningfully at all. That is to say: in order to use them, we have to refer to the very givenness of a manifold in *empirical*, and not in pure intuition, but we will not be obliged to refer to any further qualifications in empirical intuition.

VIII

If we want to try to prove a proposition, we must at least take it for granted that its subject-concept has a meaningful use of its own (we are, with Kant, no admirers of strictly dialectical propositions). If the Analogies can be proved to be synthetic a priori propositions, they will therefore have to be taken as non-pure, since their subject-concepts cannot be used meaningfully without reference to the fact that we have in empirical intuition more than one sense-impression. This fact cannot be deduced by force of any argument a priori within Kant's theory of knowledge. We should, however, take into consideration that without being aware of such a fact, the formal condition which must be fulfilled if categories of *relation* are to be predicated of subject-concepts at all, would be altogether lacking. It will be the subject-concepts of the Analogies, and not their predicates (the categories of relation), which will have to satisfy this very condition. As this condition is one and the same in the subject-concepts of all Analogies, they form a system of their own, distinguished from the mathematical principles. This system will be a system of non-pure synthetic a priori propositions within the *Critique of Pure Reason*, if it is a system of synthetic a priori propositions at all. Any attempt to give a proof that it is, should take this fact into consideration from the very beginning.

University of Heidelberg

NOTES

[1] Cf. P. Plaass, *Kants Theorie der Naturwissenschaft*, Göttingen, 1965, and the excellent application of P. Strawson's view of Kant to this problem in Ralph C. S. Walker's paper on 'The Status of Kant's Theory of Matter', published in these *Kant Proceedings*, p. 591.

² Cf. K. Cramer, *Zur systematischen Differenz von Apriorität und Reinheit in Kants Lehre von den synthetischen Urteilen a priori, Subjectivität und Metaphysik, Festschrift für W. Cramer*, Frankfurt, 1966 p. 23 ff.

³ A more elaborate account of Kant's theory of the predicables and the systematic problems connected with it in: K. Cramer *loc. cit.*, p. 28 ff.

GERHARD KNAUSS

EXTENSIONAL AND INTENSIONAL INTERPRETATION OF SYNTHETIC PROPOSITIONS A PRIORI

In the following I try to make sense of the controversy about the syntheticity of arithmetical propositions by a new interpretation. In doing so I point out that I am not of the opinion that the problem of the synthetic a priori is a dead issue as C. I. Lewis declared in 1946 and others before him and after him. I am also of the opinion that a problem which has been thought over for so long, so intensively and by such outstanding people, can not be solved by a simple yes or no decision. There must be something in the problem which justifies both answers.

Kant never speaks about arithmetical propositions in a way deviating from the idea that they are synthetical propositions a priori. But he offers different arguments at different places in his writings. In modern terminology one could group them as follows: the synthetic is located in the starting propositions and is transmitted by each demonstration; it is located in the procedure of demonstration; it is located in the arithmetical proposition itself independently of starting propositions and procedure of demonstration.[1] Occasionally he even abandons one of these arguments in favor of another.[2] Correspondingly the arguments which the critics produce against his thesis are manifold and various.

Likewise we find a variety of characterisations of 'analytic' and 'synthetic' in the texts. In spite of these fluctuations there remains one essential point, without which all the further distinctions become irrelevant for the main concern of the *Critique of Pure Reason*. This is that the predicate is or is not contained in the subject. All the other characterisations which Kant mentions (yet not all the modern ones) finally amount to this. This definition, however, presupposes a certain ontology. For, what kind of qualifications must subject and predicate have, so that the one can be contained in the other? Obviously they can not be objects or terms or expressions.

For Kant they are, following the tradition, concepts. Therefore the Kantian concept of analytic and synthetic is bound to his concept of concept. 'Analytic' and 'synthetic' are only defined for judgments which have concepts as subject and predicate. Nowadays concepts have nearly vanished from the arsenal of philosophy. No doubt this fact alone makes it difficult for modern authors to seize the Kantian problem. On the other hand this connection between the analytic/synthetic dichotomy and an ontology shows that the formal criterion of classifying propositions into analytical and synthetical can not be used to derive ontological distinctions. It is impossible to develop an ontology out of the analysis of propositions. On the contrary such ontological distinctions and assumptions are a condition for the meaningful setting up of such criteria of propositions.

The traditional concept of concept distinguishes between concept-content (*complexus*) and concept-extent (*ambitus*) and Kant took over this distinction. He is sticking to it in his usage of the expression 'contain'. "The more a concept contains *under* itself, the less it contains *in* itself and vice versa" (*Logik*, § 7). The 'under' relates to what comes under the concept-extent (i.e. the objects of the concept), the 'in' relates to what belongs to the concept-content (the marks of the concept).[3] Obviously concepts may be broader, narrower or equal both in their content and their extent; and the question will be which aspect Kant means when he calls a proposition analytical or synthetical. He himself does not explicitly put this question, nor do his interpreters as far as I can see. Nevertheless there are textual hints of what he had in mind.

Concepts for Kant are, as we know, products of the spontaneity of the understanding. The unities which are constituted by the concepts are functions of the understanding, specifying the compositional rules for representations belonging to one another. The conceptual unity, on the one hand, is a synthetic act, proceeding from transcendental apperception (which is itself constituted as a unity only by an act of synthesis); on the other hand, as a constituted unity it is detachable from the synthetic act.

The above aspects are to be recognized in the Kantian number-concept. The concept of a number is given to us only by a successive synthesis in time, but the number so constituted as object of arithmetic is detachable from the concept-constitution and independent of time. As the concepts of mathematics are all 'made' concepts both in form and matter (*conceptus factitii*), numbers must be made too. This 'making' is nothing but the synthesis of the arithmetical operations, addition, subtraction, division etc. 'Synthesis' means not only the progressive enumeration of the positive numbers; subtraction too is a synthesis (Ak. ed. X, 555). The numbers are not simply existing like Platonic ideas; but if and when they are constituted, they are independent of their generation. The objects of arithmetic, therefore, are not subject to conditions of temporal synthesis, but only their being given in representation is.[4] The precondition for the independence of numbers from the synthesis of their generation according to Kant is based on the possibility of apprehending the manifold forward and backward (Refl. 6314), i.e. in the plurality of possible syntheses that lead to the same number. "Because in the inner sense (i.e. time) everything is successive and nothing can be taken backward, the reason for the possibility of the latter (namely to apprehend forward and backward) must be based on the relation of our representations to something outside of us, which in itself is not only inner representation, that is form of appearance, but object in itself (*Sache an sich*). The possibility thereof can not be explained" (Refl. 6312). Further on Kant argues that in spite of the individuality of the synthesis of numbers "the use of the number afterwards is general" (B 205). A synthesis once performed does not need to be performed again and again. It is valid once and for all, and the symbolic construction by which it can be replaced represents the general application.

Any concept, and therefore a concept of number, is possible only by means of a judgment, but the judgment is not the concept itself but only "the act by which it becomes real" (*Falsche Spitzfindigkeit* § 6). The judgments constituting number-concepts are those equations which Kant calls number-formulae, for instance $7 + 5 = 12$. They, not the progressive sequence of natural numbers, are the true elements of arithmetic. For Kant the number-formulae have the characteristics of axioms though he does not call them axioms, because they are not general and because there is an infinite number of them whereas Kant takes for granted the traditional idea that we may not assume an infinity of axioms.[5] The number-formulae form an infinite set of individuals which can not be deduced from each other. It is not essential for the number-formula $7 + 5 = 12$ that therein we have a definition of number 12 – we could as well say that we have a definition of $7 + 5$.

Now, what does it mean to assert that $7 + 5 = 12$ is synthetic? According to the above characterisation, it means: the concept of '12' is not contained in the concept of '7 + 5'. Obviously this can not mean that 12 is more than 7 + 5. If the 12 contains anything that the 7 + 5 does not contain or vice versa, then we have no longer an equation. He explicitly declares: "...in an arithmetical judgement, that is an equation, both concepts ... must be throughout *conceptus reciproci* and objectively totally identical" (Ak. ed. X, 556). In spite of this identity the judgment is not analytical. How are we to understand this?

The key is to be found in the expression *conceptus reciproci*. According to *Logik* § 12 these are concepts that have the same extent (*Umfang*). The concepts of '7 + 5' and '12', therefore, have the *same* extent but *different* content. They are objectively identical, subjectively different (Ak. ed. X, 555). What is the meaning of 'subjective' in this context?

Kant wants to say that we can form concepts of the same quantity (*Grösse*) by different kinds of compositions, that is by different kinds of arithmetical operations, and these concepts are objectively identical because they refer to the same quantity, however subjectively different because of the different compositional syntheses through which we think of those quantities. We can think of the same quantity 8 by 3 + 5, by 12 − 4, by 2·4 or 2³. Though all these expressions determine the same objective quantity, the subjective 'thought' '3 + 5', '12 − 4', '2·4', '2³' are different. None of these thoughts is contained in the other, though they all have the same 'value' (*Wert*). If Kant maintains 3 + 5 = 8 to be synthetical, the syntheticity refers only to the subjective side. Through subjectively different compositions we refer to the same objective quantity.

Using the language of concepts this amounts to saying: the number-concepts in arithmetical propositions are reciprocal relative to their extent (objectively identical), different however relative to their content (subjectively different). Apparently when he uses the analytic/synthetic dichotomy Kant has in mind only the concept-content, otherwise he would be compelled to explain the arithmetical propositions as subjectively synthetical, objectively analytical.

This interpretation is supported by the Kantian usage of "contained in" and "contained under". In all relevant contexts he says that the predicate-concept is contained or not contained *in* the subject-concept. To be contained *in* refers always to the concept-content. Were he to speak about the extent in connexion with the arithmetical propositions, he would have to use 'contained under'; and the proper formulation would be as following: What is contained under the predicate-concept, is equally contained under the subject-concept.

This exposition of the problem which Kant presents in the letter to his friend Schultz in 1788, after Schultz had expressed some doubts about the arguments of the *Critique* seems to me the most mature and convincing and perhaps it may be considered as Kant's final standpoint on this question. He repeats it once more in the correspondence with Rehberg in 1790 (Ak. ed. XI, 205f.). Moreover, this exposition appears to me rather interesting, because Frege a hundred years later sets out from the same starting point.

Frege is starting with the distinction between sense and reference (*Sinn und Bedeutung*) of expressions. "2^4 and $4 \cdot 4$ do have the same reference, that is they are proper names of the same number, but they do not have the same sense."[6] The same number may be given to us in different ways or we have different apprehensions of it, and that constitutes a different sense. Seen from the opposite direction: the number is the identical reference of the different number-apprehensions. But the number is never given as such, and with the different apprehensions there is always connected a different sense. '16' is an apprehension too like '2^4' or '$4 \cdot 4$'. The distinction between sense and reference is to be applied not only to apprehensions of numbers, but also to propositions and equations such as the Kantian number-formulae. "Consequently $2^4 = 4^2$ and $4 \cdot 4 = 4^2$ do have the same reference, however not the same sense" (*Ibid.* p. 25). Frege continues to tell us that in each number-formula a different thought is contained (*Ibid.* p. 25). If we replace the Fregian 'sense' by the Kantian 'concept-content' and the Fregian 'reference' by the Kantian 'concept-extent', we arrive at our above interpretation.

But the difference between Frege and Kant is unmistakable. Frege is a Platonist. For him the numbers have to be given to us; they are not constituted by a synthesis of the understanding; they have objective existence in a realm of their own. For him one is mistaken to believe "that he who pronounces a judgment is constituting the connexion and the order...".[7] Whereas the transcendental philosopher is mainly concerned with the subjective aspect of the problem (sense), the mathematician is concerned with the objective (reference). Therefore the introduction of the distinction between sense and reference dos not prevent Frege from expounding, against Kant, the analytical character of the number-formulae.[8]

SUMMARY

Kant is basing his understanding of arithmetic on the number-formulae. They are propositions with concepts as subject and predicate. His concept of concept is ambiguous. This ambiguity is the reason for the appearance of the controversy about the syntheticity of arithmetical propositions. Subject-concept and predicate-concept are objectively identical, nevertheless Kant propounds the syntheticity. There is only one way out: if we assume that he uses 'concept' with a twofold meaning. Whenever he maintains identity, he is looking out extensionally for the extents, whenever he maintains syntheticity he is looking out intensionally for the content. The controversy has its origin in the fact that Kant's orientation is mainly intensional, that of his critics however extensional.

University of Heidelberg

NOTES

[1] Cf. L. W. Beck, *Studies in the Philosophy of Kant*, pp. 74ff.
[2] Cf. H. J. Paton, *Kant's Metaphysic of Experience II*, p. 130.
[3] Beck points to the difference between 'contain in' and 'contain under' (*op. cit.*, p. 77) but does not clear up its meaning.
[4] Reflexion zur Mathematik No. 13 (Ak. ed. XIV).
[5] In the letter to Schultz he calls them 'postulates' (Ak. ed. X, 556).
[6] Frege, 'Funktion und Begriff', in *Funktion, Begriff, Bedeutung* (ed. by Patzig, Göttingen, 1967), p. 25.
[7] *Kleine Schriften* (Darmstadt, 1967), p. 371.
[8] I cannot find any text where Frege expresses himself in another way, as Searle seems to believe ('Proper Names', in *Philosophical Logic* [ed. by P. F. Strawson, 1967], p. 89).

R. M. MARTIN

ON KANT, FREGE, ANALYTICITY AND
THE THEORY OF REFERENCE

One of the most famous passages in the *Critique of Pure Reason* -- among
logicians anyhow – is that in the Introduction concerned with the distinction between analytic and synthetic judgments. This passage seems not to
have been commented on to any extent, however, by proponents of the
modern semantical theory of reference, stemming from the work of
Frege, Carnap, and Tarski. History must continually be looked at in the
light of present knowledge, as Whitehead has suggested. The modest task
of the present paper is merely to examine Kant's distinction in the light
of modern semantics.

First let us remind ourselves of the distinction in Kant's own words.

In all judgments in which there is a relation between subject and predicate (I speak of
affirmative judgments only, the application to negative ones being easy)

he writes, it will be recalled,

that relation can be of two kinds. Either the predicate *B* belongs to the subject *A* as
something contained (though covertly) in the concept *A*; or *B* lies outside the sphere of
the concept *A*, though somehow connected with it. In the former case I call the judgment *analytical*, in the latter *synthetical* . . . The former might be called *illustrating*, the
latter *expanding* judgments, because in the former nothing is added by the predicate to
the concept of the subject...; while the latter adds to the concept of the subject a
predicate not conceived as existing within it, and not to be extracted from it by any
process of analysis.... (B 10)

The question arises as to whether this distinction as drawn in this way
can be substantiated on the basis of modern semantical theory. Let us
attempt to answer this question in the affirmative. But first, a kind of
'rational reconstruction' of what appears to be essentially Kant's view.

By 'semantics' is meant here merely the theory of reference, designation,
denotation, or whatever. Given such a theory, in its peroration notions of
truth, logical or analytic truth, logical or analytic equivalence, entailment,
and the like, are forthcoming by definition. But this is all an old story,
oft-told, and in many different ways.[1] One way is in terms of *multiple*

denotation, taken as a primitive on the basis of a first-order logic only. Another, that of Carnap, is in terms of *designation* on the basis of a higher-order logic. And still a third, that of Tarski and of model theorists, is in terms of *satisfaction* defined in a higher-order logic or set theory. Any one of these methods could be presupposed in what follows, although the first is the favored one, presupposing as it does a much simpler underlying logic.

It might be thought that Kant's account is quite satisfactory as it stands and that no revamping of it in the light of recent developments is needed. If one takes the account literally as it stands, however, several difficulties arise. In the first place, it is not too clear *precisely* what a *concept* is. Kant speaks of the subject *A* and of the predicate *B* as 'concepts', and he speaks of one as being 'contained' in the other, or as lying 'outside the sphere' of the other. No doubt subjects and predicates as linguistic entities, on the one hand, should sharply be distinguished from the concepts of or belonging to them, on the other. Concepts, as distinguished from linguistic entities such as subjects and predicates, are the sorts of entities we know all about until asked to give an *exact* account of them in the manner of modern semantics. And until such an account is given it is difficult to know what it means to say that one is 'contained' in the other.

In *Belief, Existence, and Meaning* a theory of various kinds of *intensions* has been suggested that may well be of service here.[2] Consider, for example, the notion of the *objective analytic intension* – roughly, the 'meaning' or 'connotation' – of a one-place predicate *a*, the ObjAnlytcInt(*a*). Strictly, this notion is defined, it will be remembered, only in contexts in which a so-called *nominal virtual class* is said to be a *member* of the ObjAnlytcInt(*a*). The problem then arises as to what it means to say that the ObjAnlytcInt(*a*) is *contained in*, say, the ObjAnlytcInt(*b*), where *b* is also a one-place predicate. One might hope to be able to define an expression for this by requiring that every member of ObjAnlytcInt(*a*) is also a member of ObjAnlytcInt(*b*). But this requirement would be meaningless, for it involves quantification over virtual classes, and even nominal ones at that. It will be recalled that the very notion of being a *virtual* class is such as to prohibit a quantifier over it. Thus the kind of definition suggested simply will not work.

There is another tack, however, that looks promising. Let us say that a one-place predicate a is *analytically included* in a predicate b provided the following sentence is itself analytic: the sentence consisting of the universal quantifier upon some variable, say 'x', i.e., '(x)', followed by '(' followed by a followed by 'x' as argument followed by ' $\supset$ ' followed by b followed by 'x' followed by ')'. Note that this clause merely spells out the structural-descriptive name of the required universal conditional. It is presupposed of course, as already remarked, that a suitable definition of 'analytic sentence' or 'logically true sentence' is forthcoming. One can then say that the ObjAnlytcInt(a) is 'contained in' the ObjAnlytcInt(b) provided, for all one-place predicates c, if a is analytically included in c then b is also.

Concepts for present purposes are being taken merely as objective analytic intensions of one-place predicates. This is a reasonable identification, for differences in intension between concepts can then be handled easily enough within the semantics involved. And one can of course pass on to concepts of two-place, three-place, and so on, predicates as needed.

If the foregoing identifications and definitions are sound, what amounts essentially to Kant's *definition* is forthcoming as a *theorem*. A universal conditional to the effect that a is analytically included in b is analytic if and only if the ObjAnlytcInt(b) is contained in the ObjAnlytcInt(a). One can prove this, going from left to right, by noting the transitivity principle for analytic inclusion, and from right to left, by noting that b is analytically included in itself. It is interesting to observe that this theorem incorporates a kind of law of *inverse variation*, 'the law of Kant', as Peirce called it.[3]

What now, strictly, is an ObjAnlytcInt(a)? Kant's law has been stated but expressions for objective analytic intensions have not been defined except in contexts in which one is said to be 'contained' in another. This is all that is required for the statement of the law itself. To get a better picture of what objective analytic intensions are, however, let us define also what it means to say that a given virtual class is a *member* of one. Roughly, a virtual class F is a member of the ObjAnlytcInt(a) if and only if a is a one-place predicate constant and there is a b such that $b = $ 'F' and a is analytically included in b. Here the 'F' occurring on the left-hand side, in the definiendum, occurs in a very special way, the 'F' on the right-hand side, the definiens, occurring only in single quotes. Hence in the definiendum, one speaks of F as being a *nominal* virtual class,

more specifically, as the virtual class *F as thus designated*. The whole
theory of objective analytic intensions may be developed then in terms of
just the two contexts introduced together with such further ones as are
definable in terms of these.

Incidentally, by 'analytic truth' here one means something quite
innocent, merely logical truth with abbreviatory definitions of complex
predicates allowing the replacement of definientia by definienda and
conversely wherever desired.

In the *Prolegomena* (§2), Kant gives the notion of analytic truth a more
pragmatic twist, on the one hand, and a more Fregean one, on the other,
than in the *Critique of Pure Reason*. "Analytical judgments express
nothing in the predicate but what has been *already actually thought*
[italics added] in the concept of the subject, though not so distinctly or
with the same (full) consciousness," he writes. The pragmatic emphasis
on what is actually thought is of course quite foreign to the purely
semantical account in the *Critique*. In the *Prolegomena* there is also the
point that "all analytical judgments depend wholly on the law of Contradiction, ..." To be sure, essentially this point is made in the *Critique*
(B.190) also, although not quite so explicitly, it would seem. It has
frequently been noted that the law of contradiction, all by itself in solitary
splendor, is rather barren of deductive consequences. If, however, one
adds to it, as Frege does in the *Grundlagen der Arithmetik* (1884), "all
laws of a general logical character," one makes analytic judgments
depend wholly on the laws of logic, a thoroughly modern conception.

Kant's two ways of drawing the distinction between 'analytic' and
'synthetic' correspond roughly with the modern distinction between the
semantical and the purely syntactical accounts. The account in terms of
'concepts' and the relation of *being contained in* is a semantical one, as
noted. The other account is in terms of the syntactical notion of dependence or logical consequence.

It is interesting that Frege, in the *Grundlagen*, states, in a footnote, it
will be recalled, that he does not "mean to assign a new sense to these
terms, but only to state accurately what earlier writers, Kant in particular,
have meant by them."[4] His actual definitions, however, seem rather
removed from those of the *Critique* and much closer to those of the
Prolegomena.

"Now these distinctions between a priori and a posteriori, synthetic and analytic, concern, as I see it," Frege writes in a famous passage worth quoting in full,

not the content of the judgment but the justification for making the judgment. Where there is no such justification, the possibility of drawing the distinction vanishes... Where a proposition is called a posteriori or analytic in my sense, this is not a judgment about the conditions... which have made it possible to form the content of the proposition in our consciousness; nor is it a judgment about the way in which some other man has come, perhaps erroneously, to believe it true; rather it is a judgment about the ultimate ground upon which rests the justification for holding it to be true.
This means that the question is removed from the sphere of psychology,

Frege goes on,

and assigned, if the truth concerned is a mathematical one, to the sphere of mathematics. The problem becomes, in fact, that of finding the proof of the proposition, and of following it right back to the primitive truths. If, in carrying out this process, we come only on general logical laws and on definitions, then the truth is an analytic one, bearing in mind that we must take account also of all the propositions upon which the admissibility of any of the definitions depends. If, however, it is impossible to give the proof without making use of truths which are not of a general logical nature, but belong to the sphere of some special science, then the proposition is a synthetic one. ...[5]

This passage contains the whole of Frege's doctrine of analytic truth. In the earlier *Begriffsschrift* (1879), there is just one reference to Kant, namely, that a "judgment as to equality of content is, in Kant's sense, synthetic."[6] This reference occurs in a context (§8) concerned with how to interpret the identity or equivalence sign, and although it flirts with the notion of analyticity, it does not come to grips with it directly.

It is interesting that when Frege returns to the subject of the proper interpretation of the identity sign, in *Über Sinn und Bedeutung* (1892), there is no reference to Kant at all.[7] Nor is there, apparently, in the great *Grundgesetze der Arithmetik*.[8] In the *Grundlagen*, to be sure, there is further reference to Kant on matters concerned with number and geometry, but none, other than that cited, on the distinction between analytic and synthetic.

Can the two accounts of analyticity, that of Kant in the *Critique* and the Kant-Frege version of the *Prolegomena* and the *Grundlagen*, be reconciled?

The foregoing 'rational reconstruction' of the view of the *Critique* is in fact an attempt at reconciliation. Kant's definition is there turned into a law of inverse variation concerning intensions or meanings, and these latter in turn depend fundamentally upon going back to 'general logical laws' including definitions. The whole theory is given systematic form within a given semantical metalanguage and for specified object languages.

The foregoing version of Kant's law is given within a semantics employing virtual classes. It is, one might say, an Aristotelian version. A Platonic version, with real classes in place of virtual ones, may also be given, as noted at the beginning, with only slight changes and using a more powerful underlying logic.

Note that Kant's law is concerned only with Aristotelian A-propositions, of universal conditional form. Can it be extended to atomic sentences in the sense of modern logic? Well, if all individual constants are eliminated in favor of additional or defined predicates, so that 'Socrates is wise' is handled as 'Everything that socratizes is wise', where 'socratizes' is the new predicate, the extension is automatic. Here it must follow from the definitions that 'socratizes' is analytically included in 'wise'. Frege queries this very point, in the *Grundlagen* (p. 100), where he remarks that Kant's

> division of judgments into analytic and synthetic is not exhaustive. What he is thinking of is the universal affirmative judgment; there, we can speak of a subject concept and ask – as his definition requires – whether the predicate concept is contained in it or not. But how can we do this if the subject is an individual object? Or if the judgment is an existential one? In these cases there can simply be no question of a subject concept in Kant's sense. ...

Although Frege regarded the truths of arithmetic as analytic, those of geometry, physical geometry anyhow, he regarded in the *Grundlagen* as both synthetic and *a priori,* as Kant did. In spite of significant differences there was much agreement on this point between the two, at least in the days of the *Grundlagen*. It is interesting to note what seems to be Frege's final estimate of his great predecessor, again in the *Grundlagen* (pp. 101-2):

> I have no wish to incur the reproach of picking petty quarrels with a genius to whom we must all look up with grateful awe; I feel bound, therefore, to call attention also to the extent of my agreement with him, which far exceeds any disagreement. To touch only upon what is immediately relevant, I consider Kant did great service in drawing the distinction between synthetic and analytic judgments. In calling the truths of geometry synthetic and a priori, he revealed their true nature. And this is still worth repeating, since even today [1884] it is often not recognized. If Kant was wrong about arithmetic, that does not seriously detract, in my opinion, from the value of his work.

His point was, that there are such things as synthetic judgments *a priori*; whether they are to be found in geometry only, or in arithmetic as well, is of less importance.

In his later discussion, in 1903, however, of Hilbert's axiomatization of Euclidian geometry, Frege drops all mention of Kant, and very likely also the doctrine that geometrical truths are synthetic *a priori*.[9] In any case, there is no further mention of the doctrine, Frege's interest having shifted to a full-fledged attack on Hilbert.

Nothing has been said thus far of Carnap's *meaning postulates*.[10] Suppose 'body' and 'extended' are two one-place predicates. Is the sentence 'All bodies are extended' – Kant's example in the *Prolegomena* – analytic or not? Much depends upon the way in which these predicates are introduced, whether by definition or as primitives. If by definition, one must expand the sentence until only primitives are reached. The sentence 'All bodies are extended' is then analytic if the result of such expansion is a logical truth. Suppose, however, that both predicates are primitives of the language. The sentence cannot then be a logical truth, but could figure as a meaning postulate if desired. One could call it 'primitively analytic', allowing it to incorporate a decision, as Carnap would put it, to use 'body' and 'extended' in such a way that 'All bodies are extended' holds wholly in view of the meanings of the constituent words. If, on the other hand, this is not the decision, and one regards the sentence merely as an empirical law and not as a meaning postulate, then it would be called 'synthetic'.

Kant's logic has frequently been accused of psychologism. No less an authority than Father Bocheński, for example, in his *History of Formal Logic*,[11] after quoting a passage from Jungius, states that

formed by this logic and its [psychologistic] prejudices, modern philosophers such as ... Wolff, Kant, Hegel etc. could have no interest for the historian of formal logic. When compared with the logicians of the 4th century B.C., the 13th and 20th centuries A.D. they were simply ignorant of what pertains to logic [and of what does not] and for the most part only knew what they found in the Port Royal Logic.

This is a severe indictment, and surely an unjust one if the foregoing account, devoid of any taint of psychologism, is even an approximative reconstruction of the purely semantical aspects of Kant's views on analyticity.

New York University

NOTES

[1] See the author's *Truth and Denotation* (1958), University of Chicago Press, Chicago.
[2] See the author's *Belief, Existence, and Meaning* (1969), Chapter VII, New York University Press, New York.
[3] *Collected Papers*, 2.400, fn. 2.
[4] F. Frege, *The Foundations of Arithmetic* (1950), §3, Blackwell, Oxford.
[5] *Ibid,*
[6] In *Translations from the Philosophic Writings of Gottlob Frege* (1952), p. 21, Blackwell, Oxford.
[7] *Ibid.*, pp. 56–78.
[8] Reprinted by Georg Olms (1962), Hildesheim.
[9] 'Über die Grundlagen der Geometrie', *Jahresbericht der Deutschen Mathematiker-Vereinigung* XII (1903): 319–324 and 368–375.
[10] See R. Carnap, *Meaning and Necessity* (1956), Appendix 2, University of Chicago Press, Chicago.
[11] University of Notre Dame Press, Notre Dame (1961), p. 258.

PART IV

SPACE

IVOR LECLERC

THE MEANING OF 'SPACE' IN KANT

My concern in this paper is with the meaning of the word 'space' –
spatium, der Raum – in Kant's usage. This is not an attempt merely at
another exposition of Kant's doctrine of space as transcendentally ideal
and empirically real. I want to get at the meaning of the word as Kant
understood it. This is worth doing, I suggest, since we tend to approach
Kant's theory with a meaning which has become implicit as a result of the
virtually complete dominance of the Newtonian inheritance from the
early nineteenth century onward. In our time the noun 'space', '*der
Raum*', implicitly carries the connotation of some sort of entity. This was
not so with the word *spatium* – 'space' in English – in its original meaning,
which persisted through the seventeenth century. In its original general
and basic sense the word meant 'an interval, a stretch or extent, between
things' – which certainly did not connote an entity. That is, originally
spatium, and 'space' in English, was an abstract noun, whereas it later
became a concrete noun.

This change in the meaning of the word was beginning to take place in
the eighteenth century and became general in the nineteenth. The original
abstract sense nevertheless persisted, though much subordinately, and has
done so to the present time. Today the prevailing presupposition is that
the term has one fundamental basic meaning, which is constant whenever
the term is used in philosophical discourse; there is extraordinarily little
appreciation of the shifts in sense in the various occurrences of its usage,
even in the same writer, and often in the same sentence or paragraph.
This variation in sense is further confounded by the use of space (and
der Raum as the German equivalent) as synonymous with 'place'.

It is clearly important for a correct understanding of Kant to avoid
implicitly importing a sense of the word which is not that which Kant
held. We need accordingly to attempt to be clear as to the meaning of the
word in Kant – for example, whether and to what extent he thought in
terms of the new concrete sense of the word. To achieve this clarification
it is necessary to go into the background of thought, to see what was in

controversy in the sixteenth and seventeenth centuries, in order to appreciate how the change in sense came about.

Now at that time what was in controversy was not 'space', as is commonly supposed. This supposition rests upon the nineteenth century sense of space as an entity, and constitutes a block to the inquiry before us. There was then indeed no concept of 'space' at all in the modern sense. The relevant controversy in the sixteenth and seventeenth centuries was concerning 'place'.

In the sixteenth century the concept of motion, i.e. locomotion, had come to the fore, and thinkers like Scaliger and Telesio argued that the concept of motion as change of place was not properly intelligible in terms of the Aristotelian definition of place. Aristotle had defined place as the innermost bounding surface of the containing body – which of course coincided with the outer boundary of the contained body. The point of the sixteenth-century criticism was that in the Aristotelian doctrine place is tied too closely to body – place not only cannot be defined except in terms of body, but if there be no containing body (as there is not beyond the universe) then there is no place possible at all. The modern thinkers argued that the concept of motion implied a body's leaving a place behind when it moved, which entailed that place must be both logically and ontologically distinct and separate from body.

The solution to the problem, put forward by Scaliger and Telesio, which later became generally accepted, was to identify place, not as by the Aristotelians with the bounding surfaces, but with the whole inner extent occupied by the body. As Scaliger put it: "Thus place is not the encompassing surface of the exterior of the body: but it is what is con-tained within this surface".[1] It is this whole inner extent, which the body leaves behind in moving, this extent itself remaining constant, as Telesio said, "itself not receding or driven away, but remaining perpetually the same and most promptly taking up succeeding entities"[2].

Because at that time the term 'place' was so predominantly understood with the Aristotelian meaning, i.e. as referring to bounding surfaces, the protagonists of the new conception took to using not simply the word '*locus*' but to speaking of '*locus internus*'.

To ensure the ontological distinction and separation of place from body Scaliger identified place and void, but redefined void as "an extent (*spatium*) in which there is body"[3] – as opposed to the Aristotelian and generally accepted meaning of void as place *without* any body in it.[4] The problem of the connection between void and place came to receive a great deal of attention from sixteenth and seventeenth century thinkers, almost all coming to the conclusion, in agreement with Aristotle, that void conceived as an extent with absolutely nothing in it, that is an extent of sheer nothingness, is a contradiction, for an extent of nothing is a non-existent extent. If there is to be any extent at all there must be something which is extended; an extent cannot exist just by itself. This argument was extremely important for and was accepted by almost all sixteenth and seventeenth-century thinkers down to and including Newton.

This does not mean that no thinkers accepted the conception of extents which are void of body. Many certainly did not, and maintained a plenum doctrine – including many of the first seventeenth-century atomists such as Sennert, Gorlaeus, and Basso, who held that the atoms are completely contiguous. Some thinkers, of whom Bruno was a notable instance, did maintain a doctrine of void extent (*vacuum spatium*). But for them all extents void of body had necessarily to be filled with some other existent, for otherwise such extents would not be possible at all. Bruno on the whole avoided the word *vacuum* because it tended to have the connotation of sheer nothingness. Instead he spoke of the extents vacant of body as *aether, aer,* or *spiritus* (the world soul). And when he was referring to this extent purely as such, in an abstract sense, and not in respect of its content (in which case it would be called *aether*, etc.), he used the Latin word for extent or interval, namely *spatium*.

In this Bruno exemplified a new technical sense of *spatium* which was beginning to come into use at the end of the sixteenth and early seventeenth century. These thinkers, as we have noted, were maintaining that place (*locus*) is to be identified, not as by the commonly accepted Aristotelian conception with exterior bounding surfaces, but with the entire extended area or room within those bounds. To put the emphasis on this internal extent or room as opposed to the boundary, the word *spatium*, i.e. extent or extended area, room, came gradually into use with the meaning, in this context, of 'the extent or room in which body is or might be as the place of body'. This was, for example, Bruno's use of the term. In general, because this use of the word *spatium* was new, it was common to explicate it by the phrase '*spatium vel locus internus*'.

What is particularly to be noted is that in the seventeenth century the term *spatium* meant *locus*, place. This is quite clear in Descartes, for example in his *Principles of Philosophy*, especially Part II, Principles X-XV, where he explicitly discusses the concept of *spatium*. In Principle X, which is headed '*Quid sit spatium, sive locus internus*', the word *spatium*, space, is quite definitely throughout the paragraph used with the meaning of *locus*, place. In the succeeding Principles he often speaks explicitly of '*spatium vel locus*', and in Principle XIV he goes on to examine "Wherein space and place differ". The difference is that 'place (*locus*) indicates situation (*situs*) more explicitly than magnitude or figure; while, on the contrary, we more often think of the latter when we speak of space (*spatium*)'. Descartes constitutes most important evidence for the current usage of the word *spatium*; he was not only a very clear writer but also a particularly clear and penetrating thinker. Further, his influence was very considerable.

It was this meaning of the word *spatium* which was accepted by Leibniz and right through to the pre-critical Kant. This was also the meaning current in England, as is clearly evidenced in Joseph Raphson, a Cambridge mathematician and younger contemporary of Newton, who was not only an enthusiastic proponent of Newton's system, but wrote a most important explication of the philosophical basis of Newton's work[5], in which *spatium* is explicitly defined and spoken of as *locus internus*.

In the latter part of the seventeenth century, as the new special meaning of *spatium* came into currency it was less and less necessary to add the words '*locus internus*'. But concomitant with this there occurred a further important development in the usage of the term, to which Newton's thought constituted a major contribution. In addition to the new general meaning of *spatium* as *locus internus* it came to be used also in a slightly more special sense, of 'all places in their totality', or 'the extent constituted by all places in their totality'. This is Newton's use of the term in the General Scholium in his *Principia*. Newton's conception of *spatium* was not, as has subsequently come to be so widely misinterpreted, that of an 'entity'. It was that of 'place', the *locus* of God's activity, i.e. *where* God is present and active. To substantiate this of course requires a much more extensive discussion[6]; in the scope of this short paper I can do no more than merely adumbrate Newton's conception.

Further and most important evidence of this later usage of the term *spatium* as the totality of places is presented by Leibniz in his controversy with Clarke. Having experienced much difficulty in getting his theory understood, Leibniz was driven, in his Fifth Letter, to an explication of the meaning of the term space (§ 47). He started this by explaining in some detail the meaning of 'place', and then went on to show that 'that which comprehends all those places is called *space*', or as he put it alternatively, '*space* is that which results from taking places together'. Space is the sum total of places. It is clearly no entity, neither for Leibniz nor for Newton. What is of first importance to appreciate is that the concept of *place* was fundamental in the concept of 'space', in both Leibniz and Newton. Basically what was at issue between them was the nature and ontological status of *place*.

Newton had maintained the conception of place as ontologically distinct from bodies and as immovable in order to have a clear and unambiguous meaning for the concept of motion as change of place. Newton's grounding of place ontologically in God was quite unacceptable to Leibniz. But Leibniz's own ontology involved difficulties in regard to the concept of place, difficulties which eventually led Kant to the position of the Inaugural Dissertation and the first *Critique*.

On the basis of his ontology Leibniz could not accept the widely current conception of place as ontologically distinct and separate from body. For Leibniz the only actual existents or substances were the monads, and it was impossible that place be a monad. Hence the only possibility for him was to define place, basically as Aristotle had done, by reference to actual existents. Now the notion of place can have no sense by reference to a single existent or monad, isolatedly and in itself. Place, therefore, Leibniz maintained, has to be defined and determined by reference to a plurality of monads. That is to say, the place occupied by any particular monad has to be defined by reference to its situation relatively to other monads. Thus Leibniz is in agreement with Descartes that place (*locus*) connotes situation (*situs*). Leibniz saw clearly that on his ontological basis place must be a relative concept; that is, place is 'where' one entity is situated with reference to where other entities are. The entities concerned here must of course be co-existent. All co-existents must be mutually external to each other, i.e. each is situated elsewhere in reference to each other. Their situation in reference to each other is quite definite, and abstractly considered constitutes a certain order of places. The total abstract order of places, Leibniz explained, is what is meant by the term 'space'.

This is the conception and meaning of 'space' which was inherited by Kant, as is clear in his first published writing, *Thoughts on the True Estimation of Living Forces*, 1747. Kant held a theory of monads at that time, but his theory differed from that of Leibniz in that he maintained a dualism: for him there were bodily or physical monads as well as spiritual ones. This treatise was primarily concerned with the physical monads. He conceived them as units of force, and in the first paragraph he made explicit his agreement with Leibniz "that there inheres in body a force which is essential to it, and which indeed belongs to it prior to its extension". Kant's monads, however, were not windowless. The forces of the physical monads act on and affect each other. If the monads did not so act on each other there would be no connection, no relation, between them. They would exist in total isolation. Indeed, as Kant said:

Since every self-sufficient being contains within itself the complete source of all its determinations, it is not necessary for its existence that it stand in relation to other things (*Op. cit.* § 7).

This means that unless and until the monads act on each other there will be no connection, no relation. Connection, and relation, are *brought into being* by their action on each other.

Now, as Kant goes on to point out a few lines later in this Paragraph 7, "there can be no place without external connections, situations and relations". This is the Leibnizian doctrine: the concept of place cannot pertain to an entity in isolation; the concept can enter only with entities in relation. Place is where an entity is in relation to other entities. Since there can be no relation unless and until entities act on each other, thereby bringing about a connection and relation, place is dependent upon the acting of the monads. Consequently the totality of order of situation in reference to each other, which is called 'space', is dependent upon the acting of the monads. Indeed, there is no extension either without that activity effecting relations and connections; extension for Kant, as for Leibniz, is not a concept which can pertain to a monad in itself. Thus, as he says in the heading of Paragraph 9, "If the substances had no force whereby they could act outside themselves, there would be no extension, and also no space". The point is, he insists, that "without a force of this kind there is no connection, without this connection no order, and without this order no space". Here it is quite clear that Kant understood 'space', *der Raum*, as meaning the totality of the order of places – the late seventeenth century meaning of the word, as it had been made clear by Leibniz.

That this was Kant's understanding of the concept of space comes out clea:ly again in his public disputation nine years later, the *Monadologiam Physicam* (1756), in which he elaborated his doctrine of the physical monads as units of activity. By their acting on each other they *bring about* connections and relations, and therewith extension (which is constituted by their 'sphere of activity' – *sphaera activitatis* [*Monadologiam,* Prop. VI]) and also place or situation in reference to each other, and therewith the totality of order of situation which is space. Accordingly, he maintained, "the ground of filled space is not to be looked for in the mere position of substance, but it is to be sought in the external relations [of substances]" (*Ibid.*). He makes the point repeatedly that space is brought about solely by external relations, e.g., in Propositio VII *passim*. This contention is only intelligible if 'space' means the order of the respective relations of the entities, i.e. 'where' they are in reference to each other.

This means that place, i.e. situation in reference to each other, and thus the total order of places or situations, is determinable only by reference to the active monads.

Twelve years after this essay Kant ran into a serious difficulty involved in this conception. If this order of relations of situation be determinable solely by reference to the physical substances, then the fact of incongruent counterparts becomes unintelligible. For example, considered thus purely relationally, the order of the parts of a left hand and a right hand are identical, but one cannot put a right hand into a left-handed glove. Kant concluded in his momentous short treatise 'On the First Ground of the Distinction of Regions in Space' (1768), that the order of places relatively to each other cannot be dependent upon, and thus follow from, physical existents and their activity of relating to each other. That order must be somehow ontologically distinct and separate, and presupposed by the activities of the existents – presupposed because unless this be so the activities will be without a sense of direction, i.e. they would have no basis upon which to act, or move, in one direction rather than another.

Kant here made a definite break with the Leibnizian doctrine. This break does not consist in the abandonment of the relational concept of space; on the contrary, Kant continues to conceive space as the totality of the order of places relatively to each other. The break consists in maintaining that order to be independent of physical existents, and not determinable by reference to them.

The problem which then arose was how that order could be independent of physical existents. Kant completely and emphatically rejected the supposition that this independence meant that that order could itself be some kind of substantial existent, some kind of entity. The solution came to him the following year, 1769, when a 'great light' dawned on him. 'Where' physical existents are in relation to each other is determinable not by reference to themselves and their activities as he had formerly thought, but by reference to the perceiver and his activity of perception. This is the new doctrine of the *De mundi sensibilis*, his dissertation of the next year (1770), and of the *Critique of Pure Reason*. Kant's understanding of 'space' remains as before, namely the totality of the order of places or situations relatively to each other. But 'where' things are relatively to each other is no longer determined by reference to things and their activities, but by reference to the perceiving activity of the observing mind.

Emory University

NOTES

[1] J. C. Scaliger, *Exotericarum exercitationum liber ad Hieronymum Cardanum*, 1557, Exer. V, 3.
[2] B. Telesio, *De rerum natura*, 1586, lib. I, caput XXV.
[3] Scaliger, *ibidem*, Exer. V, 3.
[4] Cf. Aristotle, *Physics*, 214a 13, 19.
[5] J. Raphson, the appendix to the 2nd edition of his *Analysis Aequationum Universalis* entitled 'De Spatio Reali seu Ente Infinito conamen Mathematico Metaphysicum', Def. I. Cf. A. Koyré, *From the Closed World to the Infinite Universe*, 1957, Ch. 8.
[6] I have dealt with this in detail in a forthcoming book, *The Nature of Physical Existence*.

ROBERT PALTER

ABSOLUTE SPACE AND ABSOLUTE MOTION IN KANT'S CRITICAL PHILOSOPHY*

I

In his critical philosophy Kant treats space, in varying contexts, as an intuition, as a concept, and as an idea of reason. Space as an intuition and space as a concept are familiar enough to readers of the *Critique of Pure Reason*, though the relation between them is not so easy to make out. Space – more precisely, absolute space – as an idea of reason, occurring as it does only in the *Metaphysical Foundations of Natural Science*, is perhaps not so well known. To set the stage for my discussion of Kant's absolute space I shall first try to locate it with respect to his other two spaces; after describing the markedly relativistic character of Kant's idea of absolute space, I shall then explain how Kant attempts to reconcile this idea with the reality of circular motion.

One important result of the study of Kant's idea of absolute space might be to throw some light on the general question of the role of ideas of reason in Kant's critical philosophy. Indeed, the strategic position of the MFNS in the corpus of Kant's published writings – five years after the first edition and one year before the second edition of the *Critique of Pure Reason* – makes it seem likely that careful study of any significant doctrine in the former work ought to help illuminate the latter.

I shall now introduce the terms *phenomenal space, geometric space*, and *kinematic space* for convenience in helping to classify and order some of the more important things which Kant says about space. By deliberately choosing three terms which are not used by Kant himself, I hope to avoid the implication that I am referring to some underlying set of necessary distinctions in the critical philosophy of space. Rather, my aim is simply to indicate what seem to be three more or less distinct clusters of properties which Kant attributes to space; and furthermore, I would stress the highly tentative and preliminary character of the entire discussion.

Roughly speaking, phenomenal space is the space occupied by objects of the outer sense; geometric space is the space of geometric objects; and kinematic space is any material framework with respect to which bodies can move. These three spaces are distinguished from one another and interrelated in subtle ways. First of all, phenomenal space, given us as an infinite but individual magnitude, must be an *intuition* (pure, and of the outer sense) because only by means of intuition, through its limitlessness of progression, can such a magnitude be represented. Geometric space is based on this original intuition of phenomenal space but involves in addition a synthesizing activity of the mind,[1] without which definite geometric objects could not be conceived. Finally, by introducing the pure form of inner intuition, or time, motion or change of place in time becomes possible; and the indefinite multiplicity of relative kinematic spaces is unified by a rule for generating them which corresponds to the idea of absolute (kinematic) space. Thus, the unity of phenomenal space and of geometric space, shattered in the multiplicity of relative kinematic spaces, is recaptured – but only in the sense of an indefinitely repeatable conceptual operation – in absolute kinematic space.[2]

Another way of differentiating among the three spaces depends on their respective relations to time. Phenomenal space, given its total dependence on the outer sense, must exclude any direct reference to time because time 'cannot be outwardly intuited, any more than space can be intuited as something in us' (A23 = B37). Objects in phenomenal space can, of course, be *observed* to move, and such motion serves to exhibit the interrelatedness of space and time. But the interrelatedness is, of course, merely empirical; or, as Kant puts it: "Motion of an object in space does not belong to a pure science, and consequently not to geometry. For the fact that something is movable cannot be known *a priori*, but only through experience" (B155). Geometric space is, on the one hand, even more completely divorced from time than phenomenal space, for geometric objects are timeless in their very conception. On the other hand, the crucial temporal concept [Begriff] of *succession* first arises during the construction of geometric objects (e.g., the describing of a circle). And this constitutes an *a priori* interrelatedness of space and time in two ways: first, any geometric construction necessarily involves acts of the subject and therefore the experience of subjective succession; and second, time itself – the pure form of the inner sense – can only be represented *spatially* (specifically, by the act of drawing a straight line). Hence Kant's conclusion:

Motion... considered as the describing of a space, is a pure act of the successive synthesis of the manifold in outer intuition in general by means of the productive imagination, and belongs not only to geometry, but even to transcendental philosophy (B155).

Kinematic space may now be thought of as emerging when the subjective succession implicit in geometric space is converted into an objective succession by introducing the objects of phenomenal space, which are assumed to be movable on the basis of experience. (Incidentally, the fact that in Kant's view space is in one sense presupposed by and in another sense independent of time may perhaps be reflected in the fact that time is treated *before* space in the *Inaugural Dissertation* – where we are told that 'the idea of time does not arise from but is supposed by the senses'[3] – but only *after* space in the *Critique*.)

The logical character of the sequence – phenomenal, geometric, kinematic space – may be worth noting. From phenomenal space to geometric space is not nearly so abrupt and inexplicable a transition as might appear from Kant's initial description of the former as intuition and the latter as concept; for Kant holds that phenomenal space is *also* a concept, but of a peculiar kind, namely, a singular, or 'non-logical', concept.[4] Such a concept may perhaps be thought of as mediating between ordinary intuitions of finite individuals and ordinary concepts of infinite classes of individuals. The other transition – from the concept of particular kinematic spaces to the idea of absolute space – takes place, according to Kant, by a straightforward act of abstraction whereby one simply ignores the material identity of each of the infinite number of possible relative spaces.[5]

Finally, I shall attempt to characterize the mathematical content of phenomenal, of geometric, and of kinematic space. I should emphasize that I do *not* mean to suggest in the case of any of the three spaces that all of what Kant says can be reduced to pure mathematical terms (in the sense of pure mathematics current today). However, I shall not hesitate to employ in my discussion some modern mathematical notions which, it must be remembered, are considerably more precise than most of those available to Kant. I propose, then, that we associate with phenomenal space, topology; with geometric space, three-dimensional Euclidean geometry; and with kinematic space also, three-dimensional Euclidean geometry. A few words of explanation are in order.

In a (purely) topological space such geometric notions as parallelism and distance are not defined. On the other hand, the spatial characteristics which Kant refers to by the terms *infinite* [unendlich], *continuous* [kontinuierlich],[6] and *three-dimensional* [drei Abmessungen] may all be more or less plausibly interpreted in topological terms; which is to say, they may be defined solely in terms of certain properties of sets of the undefined entities called points.[7] Specifically, I propose the following correlation: infinity with openness (of the topological space as a whole); continuity with so-called Dedekind continuity (of curves in the topological space), and perhaps also with connectedness (of the topological space as a whole). Dimensionality can also be defined in topological terms, but owing to the difficulties involved, this procedure is not now customary. The remaining three topological properties can be easily, if not always very precisely, explained by means of some simple diagrams. Openness may be illustrated by the set of points on the line-segment *l* exclusive of its two end-points (see Figure 1). This set is open in the sense that each of its members, such as *P*, is 'surrounded' (on both sides) by other points of the set.

Fig. 1.

Connectedness means that the space is, so to speak, all of a piece; thus, the space consisting of just the two sets of points in the interiors of *A* and *B* is *not* connected (see Figure 2).

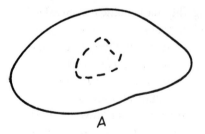
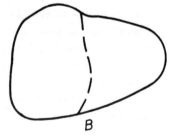

Fig. 2.

On the other hand, each of these two sets considered alone *is* connected in the sense that it cannot be partitioned (see the broken lines in *A* and *B*) into two disjoint, *open* subsets (because the partitioning curve must belong to at least one of the subsets, which could not, therefore, be open). Dedekind continuity implies that between any two points, say, P and Q, on a curve there always exists another point, X.[8] (see Figure 3).

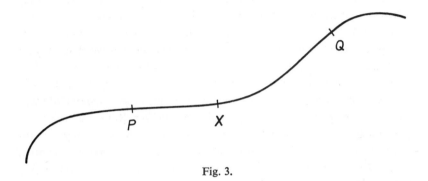

Fig. 3.

One other characteristic of phenomenal space which Kant mentions is that of being *unique* [alleinig] or *essentially one* [wesentlich einig]. In the terms we have been using, this characteristic corresponds simply to the universality or all-inclusiveness of the set of points defining the topological space.

In identifying the mathematical properties of geometric space, I have relied on the fact that in referring to it Kant cites characteristic propositions of Euclidean geometry (e.g., that in any triangle the sum of the three angles is always equal to two right angles). As for kinematic space, Kant's failure even to mention its mathematical properties means only that he took its Euclidean structure for granted.

II

I turn now to Kant's idea of absolute space. The very first Explanation of Phoronomy tells us that absolute space is 'that in which all motion must in the last resort be conceived (which is therefore itself absolutely immovable)'.[9] Now, this formulation is misleading insofar as it seems to explain absolute space in terms of a Newtonian-like absolute rest, but almost immediately Kant proceeds to a further explication in the course of which he clearly differentiates his absolute space from that of Newton. Kant's exposition here is indeed the very opposite of Newton's, for where Newton begins with absolute space in terms of which he characterizes relative space, Kant begins with relative spaces, in terms of which he characterizes absolute space. For Kant, a relative space is simply a material and therefore perceivable framework with respect to which motions of bodies may be detected, e.g., the cabin of a ship or the bank of a river.[10] Since, however, each such relative space, being material, is itself movable, the very conception of a relative space presupposes *another* relative space within which the first may move, and so on to infinity. Now, the idea of absolute space begins to emerge when, in the course of thinking about a particular relative space, one finds oneself referring to some *unspecified* one of these other relative spaces [einen jeden anderen relativen Raum] with respect to which the given relative space may be thought of as moving. By abstracting from all possible material features of such an unspecified relative space, one obtains the idea of a pure, non-empirical, or absolute space with respect to which *any* relative space may be thought of as moving. If we think of specific relative spaces as being designated by individual constants, $S_1, S_2, S_3 ...$, then absolute space may perhaps be thought of as corresponding to the variable, S_x, whose range of values is $S_1, S_2, S_3 ...$

In describing the generation of this infinite set of relative spaces, $S_1, S_2, S_3 ...$, Kant refers to successively 'enlarged' [erweitert] spaces and to any one such space being 'included' [eingeschlossen] in another, so that one tends to get the picture of an unending sequence of Chinese boxes; and Kant's example of a ball moving on a table inside the cabin of a ship, which is itself moving on a river bounded by a bank, tends to confirm this picture.

Strictly speaking, however, the actual inclusion of one relative space by another is irrelevant; indeed it is customary to think of all such relative spaces as in principle indefinitely extensible (say, in the form of a coordinate system defined by three rigid rods intersecting at a material point called the origin), and of course, it makes no sense to talk of one infinite space *including* another. That the important thing is the *state of motion* of each relative space is clear enough when Kant writes that 'these alterations in the state of motion [of a body] go on to infinity with the alterations of the relative space'.[11] Here Kant is, I think, hinting at the following more exact account of the generation of the infinite sequence of relative spaces. For simplicity we consider first only relative spaces in uniform motion with respect to one another, so that we may take the defining property of each such relative space to be the state of motion of its origin. (One set of relative spaces in uniform relative motion is of particular importance: the so-called Galilean or inertial set, with respect to any member of which the law of inertia holds.)

Consider now a set of material particles, moving along the same straight line but with varying velocities, each particle being thought of as defining the origin of a particular coordinate system and hence of a particular relative space. Arbitrarily selecting one of these relative spaces and calling it S_1, we inquire as to the velocity of S_1 with respect to a second arbitrarily selected relative space S_2. The velocity of S_1 with respect to S_2 we write V_{12}. (Note that to refer the velocity of S_1 to itself would yield $V_{11} = 0$, and would in effect single out S_1 as a privileged relative space – which we have no reason to believe it is.) Selecting now another relative space S_3, we let V_{23} represent the velocity of S_2 with respect to S_3; and this process can be thought of as indefinitely repeated. Each successive choice of a new relative space is quite arbitrary, however, so that the sequence of velocities, $V_{12}, V_{23}, V_{34}, \ldots$ is merely contingent; that is to say, there is no 'natural' initial relative space and no 'natural' principle for selecting each successive relative space. It is this contingency which is eliminated – but only in a highly tenuous and abstract way – by the idea of absolute space. This requires some explaining.

Throughout my discussion so far absolute space has been termed an *idea*. This usage – in which I am following Kant – has, of course, a very special meaning in the critical philosophy. It is only toward the end of the MFNS, in the part called Metaphysical Foundations of Phenomenology, that Kant explains exactly why absolute space is an *idea of reason* [Idee der Vernunft]. Like Kant's other ideas of (theoretical) reason, absolute space makes reference to an essentially incompletable *totality* [Totalität] of concepts, in this case the totality of possible relative spaces. And again, like Kant's other ideas of (theoretical) reason, absolute space serves as a *rule* [Regel] for unifying this manifold of concepts [Mannigfaltigkeit der Begriffe vereinigen] (A644 = B672). More specifically, absolute space is the rule for unifying the possible material frameworks for describing motion by referring them all to a single abstract framework, which itself, however, remains entirely indeterminate and beyond experience. Regulatively interpreted in this way, absolute space serves to remind us, first, that no actual material framework for defining motion can ever be more than merely *relative*: and second, that *all* such relative spaces are equally valid [gelten] for the description of any given motion.[12] (The qualification which Kant thinks is needed in the case of circular motion will be discussed below in Section III.)

Just at this point a subtle similarity between Kant's and Newton's respective absolute spaces may be noted. Even though the direction of Kant's exposition is – contrary to Newton's – from relative to absolute space, there is, I believe, an important sense in which for Kant, too, absolute space is logically prior to relative space. We can see this if we apply a general remark of Kant's about ideas of (theoretical) reason to the idea of absolute space. Such an idea, says Kant, is 'the form of a whole [Ganzen] of knowledge – a whole which is prior to the determinate knowledge of the parts and which contains the conditions that determine *a priori* for every part its position and relation to the other parts' (A645 = B673). In the case of absolute space, we may say that all possible relative motions – and therefore all motions which can fall within our experience – are in a sense unified *prior* to experience by being referred to [bezogen werden] absolute space. Also, from the logical point of view, absolute space is prior to relative space in the manner in which a higher-order rule is prior to, or subsumes, a lower-order rule. Recall that for Kant *all* concepts are rules, so that the concept of relative space must be understood as a rule for, let us say, constructing three-dimensional coordinate systems in definite states of relative motion.

Ignoring, as before, the three coordinate axes and attending only to the origin, we see that the rule for specifying any given relative space reduces to the choice of a velocity for the origin. How about the rule corresponding to absolute space? In every kinematic problem there will be some relative space whose state of motion is not specified with respect to any other relative space; this is, for the problem in question, the 'immovable' relative space, which we designate by S_x to suggest the possible variability of this space from problem to problem. (On just this point Kant's terminology is misleading: his adjective 'absolute' suggests, contrary to his intended meaning, a *unique* space.)[13] For any S_x we have $V_{xx} = 0$, which provides us with an initial term for the sequence of velocities of relative spaces, all referred to S_x. The generating rule can be specified in various ways, say, by the sequence of increasing rational numbers beginning with zero. In systematic fashion, then, each such space takes its position in a pre-determined sequence – pre-determined, that is, once S_x is determinate – but this, of course, is just what S_x can never be. The sequence of relative spaces is not even in principle objectively realizable, though it *is thinkable* as a mere idea and as such serves to unify, by interrelating, all possible relative spaces in the following way (see Figure 4).

$$V_{xx} = 0 \qquad\qquad V_{mx} \qquad\qquad\qquad V_{nx}$$

Fig. 4.

Any relative velocity V_{mn}, or its negative, $-V_{mn}$, of a pair of relative spaces, S_m and S_n, can always be expressed as the difference of two terms in the sequence of velocities: $V_{mn} = V_{mx} - V_{nx}$, or $-V_{mn} = V_{nx} - V_{mx}$. These equations embody the addition of motion principle for a set of coordinate systems moving (without rotation) in parallel lines. Consideration of the general case of coordinate systems in uniform relative motion would lead to the same law expressed in vectorial terms. A further generalization to coordinate systems in arbitrary states of relative motion would lead to the more complicated set of so called time-dependent orthogonal transformation equations.[14] Some rule for systematically varying the coefficients occurring in these equations could be taken as the defining rule for Kant's absolute space.

III

It would be only too easy now when we are all post-Newtonian relativists to conclude by celebrating the prescience of Kant's substitution of a kind of 'operational' meaning for the objective or quasi-substantial meaning of absolute space. The very role of the idea of absolute space in Kant's phoronomic and mechanical proofs is a distinctly minor one, necessary, indeed, only because of certain peculiar features in Kant's theory of knowledge. All this would suggest, correctly, that absolute space in just about any sense is fully dispensable in the classical mechanics deriving from Newton's *Principia*. Any further conclusion, however, as to the dispensability of absolute motion would, I believe, be a mistake; a mistake, moreover, which would severely limit our understanding of the full depth both of Newton's accomplishment and of Kant's appreciation of that accomplishment. In the interests of brevity, I shall have to state rather baldly the situation as I see it.[15]

The historical evolution of the concept of relativity of motion reached its culmination in Descartes' clear formulation of what is usually called the kinematic relativity principle, according to which all motions are relative and hence no reference frames are privileged for the description of motion. Subsequent developments in the history of mechanics exhibit a tension between the demands of kinematic relativity and the increasingly clear realization that there do appear to be privileged reference frames for describing mechanical phenomena, namely, so-called inertial, or Galilean, frames. The form which this tension takes in Newton's *Principia* consists in its simultaneous emphasis on the fundamental relativity of *uniform* motions (Corollary V to the Laws of Motion) and on the intrinsic meaningfulness of the absolute-relative distinction for *all* motions (Scholium to the Definitions). Now, acceleration is undoubtedly intrinsically absolute in Newtonian mechanics, but in the face of this fact opposite attitudes can be – and were – adopted: either, as with Newton, that the absoluteness of the one kinematic concept, acceleration, implies the absoluteness of the other kinematic concept, velocity; or else, as with Newton's critics, Huygens and, later, Mach, that the system of mechanics ought to be somehow reconstructed so as to eliminate all absolute concepts. (It is not widely enough known that the desiderated elimination has, in fact, never yet been achieved: in an important sense acceleration remains absolute even in Einstein's general relativity.)[16] There is, however, a third way of viewing Newtonian mechanics, and this is simply to accept *both* the absoluteness of acceleration and the relativity of velocity. Kant's successive discussions of space, time, and motion over a period of three decades seem to be – not without some hesitation and wavering – tending toward this last alternative.

Consider first one of the earliest of these discussions in Kant's *New System of Motion and Rest* (*Neuer Lehrbegriff der Bewegung und Ruhe*) of 1758. Here Kant seems to be accepting the kinematic relativity principle when he writes:

Now I begin to see that something is lacking in my expressions for motion and rest. I should never use these [expressions] in an absolute sense but rather always relatively. I should never say: A body is at rest, without adding with respect to what objects it is at rest; and never speak of it moving, without at the same time mentioning the objects with respect to which its position is changing.[17]

However, five years later, in his *Essay on the Concept of Negative Quantities* (*Versuch zum Begriff der negativen Grössen*) Kant seems to abandon his previous relativistic stance when he subscribes to the views of Euler, who, in a famous essay (published in 1750), had argued from the validity of the laws of motion to the absolute character of space. And in an essay of 1768, *Concerning the Ultimate Foundation of the Differentiation of Regions in Space* (*Von dem ersten Grunde des Unterschiedes der Gegenden im Raume*), Kant tried to supplement Euler's mechanical argument with a purely geometrical one. Finally, by the time he was engaged in creating his mature critical philosophy – that is by 1786, the date of the MFNS – his views on the relativity of motion clearly exhibit that tension to which I have earlier referred.[18] The passages I have in mind occur in the last part of the MFNS, the Phenomenology.

The problem of the Phenomenology arises in the following way. Motion as phenomenon – that is, as an object of the outer sense – is thoroughly relational [Relation]. But in order to transform [Verwandlung] such phenomena into experience [Erfahrung], or into what is the same thing, empirical knowledge [empirische Erkenntnis], it is necessary that the motion in question be predicated of a definite body. In brief, the *observed* change of relation (specifically, change of relative place) between two bodies *A* and *B* must somehow be *understood* [verstanden] as belonging to either *A* or *B*. Now, in the case of rectilinear motions it is entirely up to us whether we want to attribute the motion to *A* or to *B* (or even to both bodies). The case of circular motions, however, is more problematic, since Kant is not willing to assert the equivalence of say, the rotation of the earth and the opposite rotation of the heavens. Thus, Proposition 2 of the Phenomenology states that circular motion of a body is *real* [wirklich], whereas the opposite motion of the surrounding relative space is *mere illusion* [blosser Schein].[19] Kant's proof – which actually would apply to any non-uniform motion – depends on the law of inertia (his own 2nd mechanical law); but his crucial assumption is that there must be a centripetal force producing the body's circular motion, whereas the hypothesized opposite motion of the surrounding relative space requires no such force. Now this assumption concerning forces is just what Mach challenged when he urged that we look precisely to the *relative* motion of body and surrounding space for any possible detectable force. It would be expecting too much for Kant to have attained full clarity on this issue, but the following considerations show, I believe, how sensitively he tried to adjust the rival claims of opposed positions on the status of circular motion.

One way of putting Kant's difficulty is in terms of his own distinction between two forms of illusion: the empirical and the transcendental. Empirical illusion occurs entirely within the realm of phenomena; an example would be the optical illusion in which the moon appears abnormally large when near the horizon. Transcendental illusion occurs when one attempts to apply a mere rule or maxim of reason to determine an object which transcends experience; an example would be taking as an objective principle the proposition that the world must have a beginning in time.[20] Consider now the tendency to regard absolute space as the concept of a real object (rather than as a mere regulative idea of reason). Are we dealing here with an instance of empirical illusion (in which case there are rational criteria which will serve to eliminate the illusory concept once and for all) or with an instance of transcendental illusion (in which case, even though reason repeatedly exposes the false pretensions of the concept, it will remain a perpetually tempting source of error)? It seems clear that Kant believed the concept of an objective absolute space to be an empirical illusion, which he had eliminated once and for all by his introduction of the surrogate idea of an indeterminate relative space.

What now of circular motion? On the one hand, there is the tendency to assume (with Newton) that circular motion is objectively absolute – and this amounts to a transcendental illusion because it involves the seemingly inconsistent concept of a motion which can be fully characterized quite apart from any external material framework. On the other hand, there is the tendency to assume (with Leibniz) that circular motion is, like all other types of motion, merely subjective, classifiable at our pleasure as real or illusory[21] -- and this amounts to an empirical illusion because certain experiences do in fact enable us to differentiate real from illusory circular motions.

One of Kant's own examples can be used to illustrate the two forms of illusion with respect to circular motion. The diurnal rotation of the earth can be detected, Kant points out, simply by noting the eastward deviation of bodies falling down a vertical shaft in the earth (an effect, by the way, which had not yet been conclusively established in Kant's lifetime).[22] We have found an empirical basis for the attribution of circular motion to the earth, thereby refuting a belief in the merely illusory character of the motion. Since, however, no external surrounding space (such as that provided by the fixed stars) is required in our experiment, we may well be tempted to attribute an absolute character to the circular motion of the earth, thereby falling prey to transcendental illusion. Kant's conclusion – that 'while conceived in absolute space [the circular motion] is really only relative'[23] is just a restatement of the dilemma. For it is difficult to see how a real motion can be relative to an indeterminate, sheerly hypothetical, space.[24]

In conclusion, I would suggest that Kant's awareness of the limitations in his treatment of circular motion is probably indicated by his remark that it is 'a paradox deserving to be solved' that a circular motion can be 'empirically given' in empty space, which is to say, under circumstances when no relative space can be 'empirically given'.[25] Whether, from Kant's point of view, a solution to the paradox is even conceivable remains for me a matter for conjecture. He does say that the very attempt to conceive empty space is foredoomed to failure: 'And so ends the metaphysical doctrine of body with *emptiness* and therefore incomprehensibility' (or, in the measured eloquence of the German, 'Und so endigt sich die metaphysische Körperlehre mit dem *Leeren* und eben darum Unbegreiflichen').[26] We have thus been warned, says Kant, that we are on the verge of transgressing the boundaries of possible theoretical knowledge. But precisely in the act of pushing against these boundaries, Kant manages to locate for us some of the deepest and most subtle issues in his own – and perhaps also our own – scientific understanding of nature.

University of Texas at Austin

NOTES

* This work was supported in part by the National Science Foundation (Grant GS–2413). I am indebted for several helpful discussions to Professor Jürgen Ehlers, Physics Department, University of Texas at Austin.
References to Kant's writings other than the *Kritik der reinen Vernunft* are to the volume and page of the Akademie edition. The following abbreviations will be used: CPR for N. K. Smith's *Immanuel Kant's Critique of Pure Reason* (1933), and MFNS for E. B. Bax's translation of the *Metaphysische Anfangsgründe der Naturwissenschaft*: The

Metaphysical Foundations of Natural Science (1883). In quoting some passages I have altered Bax's language.

[1] The so-called 'synthesis of apprehension'. One puzzling feature of Kant's view here is that the synthesis in question is characterized as *pure* in the first edition of the CPR (p. 132; A100) but as *empirical* in the second edition (pp. 170–71; B160–61).

[2] I have in mind here the standard and well-known passages in the CPR and the *Prolegomena* for what I have called phenomenal space and geometric space, and certain passages in the MFNS (which will be cited later) for what I have called kinematic space.

[3] *On the Form and Principles of the Sensible and Intelligible World, Selected Pre-Critical Writings*, transl. G. B. Kerferd and D. E. Walford (1968), p. 63; II, 399.

[4] *Ibid.*, p. 61; II, 397: "pure (human) intuition is not a universal or logical concept *under which*, but is a singular concept *in which*, sensibles no matter what are thought, and so it contains the concepts of space and time."

[5] 'I abstract from [the matter of relative spaces)' and thereby represent [vorstellen] 'a pure, non-empirical and absolute space' (MFNS, p. 151; IV, 481-2).

[6] Kant characterizes continuity in different ways: as infinite divisibility, when he writes that "The property of magnitudes by which no part of them is the smallest possible, that is, by which no part is simple, is called their continuity" (CPR, p. 204; A169 = B211) and as absence of gaps, when he writes that "the principle of continuity... forbids, in respect of the sum of all empirical intuitions in space, any gaps or cleft between two appearances" (CPR, pp. 248–49; A229 = B281). What the latter passage actually asserts, to be sure, is that appearances or empirical intuitions must be continuous with respect to their spatial extension, but from this it would seem to follow that space itself must also be continuous in the same sense.

[7] The precise definition of a topological space $(S, \{\sigma\})$ is that it consists of a set, S, of points together with a class, $\{\sigma\}$, of so-called open subsets of S, such that (1) the union of any class of open sets is open, and (2) the intersection of any finite class of open sets is open.

[8] For elementary accounts of openness and connectedness, see, e.g., L. Felix, *The Modern Aspect of Mathematics* (1960), pp. 110–14, or D. Bushaw, *Elements of General Topology* (1963), pp. 9–13, 91–95. For an elementary account of Dedekind continuity, see, e.g., A. Delachet, *Contemporary Geometry* (1962), pp. 42–45, Dimensionality, as already explained, is ordinarily taken as a primitive notion in topology, as when one specifies the number of dimensions of a given topological space simply by the number of independent parameters required to fix a point in the space.

It is worth remarking that connectedness does not exclude the presence of 'holes' in a space, which Kant certainly would have wanted to exclude if the possibility had occurred to him. The relevant topological property here is that of *simple* connectedness.

[9] MFNS, p. 150, IV, 480.

[10] Here Kant is in agreement with Newton: "Relative space is some movable dimension or measure of the absolute spaces; which our senses determine by its position to bodies" (*Principia*, ed. Cajori, p. 6); "space, in which we are to institute experience [Erfahrung] respecting motions, must be perceivable [empfindbar]... and this is called *empirical space*" (MFNS, p. 151; IV, 481). Since empirical space, as material, is itself movable, it follows that every empirical space is *relative*.

[11] MFNS, p. 151; IV, 481. I have translated somewhat freely here to bring out what I take to be Kant's real point when he wrote; "diese Abänderungen des Begriffs der

Bewegungen gehen mit der Veränderung des relativen Raums so ins Unendliche fort."
[12] I have been summarizing what I take to be the meaning of a passage in MFNS, pp. 238-9; IV, 559-60.
[13] Compare Einstein's introduction of a so-called 'stationary system' [ruhendes System] 'In order to render our presentation [of relativity kinematics] more precise and to distinguish this sytem of coordinates verbally from others which will be introduced hereafter' ('On the Electrodynamics of Moving Bodies' [1905], *The Principle of Relativity*, H. A. Lorentz *et al.* [1923], p. 38.)
[14] See H. Weyl, *Space-Time-Matter*, transl. H. Brose (1922), p. 152.
[15] For a more detailed and precise treatment of both the historical and the systematic issues, see H. Stein, 'Newtonian Space-Time', *Texas Quarterly*, X, 3 (Autumn, 1967), 174-200.
[16] As a leading relativist has recently put it: "Since the days of Galileo and Newton we have regarded velocity as relative but acceleration as absolute. This is difficult to understand, but there doesn't seem to be any simple way out" (H. Bondi, *Assumption and Myth in Physical Theory* [1967], p. 20). Furthermore, space-time itself in an important sense remains absolute in general relativity (see A. Grünbaum, *Philosophical Problems of Space and Time* [1963], Chap. 14.
[17] *Neuer Lehrbegriff der Bewegung und Ruhe*, II, 17.
[18] M. Jammer mistakenly suggests that Kant continues to maintain the Eulerian position with respect to absolute space in his MFNS (*Concepts of Space*, 2nd ed. [1969], p. 131). Furthermore, according to Jammer, "... in the eighteenth and early nineteenth centuries, primarily as a result of Leonhard Euler's justification of absolute motion on the basis of the principle of inertia (*Mechanica; Theoria Motus*, Secs. 84, 99) and Kant's argumentations in his 'MFNS' (*MAdN*, 1786), absolute motion was regarded by the majority of philosophers as a meaningful concept, not only in physics but also in philosophy" ('Motion', *Encyclopedia of Philosophy*, ed. Paul Edwards, V [1967], p. 399). Since Jammer cites no evidence as regards Kant for this claim, I can only say that it seems highly dubious in view of the fact that, as we have seen, in his MFNS Kant disclaims both the concept of absolute velocity (which cannot survive his rejection of Newtonian absolute space) and the very term 'absolute' as applied to circular motions. People do, of course, misread even the most clearly written texts, and it is possible that the influence of the MFNS was indeed to foster a belief in absolute motion.
[19] MFNS, p. 235; IV, 556-7.
[20] Both of these examples are from CPR, pp. 299-300; A297-9 = B353-4.
[21] 'As for absolute motion, nothing can determine it mathematically, since everything ends in relations. The result is always a perfect equivalence in hypotheses, as in astronomy, so that no matter how many bodies one takes, one may arbitrarily assign rest or some degree of velocity to any one of them we wish, without possibly being refuted by the phenomena of straight, circular, or composite motion' ('A New System of the Nature and the Communication of Substances' [1695], G. W. Leibniz, *Philosophical Papers and Letters*, ed. L. Loemker [1956], Vol. II, p. 750). In his very next sentence Leibniz adds, somewhat inconsistently, that 'it is reasonable to attribute true motions to bodies if we follow the assumption [of pre-established harmony] which explains the phenomena in the most intelligible way, for to do this is in conformity with the concept of activity which we have just established' (*ibid.*).

H. Reichenbach finds similarities in Leibniz's and Kant's views on circular motion, but suggests that 'One advantage of Kant's interpretation [over Le'oniz's] ... seems to me to be that he does not regard the distinction between true and apparent motion as an objection to Newton' ('The Theory of Motion According to Newton, Leibniz, and Huygens', *Modern Philosophy of Science* [1959], pp. 58–9, footnote).

[22] MFNS, p. 240; IV, 561. J. F. Benzenberg successfully performed such experiments in 1804 and F. Reich in 1831.

[23] *Ibid.*, p. 241; IV, 561.

[24] Huygens saw further here when he showed how the rotation of a body could be construed in terms of mutual relative motions of its parts, *without* at the same time ascribing 'real' or 'absolute' motions to any of these parts. See Stein, *op. cit.*, pp. 183–84, and Reichenbach, *op. cit.*, pp. 63–66.

[25] MFNS, pp. 236–7; IV, 557–8.

[26] *Ibid.*, p. 244; IV, 564.

ROBERTO TORRETTI

ON THE SUBJECTIVITY OF OBJECTIVE SPACE

Kant maintains that space is "empirically real," but is nevertheless "transcendentally ideal." He explains this saying that space "is nothing, as soon as we lay aside the condition of the possibility of all experience, and look upon it as something that underlies things in themselves" (KrV, A 28 = B 44). "It is therefore solely from the standpoint of man that we can speak of space, of extended things, etc. If we depart from the subjective condition under which alone we can have outer intuition... the representation of space means nothing at all" (KrV A 26 = B 42). This doctrine of the transcendental ideality of space (and of time) is, he writes, one of the two hinges upon which the whole of metaphysics turns (the other is the reality of freedom – Ak., XX, 311; XVIII, 669). The importance of this doctrine in the architecture of Kant's philosophy should therefore not be underrated. There seems to be, however, some difficulty in understanding what it means. This difficulty continues to generate misunderstandings in spite of the many scholarly accounts of this matter. I feel therefore that a concise review of this question, bringing together within a short compass a few points essential to clarify it, will not be altogether useless.

It should be clear to all, in the first place, that Kant's doctrine concerns the nature of real physical space, the space where stones fall, and plants grow, and all animals, including ourselves, move, live and have their being. His words might at times suggest that he speaks rather of what we may call psychological space, the space of colours, or the space of sounds, or the space of tactile sensations, or a conflation of all these. But we can easily see that this cannot be so. If Kant wished to maintain merely that one or all of these "fields" of perception are dependent on the human subject, his doctrine would be most certainly true, but quite trivial and uninteresting. Besides, Kant held that that space which he said was transcendentally ideal possessed the metrical structure of Euclidean space, which the most clearly structured of perceptual spaces, the visual field, evidently does not possess. We may state therefore that when Kant says that the representation of space means nothing at all apart from certain condition of human experience, he is maintaining the subjectivity of objective space.

The difficulty, however, lies in determining how we are to understand this subjectivity. For it is quite obvious that it does not refer to what we may call the empirical existence of man, man insofar as he is an object of biology, or sociology, or scientific psychology. The existence of man, in this sense, is a bodily existence, of which we may rightly say that it is nothing apart from space. Kant could hardly maintain therefore that space depends on man, if we understand human existence in this first and most obvious sense.

But on the other hand, Kant cannot maintain within the bounds of his critical philosophy, that space depends on what we could call the metaphysical existence of man, that space is an attribute, or a consequence of the platonic *psyche* or the cartesian *res cogitans*, or is in any way essentially connected to some kind of spiritual substance. Not that Kant would have denied that man also exists metaphysically, and not just empirically as a living and talking body. But he was bound to maintain that we can know nothing whatsoever about the nature and attributes of metaphysical man (except possibly that he is free), and could not therefore have asserted that space depends on him or somehow belongs to him.

Since empirical man and what I have vaguely described as metaphysical man were the two ways of conceiving the human subject in the philosophical tradition before Kant, we must conclude that this doctrine of the subjectivity of objective space can only be understood in the light of a new way of conceiving subjectivity itself. This new conception of subjectivity has been brought about in part by the very development of Kant's philosophy of space, so that when he maintains that objective space is subjective he is saying not only something new about space, but also and mainly something new about the human subject. In fact, this new conception of subjectivity is developed through a consideration not only of space, but also of time, and of objective experience. We cannot however within this paper do much more than suggest the connections that bind Kant's doctrine of the subjectivity of space to the whole of his philosophy of experience.

The turning point in Kant's philosophy of space appears in his essay of 1768 on incongruent counterparts (*Von dem ersten Grunde des Unter-*

schiedes der Gegenden im Raume, Ak., II, 377–383). Here he concludes, against his former opinion, that spacial things depend on space for their very being, and are not therefore presupposed by space. The difference between a right-winded snail and its left-winded mirror image can only be determined, according to Kant, through a reference to the whole of space, and it is a well-known fact of zoology that the sense of the spiral shape of a snail's shell is a characteristic of each species of snail, which in Aristotelian ontology would have qualified as *symbebekós kath'autó* (*Metaph.*, V, 1025 a 30), a "proper" accident, depending on the snail's substantial form. Space, therefore, is not just a net of relations abstracted from the set of spatial things; space is rather the universal ontological condition of the possibility of such things. This implies a rejection of Kant's earlier doctrine, according to which space and its structure depend on the actual interaction of physical substances which fill space but are not determined by space (Ak., I, 480ff; II, 287). Things that fill space are now to be regarded as thoroughly spatial, spatially structured in their very being.

It might be thought that Kant in 1768 was defending the Newtonian conception of real, infinite, absolute space, an empty receptacle wherein God places bodies. But in his later writings, while abiding by the essential conclusion of 1768, namely, the ontological priority of space over bodies, he openly rejects the Newtonian theory, which, he fears, leads inevitably to the Spinozistic thesis that space is divine (Ak., V, 101f.; XVIII, 626; Kowalewsky *Metaphysik-Vorlesung*, 586; Pölitz *Metaphysik-Vorlesung*, 62). According to Kant it is absurd to conceive space as actually subsisting even in the absence of all spatial things. Pure space as such is an 'Unding'. It has no actuality except through the actual existence of bodies and processes *in* space. The full actuality of the whole of space implies therefore the actual, fully determined existence of bodies and bodily processes filling up its entire infinite expanse. According to Kant this is altogether impossible. Such is the upshot of the discussion of the first two antinomies. An infinite totality of bodies cannot exist simultaneously because if it did, it would be a collection at once complete and incompleteable, which, he says, "would provide eternity with inexhaustible matter for successive progress through its innumerable parts towards infinity, which series however would be actually given in all its numbers in the simultaneous infinity, whereby a series which could never be completed through successive addition could nevertheless be given as a whole – *tota esset dabilis*" (Ak., II, 391f.). Moreover, not even an ordinary, small body can enjoy a fully determined actual existence; being spatial, a body is infinitely divisible; if it were fully determined, it would be infinitely divided, wherefrom the well-known absurdities discussed in the second antinomy would ensue.

The ontological priority of space over bodies implies therefore the priority of the virtual over the actual, the priority of an *Inbegriff* of possible relations over the bodily substances actually sustaining those relations. Kant reverses thereby, at least in the case of physical objects, the tradition of western metaphysics, which had understood the virtual as depending upon the actual. Kant's new conception of bodily existence is intimately bound to this reversal of ontology: Bodies do not actually exist as fully determined entities (*entia omnimode determinata*), but only *in the process of becoming determined*. This, I deem, is the decisive step leading to the subjectivity of objective space.

I find the cue to this last step of our argument in the much discussed sections of the first edition of the *Critique of Pure Reason*, where Kant develops the doctrine of the threefold synthesis (KrV, A 98/110). The objection has been frequently raised, that this doctrine is psychologistic. In fact, Kant starts from an examination of familiar psychical processes – namely, the apprehension of sense-data – to reach the transcendental views which he wants to put forth. However, his critics have failed to see that psychical facts, being just as real as any other kind of facts – a part, so to speak, of the "furniture of the universe" – may be shown to involve ontological truths. Such truths will apply to any entities which share with those psychical facts the traits relevant to the proof of the said truths. Kant maintains that the apprehension of a plurality of sense-data is a necessarily temporal process, which cannot take place in an instant; therefore, it requires steady reproduction of the material already apprehended; such reproduction would be pointless unless accompanied by recognition, that is, identification of the variegated sensuous material as facets of one and the same object; recognition, on the other hand, involves at least the possibility of self-awareness, that is, the possibility of taking notice of the identity of the very activity of apprehending, reproducing, recognizing. Now I hold that this well-known argument contains an ontological kernel, by virtue of which it may be applied, *mutatis mutandis*, to spatial things. If bodies are fully determined at a given instant, they may preserve their being through time while remaining indifferent to the course of time; each moment they are what they are, lacking nothing for their full actuality. We have seen that this conception of bodily existence, which may be said to be that of contemporary common sense, was rejected by Kant. In his view the being of bodies is always becoming: becoming integrated in a network of spatial relations with its proximate and distant neighbours, becoming articulated as a network of spatial relations of its immediate and mediate parts. At any moment a mere stage of this development is present, a thoroughly incomplete stage, which only on the strength of its relations to previous and later stages may be described as the actual presence of a body. Bodily being is therefore synthetic being, depending somehow on the retention of the past, the anticipation of the future, held together through the identification of its several stages, varied and united in time. We must not conceive such identification as a self-conscious mental act. Indeed, Kant will maintain that actual "empirical" self-consciousness presupposes the existence of bodies (KrV, B 274ff.); it cannot therefore be required for the constitution of these. But the synthesis constituting bodies is, as we have seen, structurally equivalent to the triple synthesis constituting unitary self-conscious experience in time; if this is so, the being of bodies so constituted necessarily agrees with the conditions under which alone their intrinsic multiplicity and variety can come together in one consciousness, and is therefore essentially referred to a *possible* self-consciousness, to apperception regarded as *Vermögen* (cf. KrV, A 117n.). Moreover, we have seen that the synthesis of bodies can never be completed in a finite time, since its completion would imply full internal articulation of each body in all its infinite parts, plus external interconnection of all bodies through the whole of infinite space. But if it can never be completed, and nevertheless bodies may be said to exist effectively at any moment, we must conclude that the *idea* of the complete synthesis, the idea of bodies fully articulated in a system of the universe, is an essential ingredient of actual bodily being. Now this idea need not be actually thought by some particular subject, need not be actually guiding a mental process of inquiry and construction of experience. But it is certainly a pure idea, and as such purely ideal: a rule addressed to a possible subject concerning a possible construction of experience. In this sense, therefore, and within these limits, Kant may claim to have established the ideality of bodies and bodily processes.

This conclusion is readily transferred to space as such. Space is, after all, nothing but an *Inbegriff* of virtual relations which are partially realized in bodies; whatever is a condition for the subsistence of each and every body is a condition for the reality of space. We might go deeper into the matter and try to show that this peculiar relation between actual bodies and virtual space, whereby each cannot be without the other, requires mediation between the virtual and the actual, and that such mediation is the role devolved upon the subject by the theoretical philosophy of Kant. But this would take us too far. It may suffice here to have shown that the subject Kant is talking about is not the object of empirical or rational psychology and that his doctrine of the subjectivity of objective space is indeed a doctrine of the objectivity of the human subject, teaching as it does the essential agreement of physical existence and mental experience, and thereby justifying the vocation of man for objective knowledge.

Universidad de Puerto Rico

PART V

CAUSALITY AND THE
LAWS OF NATURE

HENRY E. ALLISON

TRANSCENDENTAL AFFINITY –
KANT'S ANSWER TO HUME

Kant's rather obscure and scattered references to the doctrine of *transcendental* or *objective affinity* in the first edition version of the Transcendental Deduction are generally regarded as directed against Hume, and specifically against the latter's sceptical reflections on the principle of the uniformity of experience, i.e. the claim that future associations of events will necessarily conform to past ones.[1] The gist of Hume's contention is that this principle is neither demonstrable *a priori* (since its opposite is conceivable) nor a valid empirical inference (any such inference being obviously circular). But since these are the only two ways of acquiring knowledge, Hume concludes that we can have no rational insight into the necessity of this uniformity, and that our belief therein is due solely to custom or habit. As Kant himself was well aware, Hume's argument is not directed against the practical necessity or indispensability of this belief, but against its objective validity or foundation in reason. From Hume's sceptical standpoint this uniformity, and consequently the continued conformity of experience to our custom-induced expectations remains a brute and inexplicable fact in which we must believe, but can never understand.

The argument for *transcendental affinity* is intended to demonstrate that the uniformity of experience, or in Kant's terms the 'associability of appearances', is indeed necessary and objectively valid, and thus, that nature, as the object of experience, not only does, but *must*, stand under unchanging laws. The aim of this paper, however, is to show that although in the actual form in which we find it in the sections devoted to affinity, Kant's argument fails to do the job, its reformulation in terms taken from other portions of the *Critique*, not only provides a decisive answer to Humean scepticism, but also some clues as to the nature and significance of Kant's transcendental idealism.

I

Although much of Kant's argument is entangled with his discussion of the reproductive function of the imagination, it seems possible to largely divorce its logical structure from these quasi-psychological considerations. This involves the piecing together of materials from three different portions of the first edition *Deduction* (A100–101, 110–14, 120–22). Thus reconstructed, the argument is typical of Kant's analytic or regressive approach. Beginning with what amounts to an acknowledgement of Hume's point: "It is merely an empirical law that representations which have often followed or accompanied one another finally become associated, and so are set in a relation whereby, even in the absence of the object, one of these representations can, in accordance with a fixed rule, bring about a transition to the other", Kant proceeds to point out that the possibility of such association or reproduction presupposes that 'appearances are themselves actually subject to such a rule'. This is necessary, for:

If cinnabar were sometimes red, sometimes black, sometimes light, sometimes heavy... my empirical imagination would never find opportunity when representing red colour to bring to mind heavy cinnabar. (A 100).

This again does not seem to mark a significant advance beyond Hume. Both hold that the imagination functions according to rules of association, and that this requires a certain orderliness in experience. However, whereas Hume regards this orderliness as a fact to be wondered at, Kant treats it as a necessity to be explained. This associability or 'empirical affinity' of appearances, he holds, requires an objective or transcendental ground, by which he means a principle in terms of which this necessity can be understood.

Kant's argument for the necessary affinity of experience is indirect, amounting essentially to an attempted *reductio ad absurdum* of the Humean position. If one maintains, he argues, that the affinity of appearances is merely a contingent fact, he must further acknowledge that "it be entirely accidental that appearances should fit into a connected whole of human knowledge". Such a consequence, however, which the Humean sceptic might very well cherish, is impossible; for if appearances were not associable, i.e. unifiable in consciousness, "there might exist a multitude of perceptions, and indeed an entire sensibility, in which much empirical consciousness would arise in my mind, but in a state of separation, and, without belonging to a consciousness of myself". But this, Kant continues is impossible: "For it is only because I ascribe all perceptions to one consciousness (original apperception) that I can say of all perceptions that I am conscious of them" (A 122).

Thus the Humean thesis concerning the lack of necessity in the uniformity of experience is shown to entail an impossible consequence, and Kant's next step is to supplement this refutation with a positive statement of the ultimate basis of this necessity. In Kant's own words, we must: "...make comprehensible to ourselves the thoroughgoing affinity of appearances, whereby they stand and *must* stand under unchangeable laws" (A 113). This basis is to be found in principle of the transcendental unity of apperception: 'According to this principle,' Kant writes, "all appearances without exception, must so enter the mind or be apprehended, that they conform to the unity of apperception" (A 122). This requires that they be unifiable, for it is only under this condition that they can be held together in the unity of one consciousness. Unassociable, ununifiable, unsynthesizable appearances (all three being synonymous in this context) could not be brought to consciousness. However, since appearances which do not stand in relation to a possible consciousness "would be nothing to us", and indeed "nothing at all" (A 120; cf. A 111, 112, 116, 127), Kant can conclude that the necessary synthetic unity of appearances is "objectively necessary" (A 120), and even more strongly: "Thus all appearances stand in thoroughgoing connection according to necessary laws, and therefore in a transcendental affinity, of which the empirical is a mere consequence" (A 113–114).

Furthermore, the 'objective necessity' of this affinity provides Kant with a basis for the introduction of the Copernican thesis that "the order and regularity in the appearances, which we entitle *nature*, we ourselves introduce" (A 125). Since the unity of nature has to be a necessary one it cannot be accounted for in realistic terms. Any such explanation would reduce that unity to a contingent fact, knowable only *a posteriori*. It is therefore only in light of the idealistic principle that this unity is imposed by the mind, and that nature is 'merely an aggregate of appearances, so many representations of the mind" rather than a realm of things in themselves that this necessary unity is explicable. Given this standpoint, the unity of apperception becomes the "transcendental ground of the necessary conformity to law of all appearances in one experience" (A 127). But since the categories are the rules of functions of synthesis "in which alone apperception can demonstrate *a priori* its complete and necessary identity" (A 112), it follows that the categories are likewise objectively valid.

Thus we can discern in the first edition of the *Deduction* a response to the Humean scepticism which endeavors to prove: (1) that nature is not only lawful, but *necessarily* so; (2) this this necessity can only be explained from the standpoint of transcendental idealism; and (3) that the categories provide the universal rules governing this affinity. Moreover, this is accomplished by means of an argument which begins where Hume ended, i.e. with the fact of association, and which shows that the above three results express the necessary conditions for the possibility of this fact.

II

In reality, however, this argument involves an equivocation and a *petitio principii* which casts serious doubt upon the feasibility of the whole program of the Transcendental Deduction. The equivocation concerns Kant's use of *Erscheinung*. Throughout the *Critique* as a whole, and in the present passages in particular, Kant uses the term in two distinct senses. At times it is synonymous with *Phenomenon* referring to the object of human experience. In other places it is equivalent to *Vorstellung*, *Anschauung*, or even *Wahrnehmung*. These latter usages reflect the 'official' definition of *Erscheinung* as the "undetermined object of empirical intuition" (A20–B34), and points to its subjective or private character.[2] The above argument, however, is largely based upon the surreptitious move from the first to the second sense of the term, and although this may have a certain *ad hominem* justification, being directed against Hume, whose confusion of objects and impressions is notorious, it nevertheless destroys the cogency of Kant's claims.

The illicit nature of Kant's move can be easily gleaned from a brief review of the argument. In the formulation of the problem of uniformity, where he asserts that the association of appearances is a necessary condition for the empirical functioning of the imagination, he is clearly using *Erscheinung* in the first of the above senses (for example he refers to cinnabar, men, snow, ice, etc.). The move, however, from the affirmation of this *de facto* regularity, and the subjective laws of association which follow upon it, to the affirmation of the *necessity* of this regularity involves a shift from the first to the second sense. For why, after all, is such regularity necessary, and thus exempt from Hume's sceptical reflections? Only because, as we have already seen, unassociable appearances could not be brought to the unity of consciousness, and an appearance *qua* representation, which cannot be a possible object of consciousness 'would be nothing at all'. The argument here is close in spirit to Berkeley. It amounts to the claim that the *esse* of an *Erscheinung*, *qua* representation, is *percipi*, and consequently that all *Erscheinungen* must necessarily be subject to those conditions under which they can be perceived. This follows analytically from the subjective conception of *Erscheinung*, but it hardly applies to *Erscheinung* taken in the objective sense. It therefore fails to establish the necessity of the regularity of nature, and its continued conformity to our custom induced expectations.

Now it may be true that from the standpoint of transcendental idealism, it is legitimate to use *Erscheinung* in these two senses. The problem, however, is that the general purpose of the argument is to demonstrate the validity of that standpoint, and it therefore seems clear that the equivocation in the use of *Erscheinung* leads Kant into a *petitio principii*. Hence a Humean, or better, a sceptic who is not guilty of confusing statements about impressions with statements about objects, could quite well, and would indeed have to, grant Kant's analytic claim about the relation between *Erscheinung*, *qua* representation, and consciousness. He would, however, have no compunctions in denying that this has any bearing on the uniformity of nature. By arguing in this manner the sceptic becomes, in Kantian terms, a transcendental realist. Nature is regarded as a realm of things in themselves existing independently of our merely subjective conditions of apprehension. On this assumption, Kant tells us, all knowledge of nature would be *a posteriori*, and "as this could take place only empirically, none but a merely accidental unity could be obtained, which would fall short of the necessary interconnection that we have in mind when we speak of nature" (A 114). But it is precisely the alleged necessity of this connection which the sceptic is questioning in the first place. Certainly, if past associations ceased being a reliable guide to future expectations we would not be able to act with any degree of rationality, and as Hume admits our knowledge would be "limited to the narrow sphere of our memory and senses".[3] Nevertheless, such considerations fail to show that this uniformity is necessary in any but the pragmatic sense which Hume readily acknowledges, and with which Kant was not at all concerned.

In fact, the necessity which Kant claims can only be explained in terms of transcendental idealism is one which is only required by that idealism. As we have already seen, the alleged contradiction in the sceptical reflection that nature might not conform to our subjective conditions of experience is dependent upon the idealistic conception of nature as *Erscheinung*. If we deny that with either the sceptic or the realist, we deny not only the distinctively Kantian solution to the 'problem of affinity', but the very existence of the problem as Kant here defined it.

III

Against such an attack it would seem that the Kantian has two lines of defense. He can claim that the argument for affinity only appears to be question begging because it is taken out of context; for the thesis that objects of human experience are only appearances and not things in themselves has already been established in the Transcendental Aesthetic. This, however, would be to place an undue amount of weight upon what is generally regarded as the most dubious section of the *Critique*, especially since the arguments for transcendental idealism contained therein can easily be shown to be subject to a similar dialectic.[4]

A considerably more promising approach involves the reformulation of Kant's argument in such a manner that it is no longer dependent upon the equivocal notion of *Erscheinung*. This requires the translation of claims about appearances into claims about possible experience, i.e., the consciousness of a public objective world, distinct from the self. Furthermore, it is essentially this approach which characterizes the second edition of the Transcendental Deduction and the Analytic of Principles. This line of argument is based upon the correlation between self-consciousness and the consciousness of an objective world, or more specifically, upon the fact that experience requires both an object to be experienced and a self-conscious subject who does the experiencing. This subject-object structure of all possible experience is the ultimate ground of the claim that experience requires a synthesis according to necessary rules, i.e. the categories. Only under these conditions can the manifold be united into the representation of one public, spatio-temporal world, and only under the same conditions can it conform to the necessary unity of consciousness, i.e., be an object of a possible experience by an abiding and identical self. The latter, Kant tells us, is because "only in so far...as I can unite a manifold of given representations in *one consciousness*, is it possible for me to represent to myself *the identity of the consciousness* in these representations. In other words, the *analytic* unity of apperception is possible only under the presupposition of a certain *synthetic* unity" (B 133). That is to say, the very possibility of self-consciousness, and thus even experience of a subjective sort, is dependent upon a necessary and 'objectifying' synthesis. It is this conception which finds its culmination in the Refutation of Idealism where Kant shows that the awareness of an abiding and identical self is correlative with and dependent upon the awareness of an abiding world. Now since without such necessary synthetic unity neither self-consciousness nor consciousness of an object (or an objective world) would be possible, Kant can hold that the uniformity of experience, or of nature as an object of possible experience, is indeed necessary. This, of course, does not apply to nature regarded as a realm of things in themselves, but such a nature, existing by definition apart from all possible experience, would indeed be 'nothing to us'. Thus the necessary synthetic unity or lawfulness of experience assumes the role of a kind of *Urprinzip* defining its very possibility, and it is in light of this conception that Kant proceeds to demonstrate the necessity and hence objective validity of the separate principles as the general laws which determine this uniformity (cf. A 156–58 = B 195–97).

Furthermore, this better enables us to understand the misguided nature of Hume's doubts. The great sceptic had admitted that without such uniformity, which alone renders association possible, our experience would be limited to the immediate evidence of sense and memory. Kant, however, has argued that in the state of affairs envisioned by Hume's sceptical imagination there could be no experience at all. Not only would there be no awareness of an objective world apart from the self, and no possibility of distinguishing past, present, and future events, and hence remembering, but there would be no unified consciousness capable of distinguishing between impressions, or of being aware of itself as 'having' impressions. Thus Hume was right in pointing to the contingency of particular associations within experience, but he was wrong in generalizing from this to the contingency of the principle of uniformity or lawfulness itself. This uniformity is not a contingent fact on the same level as particular uniformities, but rather constitutes the framework within which we can alone discern what are the facts (cf. A766 = B794).

Now it should be noted that *this* line of argument which I have only sketched in bald terms, and which has been analyzed with great subtlety by Strawson,[5] is not at all dependent upon the equivocal notion of appearance. It still appeals to the transcendental unity of apperception, but its force does not derive from the claim that appearance, as mere representations, are nothing apart from consciousness, and thus necessarily subject to its conditions. Rather, as we have seen, the basic claim is that without uniformity in experience, i.e. necessary synthetic unity, consciousness itself would not be possible. The first argument for affinity seems to have been inspired by the model of consciousness as a kind of container in which appearances (representations) must be ordered in certain relationships. The second argument, on the other hand, operates with a dynamic conception of consciousness. Rather than being a place in which representations are contained, consciousness is itself the product of a conceptual activity. Moreover, if the former conception points backward to Berkeley, the latter points forward to Fichte and Hegel.

The juxtaposition, however, of these two conceptions and the arguments based upon them, raises some interesting questions about Kant's idealism. Strawson, for one, has denied the relevance of this idealism to the 'analytic achievement' of the *Critique*,[6] and other empirically minded critics have likewise tried to separate the 'true Kant' from this idealism with its alleged subjectivism and rigid a priorism. Furthermore, Kant himself defines transcendental idealism as "the doctrine that appearances are to be regarded as being, one and all, representations only, not things in themselves..." (A 369), and it is precisely this conception, which, as we have seen, underlies the question-begging discussion of transcendental affinity.

Nevertheless, it must be admitted that although apparently independent of the specific teachings of the Aesthetic, the argument which we have just sketched is clearly idealistic in orientation. The ultimate appeal is to the transcendental unity of apperception, and the necessary features of any possible experience, or the forms of objective validity, are not determined realistically by an examination of the nature of things, but by a consideration of the conditions of our consciousness of things, and therefore by the nature of consciousness. But if we can indeed so distinguish between two lines of argument in the *Critique*, both idealistic, but the one dependent upon, the other independent of the results of the Aesthetic, does not this suggest the intriguing possibility that perhaps the myriad attempts to distinguish between the idealistic and realistic tendencies in Kant, or to save the 'true Kant' from his erroneous idealistic preconceptions, are fundamentally misguided? Perhaps the real task is to distinguish between two strands of idealism, one genuinely critical and transcendental, and the other, for all Kant's protestations to the contrary, basically subjective and dogmatic. Let us call the former the idealism of apperception and the latter the idealism of sensibility.

University of Florida

NOTES

[1] Cf. Robert Paul Wolff, *Kant's Theory of Mental Activity*, Cambridge, Mass., 1963, pp. 162–64.
[2] Cf. N. K. Smith, *A Commentary to Kant's Critique of Pure Reason*, 2nd edition, New York, 1962, p. 83.
[3] Hume, *Enquiry*, Library of Liberal Arts edition, edited by C. W. Hendel, 1965, p. 68.
[4] Cf. *Critique*, B70, H. J. De Vleeschauwer, *La déduction transcendentale dans l'oeuvre de Kant*, 3 Vols., Paris, 1934, Vol. II, p. 559.
[5] P. F. Strawson, *The Bounds of Sense*, Methuen & Co., Ltd. London, 1966, esp. pp. 97–112.
[6] For a detailed analysis of Strawson's interpretation, see my 'Transcendental Idealism and Descriptive Metaphysics', *Kant-Studien*, Heft 2, 1969.

GERD BUCHDAHL

THE CONCEPTION OF LAWLIKENESS IN KANT'S PHILOSOPHY OF SCIENCE

I

If we want to grasp Kant's approach to the philosophy of science we need to be clear about the demarcation between the latter and his general transcendental approach as formulated in the 'Analytic of Principles' of the *Critique of Pure Reason* (A130 = B169). The lines of demarcation have not been usually appreciated very clearly. Common to many scholars is the belief that Kant *intended* to lay the foundations of *Newtonian* 'nature' in the analytical portions of the first *Critique*. In reality, there is a considerable gap. Many scholars do not even notice this gap. Others do, but they then think that Kant did not. and proceed to charge him with the failure of having appreciated the gap, thus misconstruing his *intentions*. Naturally there must be a reason for this state of affairs which can be traced partly to Kant's language and mode of presentation. Yet, the result of overlooking this gap, this looseness of fit, between Kant's theory of Newtonian science and the Transcendental Analytic, has the additional baneful result of causing us to misrepresent the significance and limitations of the latter itself. In particular, this affects our ideas about the relevance of the Analogies of Experience whose bearing in this connection is frequently misunderstood.

Since I have already attempted elsewhere to interpret Kant's intentions in the Analytic, I may perhaps be brief.[1] I assume – and this has certainly the backing of some of Kant's *ipsissima verba* – that the Analytic purports to establish no more than the experiential notion of an objective 'nature' in general, regarded as a series of singular contingent happenings and things, a notion which according to Kant essentially involves certain categorial concepts, some of which – especially the categories of relation, including those of causality and interaction (mutual causation) – have a lawlike character.

Thus something 'lawlike' is built into the notion of an objective nature, considered as a series of contingent happenings and things.[2] What is not thereby determined, and what requires a special account is whether this 'nature' is also lawlike in other senses, and further, whether nature is 'Newtonian'. As to the former: this concerns the question whether nature can be represented through a system of empirical laws, under higher-level hypotheses, the laws being regarded as principles of necessity. (I propose to call this 'empirical lawlikeness'.) A distinction which is here frequently overlooked is that between Kant's 'nature', contrasted with the 'order of nature', a parallel distinction at the level of experience being drawn by Kant between 'experience' and 'systematic experience' (cf. MPS 481–2, 499–506; 503–4). Though Kant's very fluid and technically narrow language makes it very easy to overlook these distinctions, they are quite clearcut. They manifest themselves moreover in yet another dichotomy, that which distinguishes between the unity of the manifold of perceptions and the unity of the manifold of empirical laws (MPS 518).

As to 'Newtonian nature': this is the *material* universe whose primary constituent, 'matter', is governed by certain 'laws of motion', whose 'possibility' is purportedly demonstrated in Kant's *Metaphysical Foundations of Natural Science* (hereafter called *Foundations*). Now this 'demonstration', according to Kant, explicitly involves the ingression of a concept, viz. 'matter', the interpretation of which employs 'empirical' considerations.[3] Moreover, the idea of 'construction', which in the Analytic appears under the guise of 'synthesis', and is *implicit* in the resulting notion of objective happening, or objective thinghood (in the sense either of an individual, or of a plurality of *coexisting* bodies) is in *Metaphysical Foundations* employed *explicitly* for the purpose of representing such things as the combination of motions (cf. M.489–93/160–64), or again the process of action and reaction between bodies in collision (cf. M.544–47/223–5), both belonging to quite a different level of concerns, thereby resulting again in a considerable logical gap, as will be shown below.

We may summarize these remarks by saying that there is in Kant a sharp distinction between what we may term 'transcendental lawlikeness', on the one hand, and 'empirical lawlikeness' and 'metaphysical lawlikeness' on the other. (By 'metaphysical' I simply mean the kind of lawlikeness demonstrated in *Foundations*. 'Lawlikeness' is used in the sense of conformity to law [*Gesetzmässigkeit*].)[4] Moreover, to these distinctions there correspond a variety of logical gaps of varying width which are bridged by Kant in a number of different ways.

In what has preceded I have intentionally spoken only of 'lawlikeness'. For every reader of Kant is probably aware of his basic position that our evidence for *actual* empirical *laws*, as distinct from their lawlikeness, and from the problem of the lawlikeness of nature in principle, is inductive.[5] But this is even true, I think, of the 'metaphysical' case. Thus, in one of his *Reflexionen* Kant writes: 'All metaphysical principles of nature are no more than grounds of lawlikeness.'[6] And whilst in the *Foundations* the contrary doctrine may sometimes seem defended, Kant programmatically insists that he is concerned with establishing the 'possibility' of certain Newtonian formulations, e.g. of the possibility of matter acting at a distance; of two material bodies interacting, either through impact or gravitationally, and so on.[7] Inductively, he always says, we can establish only the 'probability' of hypotheses. 'Certainty' belongs only to that which establishes 'possibility'.[8] And this is true both of 'metaphysical' and of 'empirical' lawlikeness. In both cases, the 'certainty' involved is vouchsafed by Kant's peculiar method of 'subjectivization' of procedure, whether this concerns the 'projective' (cf. A647 = B675) activity of 'reason' generating the system of empirical laws (in respect of their lawlikeness), or 'constructive' activity at the level of the understanding, where we are guided by and apply transcendental principles to the empirical concept of matter (see Note 3).

To some, the recognition of the gaps that exist between transcendental, empirical and metaphysical principles may be distressing. To others, however, this will come as a liberation, indicative of the fact that Kantian philosophy is less systematic than appears at first sight, and more tentative and exploratory than often suspected. What is important is that we should have a less crabbed and rigid approach to the different fields covered by Kantian philosophy; above all that we should not think of it as a more or less deductive enterprise, leading from transcendental principles straightway to a Newtonian physics of nature.

Yet that is the view one finds only too often in the literature, early and modern. Thus a perceptive writer on the philosophy of science like A. F. Apelt, by no means inimical to the Kantian point of view as such could say, in 1854, that Kant "demonstrates the metaphysical axioms that arise out of the mathematical schematism of the categories, as the principles of the possibility of experience. *With this*, the firm basis for a correct theory of induction was really achieved."[9] Notice the coupling of the schematism of the categories, generating 'possible experience', with 'induction'. About a hundred years later, in Heidegger's *Frage nach dem Ding* we find a similar slide. Kant's conception of 'nature' is declared, without blush, to be 'Newton's nature'.[10] And whilst on the one hand Heidegger quite correctly identifies the Kantian notions of 'possibility of experience' and 'possibility of nature', the strict sense of the Kantian term 'nature' here involved, and which we have noted before, is immediately watered down. Taking the two, for Kant, equivalent expressions, 'object of possible experience' and 'object in nature' (*Naturding*), Heidegger spontaneously interprets the latter as 'object of mathematico-physical science', the surreptitious slide from the 'transcendental' to the 'metaphysical' level concealing again the gap between the two cases (*op cit.*, 100/128). For the demonstration of the possibility of a 'Newtonian Nature' and of Newton's 'system of the world' (*Ibid.*, 98/120) to which Heidegger here refers involves both the *explicit* processes of 'metaphysical' and 'mathematical construction' developed in the *Foundations*[11] (in respect of the proper construal of Newtonian 'matter') and the regulative employment of reason (or judgment) of the first and third *Critiques*, respectively, whose intended 'project' is moreover not 'nature' but (as already mentioned) the 'order of nature'. Unless these divisions are constantly kept in mind, the structurelines of the Kantian edifice become fuzzy and its edges blunted, with consequent loss of understanding of the general nature of the enterprise.

On the other hand, as already anticipated, for lack of awareness of these structurelines some commentators in their turn charge Kant with a series of *non sequiturs*. This happens particularly with respect to the special case of causal lawlikeness. For instance, Peter Strawson has accused Kant of engaging in an impermissible slide from causality as a transcendental condition ('transcendental lawlikeness') to causality as a principle justifying actual causal inferences ('empirical lawlikeness').[12] A similar objection is found in Jonathan Bennett, who censures Kant's argument of the Second Analogy by interpreting it to imply that knowing that X precedes Y presupposes knowing that X and Y are completely causally determined.[13]

II

I will now develop these outlines in greater detail. Clearly, to perceive the distinctions just referred to, we require two things. First, a proper perception of the nature and limits of the transcendental argument, especially as involved in the Analogies. Secondly, we need to appreciate that Kant did actually intend something akin to a separate justification of empirical as well as metaphysical lawlikeness; though 'justification' is perhaps too strong a term: the arguments involved are rather looser, less logically binding than we should normally expect. Moreover, the two enterprises go together. A realization that there *are* independent arguments may prevent us perhaps from reading too much into the intentions of the Analogies, and this is particularly necessary since in the light of the traditional claims about Kantian confusions (a few of which have just been mentioned) we may suspect that the language of the Transcendental Analytic (and this is even more true of the whole presentation in the *Prolegomena*) does rather tend to conceal the true situation.

I will first of all turn to the distinction between transcendental and empirical lawlikeness, the latter covering empirical causality in particular, and empirical lawlikeness in general. As regards *transcendental* causality, limitation of space will permit only a very brief summary and somewhat dogmatic presentation of my reading of Kant's Second Analogy.[14] The object of Kant's enterprise, as I see it, it to provide our 'representation' of an otherwise 'accidental' concatenation of 'perceptions' with a concept that will convert the 'accidental' into an 'objective sequence'. The notion of 'accidental' here involved is entirely Pickwickian; it has to do with the Kantian doctrine which assigns to the object (or objective situation) the status of an 'appearance' whose structural elements are 'perceptions' which, though they are regarded as 'order*able*' in terms of spatio-temporal form ('forms of intuition'), stand in need of a simulacrum of objective order, intended – as Kant occasionally puts it – to correspond to an 'absolute time' which can itself never be 'an object of perception'.[15]

For the special case of objective sequence, the crucial point is that the members of such a sequence, generated through the injection of the concept of causality, are not as such related by any causal connection – not even in principle. The experiential sequence may be wholly contingent; indeed, this *must* be so, since anything more could not be 'given' experientially and would hence not be unproblematical – with the consequential destruction of the transcendental argument. Kant actually does note explicitly that the members of such a sequence, being contingent, do not "belong necessarily to one another in the empirical intuition, but [rather] that they belong to one another in virtue of the necessary unity of apperception in the synthesis of intuitions" (B142). The foundational force of causality exhausts itself thus entirely in providing a categorial clamp between the 'perceptions' that is meant to generate a contingent sequence at the level of experience. In that case, the transcendental context can evidently not yield any 'validating ground' (some general justificative principle of induction) that might prop up the empirical (inductive) context of causation. (Nor, let us here anticipate, is it likely that the Analogies will be available to provide in any strictly deductive fashion a ground for Kant's demonstration of the various laws of mechanics which Kant elucidates in the third section of *Foundations*.)

III

If the reading just given is correct, the question remains: What *is* the relation between the transcendental structure and the foundations of physical science? In line with the foregoing, I shall understand this question to be concerned with the problems of empirical and metaphysical lawlikeness. For the moment I will consider the former. Here it seems to me that we can distinguish four indications in Kant's writings that on the one hand make it clear that he was aware of the need for an independent foundation, and which, on the other, offer suggestions about the logical nature of the arguments that are meant to back up the requisite formulation. I will first enumerate these four indications and then add some very brief explanations – restriction of time again forbids any detailed textual backing. The four indications are as follows:

(1) The distinction between causality as a regulative principle of the understanding, and as a regulative principle of reason, with reason invoked as a spontaneous source commanding the search for causes.

(2) The second indicator has to do with a distinction similar to the first, with the added suggestion of some kind of 'analogy' existing between the two.

(3) The third indicator concerns systemicity of scientific theory as a source of the lawlikeness of empirical laws. Here, Kant is quite explicit that we require the regulative and systematic activity of reason for an independent foundation of empirical lawlikeness in general.

(4) The last indicator concerns the contention sometimes expressed quite explicitly that the concept of causality, whilst 'founded' or legitimized in the transcendental argument, is, at the level of empirical lawlikeness, only *applied*. In other words, at this level causality provides us with conceptual form, not transcendental foundation.

Let me give some very sketchy backings to these 'indications'.

(1') Causality as a regulative principle of reason (contrasted with a principle of the understanding) occurs prominently in the Fourth Antinomy (A561 = B589). At the level of reason, this principle is said to require us to 'expect and to seek out' the empirical conditions responsible for change. It thus functions as a kind of postulate of empirical science. It would however make no sense to say that we 'know' the principle to be universally binding; Kant explicitly recognizes this when he contrasts the force of reason with that of the understanding:

> That *everything* which happens, has a cause is not a principle *known* and *prescribed* by reason. That principle makes the unity of experience possible, and borrows nothing from reason, which... could never, from mere concepts, have imposed such synthetic unity. (My italics) (A307 = B 363).

Reason is thus not *bound* to a universal application of the rule of causation (except of course in terms of its own spontaneous needs), for the only place which necessitates its universality is at the level of the understanding, where it functions as a transcendental condition of possible experience in general, and thus of the possibility of objective events (sequences).

On the other hand, there does exist some *connection* between the two levels, as becomes explicit in a passage that occurs in the context of the Third Antinomy, where Kant contends that we stand in need of the principle of causal connection, for the purpose of 'searching after and formulating' causal connections in the realm of phenomena (A544 = B572). He thereupon continues that provided we 'allow' this principle, and 'weaken it through no exceptions', then the understanding [which – he reminds us – sees causality built into *every* item of 'nature', in the sense of objective happening, contingent or otherwise] 'has all it can demand'; and 'physical explanations may proceed on their own lines without interference'.

Here, you see, the understanding, so to speak, holds up a mirror to reason. But where the former is bound by the conditions of possible experience in general, the latter is only constrained by the need to formulate 'physical explanations' – quite a different matter. Two things stand out: The universality of the causal principle at the level of reason (physical science) is only 'demanded', and not a transcendental ingredient. Secondly, *that* no exceptions are allowed, whilst a *requirement* of reason, is at best only helped along by the 'bidding' of the understanding. The justification of empirical lawlikeness is as such a function of reason, and not the understanding.

(2') I proceed to the *analogy* that holds between understanding and reason. One important passage occurs in the Appendix to the Transcendental Dialectic (A642 = B671ff.). Kant there contrasts the unity of the perceptual manifold of the understanding, achieved by the help of its categorial concepts, with the unity of empirical laws which results from the regulative activity of reason, the latter being called the 'analogon' of the former. Analogy involves identity as well as difference. And it is the difference that is here important. The categorial principles, writes Kant, "prescribe *a priori* to the understanding thoroughgoing unity", but (note well!) they hold "only indirectly of the object of experience", namely by indicating "the procedure whereby the empirical and determinate employment of the understanding can be brought into complete harmony with itself" (A665 = B693). Once again we note the contrast between '*a priori* prescription' at the level of the understanding and 'the procedure' of systematization of empirical laws at the level of reason, – not a transcendental matter but one possessing merely methodological import. At the same time, as we shall indicate in a moment, it is this logically rather weaker form of methodological activity of systematization that (according to Kant) first generates the notion of empirical lawlikeness.

Other passages, implying the relation of analogy between the two levels, occur also in the First Introduction to the Critique of Judgement. Thus in Section II, an explicit analogy is drawn between the categories in relation to particular experience, and the systematic power of judgment (another name for theoretical reason) in relation to its particular empirical laws. But whilst the category 'determines... synthetic unity objectively', reason 'yields [only] subjective principles that serve as guiding thread for our enquiry into nature' (IJ 204.26–8/10). Once again, the transcendental compulsiveness at the level of the understanding is contrasted with the merely methodological prescriptiveness at the level of reason, with the former throwing its analogical shadow on the latter. The category yields mere contingency, and only indirectly, and *via* its analogical power, does it suggest a systematically unifying approach at the level of reason, an approach which reason as such imposes upon itself, but only 'subjectively', not 'objectively'. For whilst the unifying act of the understanding is balanced by an 'object' which is 'given', the corresponding act of reason is not balanced by any 'object', but on the contrary *creates* its 'project': 'Systematic unity is... only a projected unity, to be regarded not as given in itself, but as a problem only' (A647=B675).

(3') The indicators, which I have sketched so far evidently cut down severely the power of the understanding to yield empirical causality and physical explanation. It remains to show that reason in its 'hypothetical employment' (or the reflective judgment of the third *Critique*) is actually regarded by Kant as the source of empirical lawlikeness. I have already alluded to Kant's oft-repeated reminder that the categories do not yield particular empirical laws without recourse to experience (cf. B165). What I am maintaining is that according to his less frequently noted view, they do not even yield lawlikeness,[16] which requires an independent foundation, to be shunted between the transcendental principle and the actual empirical law. Since this is made properly explicit only in the two introductions to the *Critique of Judgment*, it is not surprising that it has often been overlooked.

Empirical laws qua empirical, Kant tells us in Section V of the second Introduction, are contingent. Yet they must be *thought as necessary*. The reason Kant gives is that 'otherwise they would not constitute an order of nature' (J. 184.30–1, 184.36 and 185.3/21). Evidently, this ties their necessitarian status to scientific systematization. Section IV completes the argument: In so far as empirical generalizations are to be 'called laws they must be regarded as necessary'. And why? 'In virtue of principles of the unity of the manifold' – which is here a reference *not* to the unity of the understanding but to reason or reflective judgment (J.180.4/16)

The fourth section of the First Introduction supplements this further. An infinity of uniformities is always possible; it is our 'need' alone to 'think experience as a system' that limits this infinity, by demanding that 'nature' should be 'characterized as experience qua empirical system', by for instance putting particular laws under more general ones (IJ. 209.29/15). Once more, then, the necessitarianism of empirical laws, their lawlikeness, is a function of the unifying procedure of reason or judgment, and this procedure is one which reason is driven to procure, especially under the guidance of its 'ideal' – God.[17]

Let me finalize the argument by returning to the sixth section of the second Introduction. Here Kant explicitly states that the understanding is not in a position to '*pre*scribe any [empirical] law' to nature; rather, it is 'judgment [which] *a*scribes to nature' an order which mirrors the systematic activity of science (J. 188.9–10/23). Within the Kantian system, the phrase 'nature is subject to law' has thus two quite different senses: once, as a reference to the fact that transcendental necessity is built into the concept of possible experience in general (or objectivity or thinghood); a second time, that reason or judgment *ascribes* to nature an order which is the source of empirical lawlikeness.

(4′) This is the place briefly to refer to our fourth and final indicator of the gap that divides transcendental from empirical lawlikeness. It occurs in connection with the special case of the concept of causality. Here we can again distinguish two cases: (1) causality as a transcendental concept which converts an 'accidental' series of perceptions into an objective sequence of events; (2) causality as a concept employed in an inductive context, when it supplies a formal means of converting a judgment concerning a uniformity of sequence into a judgment of causation. Thus, a passage at A159 implies that whilst the concept of causality, for instance, is a transcendental ingredient of every empirical statement, whether lawlike or not, in the special case of empirical laws the very same concept is *applied*, a second time over, viz. in order to yield the form of empirical lawlikeness. *Per contra*, as it is put in this passage, the necessitarian character of empirical laws contains a suggestion [Vermutung] (though note: it is *only* a suggestion!) of the transcendental concepts which antedate all experience. Clearly, the two are not identical; they run only in parallel. (This is not to say that Kant does not sometimes conflate the two cases, especially for the sake of popular exposition, as in *Prolegomena*, the two footnotes to paras. 20 and 22, with their example of the sun warming the stone. Kant could perhaps defend his procedure by saying that the 'applied' case is an analogy for the 'transcendental' one.)

Again the third *Critique* makes this more explicit. According to Section V of the second Introduction, all causal situations, as being part of 'nature', have in common for instance the transcendental ingredient of causality. But the specific way in which 'different natures' have their causes 'must have its rule, which is a law and therefore brings necessity with it, although we do not at all have any insight into this necessity' (J. 183.20–22/19). The association between the transcendental and the empirical context is implicit, but nonetheless quite clear: each empirical case is treated 'in accordance with the concept of cause' [nach dem Begriffe einer Ursache, überhaupt] (J. 183.19–20/19). Here the case of purely formal application, rather than of transcendental presupposition, of causality is made perfectly evident.

Let me summarize the results of our survey of the four indications which Kant supplies concerning the 'foundation' of empirical lawlikeness. Evidently, there is no interest in providing something like an 'inductive' justification of the kind called in question by Hume, and subsequently attempted by the whole stream of inductive logicians from Mill to Keynes. If anything, Kant (like some modern deductivists) is more concerned with defining the conditions under which empirical uniformities (be their inductive foundation what you like) may be regarded as possessing the character of laws, i.e. statements with necessitarian import. His solution is twofold, with either formal or material import. Formally, lawlikeness is generated by employing the category (mostly causality) to cast statements of uniformity in causal form (Indicator 4). This procedure is 'a priori' only in the Pickwickian sense (a) that the concept of causality has the transcendental function of defining 'nature in general'; (b) that the explicit form of *causal* statements is not (as with Hume) derived from, nor produced by, statements of uniformity, but is injected or applied as a quasi-grammatical act 'from outside'. Materially, lawlikeness is the result of the legislative or regulative function of reason, answering analogically to the suggestions of the understanding (Indicators 1 and 2). More specifically the procedure of reason occurs in the context of its systematic and constructive employment (Indicator 3). As Kant writes:

If empirical laws *are to be called* laws…, they must be regarded as necessary in virtue of a principle of the unity of the manifold [supplied by reflective judgment]…. Without this presupposition we should have no order of nature in accordance with empirical laws, and consequently no guiding thread for an experience ordered by these in all their variety. (My italics) (J. 180.2–5/16; 185.19–22/21–2).

IV

The lawlikeness of the empirical laws of Newtonian science (e.g. of Kep-

THE CONCEPTION OF LAWLIKENESS

ler's laws, Galilei's laws) have now been seen to be a function of the architectonic of reason; it is injected, so to speak, 'from above'. There are, however, certain privileged principles whose necessitarian character is established 'from below'. They are part of Kant's 'special metaphysics of nature', being contrasted with his 'general metaphysics' (i.e. the doctrine of the Transcendental Analytic) where the former, instead of being occupied only with the concept of nature in general, involves the introduction of a *specific* aspect of nature, viz. nature qua 'matter' – a concept which Kant declares to be 'empirical'.

In the *Foundations* this concept is 'analysed' under the guidance of the categories and transcendental principles, an analysis which in turn involves what Kant once called a 'metaphysical construction' whose aim it is to allow the application of 'mathematical construction' to the result of the analysis.[18] Such a construction is necessary in order to obtain the intuitional aspect of the concept of matter, for only in this way can we explicate the 'real possibility' (as contrasted with the purely logical possibility) of a mechanical science (M. 470.26–18/140).

There is here once again a parallelism with the procedure of the Transcendental Analytic. There, 'possibility' also requires something akin to 'construction', viz. transcendental synthesis, which is indeed implicit in the very notion of nature in general. It is something contained in that *conception* of nature (or 'possible experience in general'), the 'objectivity' of the transcendental argument being guaranteed by the fact that the conception is 'balanced' by there *being* such an 'experience' and such a 'nature'.[19] In the case of special metaphysics, matters are slightly different. Here we are more 'creative', we literally and 'explicitly' construct a conception in order to *bring about* a possible science of Newtonian mechanics. It is true that the notion whose 'possibility' is thereby again demonstrated is likewise 'balanced' by a previously existing element, viz. what Kant takes to be Newtonian mechanics. But evidently this is a body whose character is more 'problematic' than is the fact of 'experience in general' of the first *Critique*. We may anticipate that this parallelism again opens the way to a misleading conflation of two quite different cases. For instance, in the famous paragraph of the Preface to the *Foundations*, which contends for the necessarily mathematical nature of science proper, it is argued that the real possibility of the objects of nature (i.e. Newtonian mathematizable matter) requires an 'intuition' corresponding to the concept, an 'intuition' which is said to be tantamount to 'construction' (metaphysical and mathematical (M. 470.25–6/140; 473.7–8/143). Not that Kant is unaware that he is here conflating two different levels, for he suddenly slips in the reminder that the 'general' case, on which the special case is here modelled, is concerned only with the notion of 'the concept of nature in general', and does thus not actually require *mathematical* construction. Unfortunately, Kant's *examples* of transcendental synthesis sometimes involve mathematical models, as for instance his example of the drawing of the line in the Transcendental Deduction (B138). This contributes further to the possible confusion in the mind of the unattentive reader.

There appears thus again a gap, this time between the treatment of the Transcendental Analytic and the special metaphysics of nature. And more than likely the principles elucidated in the latter, universal repulsion and attraction, the conservation of matter, its laws of inertia, and of action and reaction, will not grow smoothly and deductively out of the transcendental principles. Let us follow this up by looking at the *Metaphysical Foundations* more closely.

First of all, Kant recognizes explicitly that the metaphysical construction of the concept of matter is 'empirical' (M.470.2–5/140; 472.8/142). True, the categorial table is used as a classificatory guide to the four-fold analysis; Kant speaks of the analysis being 'in accordance with' the transcendental principles [*nach Gesetzen*] (M.472.10/142). Thus, the category of quality is associated with the second chapter, Dynamics. The subdivisions of that category, 'reality, negation and limitation' suggestively parallel Kant's analysis of the 'filling of space' in terms of repulsion, attraction and the balance between these, leading to the notion of 'degrees' of the filling of space which links up with the second transcendental principle, the 'Anticipations of Perception'. But such classificatory guidance does not provide a shadow of justificative power in any *a priori* sense. And still less is this true of Kant's interpretation of the 'quality' of matter, its power to 'fill space', as a 'particular motive force' (M.496.6/169; 497.16/170). For this analysis, as we have noted already, is said to be basically 'empirical'.

What does Kant here mean by 'empirical'? [20] For an answer we need to go back to the 1763 tract on the *Clarity of the Principles of Natural Theology and Ethics*, where Kant emphasizes that metaphysics cannot start (unlike mathematics) with clear (because autonomously constructed)

definitions of essences. Indeed it must begin with 'confused' concepts, the
task of metaphyscis being their clarification by some kind of logical
analysis; 'in metaphysics one must proceed entirely by analysis'.[21] Such
an analysis operates on what is part of our 'internal experience' and what
is given in an 'immediate evident consciousness' (CP286.16–18/18). Moreover, the concept which we thus seek to clarify is not given all at once, nor
once and for all; we need (as Kant notes) to develop the analysis through
a continual and widely extended survey of its use, taking 'note of every
changed application of the concept' (CP.289.32/22). His example is particularly pertinent to our topic. An attempt to clarify the nature of action
through impact or attraction-at-a-distance, soon leads us to ask such
analytical questions as 'what do we mean by touch?' And the resulting
conceptual explication will show that what is involved (for the case of
impact) is the 'resistance of impenetrability' of a body.[22] But this reference
to resistance at once suggests that the operative notion here is that of a
force. In consequence it is also quite possible to speak of the action of a
body at a distance since the operative aspect of all material being is
evidently the notion of force.

   Though this way of construing 'metaphysical enquiry' *as a method* is not
explicitly referred to in the later *Foundations*, its application is evident
from many of its pages. We need only name the Note to Theorem 1 of the
second chapter (Dynamics) where Kant criticizes the approach of 'Lam-
bert and others' who identify the 'real in space' (its 'existence') as 'solidity',
and imply that resistance to interpenetration is true analytically ('in
accordance with the law of contradiction'). Instead (Kant argues) we should
build into matter the property of force itself, for only in this way can we
apply the vectorial methods of mechanics, enabling us to add and subtract
forces in space (M.497.30–498.15/170–71). 'Empirical' has here a generalized import which includes those observations and hypotheses that led
Newton, for instance, to the elucidation of his theory of dynamics.

   Evidently Kant is here utilizing the scientific tradition (Newtonian)
of history by building the notion of force into the very conception of
material body. His argument is that metaphysics cannot fall back on any
idea of 'real essence' but needs to take its survey from 'experience' –
reminiscent of some of Kant's predecessors and contemporaries, e.g.
Locke, John Keill, Maupertuis etc.[23]

   Kant's analysis is however 'empirical' in yet a further sense, which contrasts *a priori* with *a posteriori*, since for Kant the presence of forces is pre-eminently never an *a priori* item of knowledge. 'Actual forces', he notes in the Second Analogy, 'can only be given empirically', and this is because 'the possibility of fundamental forces' can never be made comprehensible (A207 = B252). The reason is that forces as such cannot be constructed, they are only 'first data' for such a construction,[24] e.g. when we coordinate corresponding spatio-temporal notions with such forces; but the *existence* of these forces nevertheless remains opaque to the intellect. So the most we can show (as Kant says in the General Note to Dynamics) is that force unavoidably belongs to the concept of matter, and even this attribution is only an 'assumption' (M.524.29/200).

This whole 'metaphysical construction' has hence only the 'negative' purpose of showing that it is possible to build the conception of repulsive and attractive force into the very idea of matter itself, thereby indicating that it is not necessary (as for instance was the case for Newton) to 'add' attractive force secondarily, as something 'foreign', to a concept of matter that has previously been declared *essentially* to lack the power of attraction.[25] All this is evidently a very tentative and exploratory activity, proceeding merely architectonically under the guidance of the categories, together with certain conceptual analyses which borrow heavily from the result of the Newtonian tradition – not however, let us insist, by way of a sleight of hand, but on Kant's own admission. Once again we see that certainly the transcendental portions of the *Critique* are by no means sufficient to yield a '*Newtonian* nature'; the relations between the 'general' and the 'special' metaphysics are extremely loose. Nor can there be any question of Kant having claimed any ability to provide an *a priori* demonstration of any laws of force, for instance of the law of gravitation.

Here, the language of the Preface to *Foundations* which is again extremely fluid can easily be misunderstood. This claims that science proper requires a 'pure part' whose laws should 'involve a consciousness of their necessity' – unlike for instance the laws of chemistry. Kant then shunts in the consideration that the 'term nature already involves the concept of laws' which itself has a necessitarian grammar. (These 'laws' are of course the transcendental principles of the Analytic.) Hence, he goes on, science proper can '*derive the justification* of this appellation [sc. science] from its pure part only, viz. the one containing the principles *a priori* of the remainder of its explanations'.[26]

But 'deriving the justification of an appellation' is not the same as a logical derivation of lower-level laws from higher-level *a priori* principles. Nor should the term 'principles' be understood here as being simply tantamount to *a priori laws*. For although it involves, no doubt, reference to the transcendental principles so-called, it also includes Kant's 'empirical analysis' together with his 'metaphysical and mathematical constructions' of matter. True, there will be as much 'purity' in the resulting science as this contains 'principles' in the sense here understood. Nevertheless, the emphasis is not on complete deductive development but on 'insight'. Kant's interest, as often as not, is with 'understanding' and not 'knowledge'. Clearly therefore, his language is meant to be consistent with his subsequent affirmation that one cannot, and must not even 'dare' to, formulate laws of attractive and repulsive force on the mere strength of 'a priori conjectures', of the kind suggested in Kant's own geometrical analogies which were meant to lend plausibility to the form of certain laws of force (M.534.15–18/212). These are certainly 'thinkable', but not even their 'real possibility' has been demonstrated (M.524.36–40/201), so that the only proper and correct procedure is to 'infer' such laws (including that of the inverse-square) 'from the data of experience' (M.534.18/212). A *logically* possible ('conceivable') construction (*via* models) must not be confused with the quite different notion of the 'construction' of a concept yielding 'real possibility' – a confusion which Kant's somewhat complex presentation has led generations of readers astray.

V

If there is a *visible* gap between the law of gravitation and the concept of matter as involving attractive force, that between the 'laws of mechanics' (conservation of mass, inertia, action and reaction) and the corresponding principles of possibility, enunciated in the third chapter of *Foundations* (Mechanics) is much less apparent. Let us pursue this by concentrating on the Third Law: 'In the communication of motion, action and reaction are always equal' – Newton's Third Law of motion, since this involves interesting problems of interpretation that have been less frequently dealt with in their entirety (M.544–M/223–5).

The situation here is different from that in the chapter on Dynamics, for Kant now employs the transcendental principles explicitly; in the

present case, the principle of the Third Analogy. To develop the proof of
the Third Law, that principle (Kant tells us) is 'borrowed' [*entlehnt*] from
general metaphysics. The rest of the proof cannot be discussed here as it
would lead us too far afield. It involves the contention that the principle
of interaction, when represented through a process of mathematical 'construction' yields the notion of equality between reaction and action. (For
instance, using the case of collision, one apportions the momenta between
colliding bodies equally between them, which Kant achieves by a 'relativi-
zation' of 'empirical space', suspended in a framework of 'absolute
space'. The result is then further extended to the case of 'attraction'.)
(M.548.25–449.4/227).

Now Kant says that the proof 'borrows' the transcendental principle.
What he does not make clear is that he thereby really transfers it to a
different logical level. Consider the Third Analogy. Its principle is that a
plurality of bodies coexisting in space stand in mutual interaction. Speaking more in line with the argument of the transcendental method, this
means that the notion of an objectively coexisting plurality of physical
things presupposes, or contains, the categorial concept of interaction.[27]
Where before the concept of causality yielded objective contingent sequence, the concept of mutual causation, or interaction, yields contingent
simultaneity and coexistence. And just as before causality yielded a model
replacing 'absolute time', so now interaction replaces 'absolute space' –
a fact which is obscured by Kant's emphasis on time in the Third Analogy,
but which becomes much clearer if we consider the corresponding discussions of the problem of coexistence in *Nova Dilucidatio* and the *Inaugural
Dissertation*, where we can trace the historical roots of Kant's at first sight
somewhat surprising choice of the concept of interaction as such.

Kant throughout his life held to the doctrine that space and time are not
available for yielding the notion of coexistence of a plurality of bodies.
The *Inaugural Dissertation* says that space and time are wrongly conceived
as 'some real and absolutely necessary bond', which might *per impossibile*
assign the required positions to the different bodies.[28] Even if we regard
(as already in the *Dissertation*) space and time as *forms* of intuition, this
only gives us the '*possibility* of universal coordination' (or as we might say;
spatiality and temporality) but not 'the relation ... called space' (the '*formal*
intuition' aspect of the *Critique*).[29] On the contrary, Kant implies, the
question of coexistence of a plurality has to be shunted *via* the notion of

'mutual interaction', and it is the possibility (or rather, assumption of validity) of the latter that is really in question. Indeed – and this is developed in greater detail in the *Nova Dilucidatio* – it is the mutual interactions between independent substances that give us the notion of space.[30]

Now what is the status of this 'interaction'? Both *Nova Dilucidatio* and the *Dissertation* emphasize that it is not some kind of 'crude' *influxus physicus*.[31] Rather – and here Kant follows a doctrine very characteristic of some of Newton's speculations – God must be regarded as the ground of the harmonious mutual adjustment of what would otherwise be altogether independent physical substances; something that manifests itself for instance as a 'basic law of nature' (the law of attraction) (ND.415.14/ 505). As in Newton, interaction is regarded teleologically, or even nomologically, rather than physically. It follows that God provides the ground or rationale for the *possibility* of interaction and – what comes here to the same thing – of coexistence.[32] We are not concerned with its status as physical fact, however this may be obtained or interpreted – i.e. whether you hold that it is 'derived inductively from the phenomena' or has the status of an hypothetical construct, or whatever.

Still, the argument *is* meant to yield support for the possibility of conceiving interaction between fully-fledged physical substances. Now consider the situation in the first *Critique* and subsequently. In the earlier period the atomic independence of individual substances was due to their being regarded as a kind of monads. In the critical argument, the logical independence relates to 'perceptions'. It is because these are set (prior to categorial processing) only in space and time in general (forms of intuition) that they will stand in need of linking *via* a synthetic process in accordance with categorial concepts – in the present case the concept of interaction (cf. A211 = B256ff.). Where in the earlier period, interaction was grounded in God, the whole conception yielding coexistence, it is now validated by its power to generate 'possible experience', in the sense of yielding the notion of (our perception of) objective coexistence. Ontological has been replaced by epistemological grounding; but we still are not concerned with any putative physical reality of interaction. (This by itself shows that we should be careful not to saddle Kant with the claim of having proved the existence of physical forces between material bodies.)

However, and furthermore, the considerations already advanced in connection with the Second Analogy now apply again. Kant must not say (and we have seen that he repudiates the suggestion explicitly, for instance in the passage at B142) that there *is* interaction (even in the rarefied sense evolved in the pre-critical writings) between the members of the empirical intuition, but rather, that interaction is a concept which exhausts its logical force by creating the possibility of cognition of spatial togetherness, whatever the connections (if any) between the thereby resulting plurality of bodies may be. What is really involved is a dual and successive jump in levels. The first jump occurs in moving from the 'manifold of perceptions' to 'plurality of coexisting bodies'. (First to second level.) The concept of interaction here props up the notion, not just of coexistence, but of a coexisting plurality of physical bodies existing objectively in space and time. But this does not entail its availability for the purpose of the 'special metaphysics of nature', for supplying the grounds of lawlikeness. It is however easy to construe Kant as having jumped to this third level without further justification, involving something of a logical slide; a slide made all the easier by being apparently sanctioned in the pre-critical position, where 'interaction' functions between fully fledged 'substances', and not 'perceptions'.

The situation is then as follows. Kant has now shown that the concept of interaction has a transcendental validation; that it connects trans-cendentally or *a priori* with the notion of plurality of contingently coexis-ting bodies. Whether this has further relevance also for such bodies in actual physical interaction, is quite another question – although the nature of that interaction (and the whole outlook this involves) will no doubt be conceived much on the lines of the pre-critical argumentation. Hence, the question of the *possibility* of real interaction between bodies can only be broached through an additional premise, i.e. the application of what I have called 'explicit construction' and the corresponding Kantian con-strual of matter as 'the movable which possesses moving force';[33] a definition which we have shown for Kant to be the result of an 'empirical' analysis, in the sense of 'empirical' previously elucidated; i.e. nothing 'transcendental' but purely conceptual, and moreover involving the postulation of the 'opaque element' of force as an ingredient in the conception of matter.

Our result is this. Interaction first occurs as a transcendental component of the notion of objective coexistence of a plurality of bodies. The tran-scendental argument (Third Analogy) provides its *validation*, a validation which simultaneously yields demonstration of the real *possibility* of co-existence. The *Foundations* however are meant to demonstrate, not the *validity*, but the *possibility* of interaction between this plurality of bodies, and it does this by 'borrowing' the transcendental principle, and applying it to material bodies metaphysically construed as endowed with forces. The argument is hence once again far looser than one might have expected; it is quite wrong to saddle Kant with the view, expressed by some commentators, that the Third Analogy was meant to demonstrate or that it was meant to entail (and if so, entirely fallaciously) the conclusion that between all physical bodies there act forces. Rather, the argument of the *Foundations* only contends that whilst interaction is an essential conceptual component of our notion of coexistence (part of the notion of nature in general), the corresponding principle of interaction *may* be *applied* to yield the construction as given in the proof of the Third Law of motion. I say '*may*', not *must*; the employment of the principle of the Third Analogy is just as tentative as is the construal of matter that endows it with moving force. The argument is just as limited as that in the section on Dynamics (in relation to the conception of matter as force), i.e. essentially 'negative', as we have found Kant actually to tell us. It seeks to supply contentions which suggest possibilities and insights, not physical actualities. It seeks to show that there are considerations that speak in favour of Newton's Third Law which are not simply crudely empirical; the law is not simply derived from observation. A view which on general and somewhat different grounds has found favour in recent times with a number of interpreters of Newtonian dynamics.[34]

Here, as in our previous cases, Kant's philosophical procedure can be seen to be creatively exploratory and even tentative, rather than crudely deductive. The architectonic display serves as a guideline, not as a foundation for logical demonstration, though no doubt the psychological effect of the introduction of the table of categories can easily produce the false impression of logical conclusiveness where none is to be found nor intended. What *is* clear, is that the transcendental principles of the *Critique* yield neither empirical lawlikeness nor a Newtonian nature defined in terms of the basic concepts and laws of motion. To obtain this result, concepts and constructions have to be added which have an analogical resemblance to the critical apparatus but which sit very loosely on the ensuing result. *Per contra*, any change in the picture of physics, for in-

stance from the Newtonian to post-Newtonian period would as such seem
to leave the core of the critical arguments intact, unless it is shown that
more basic 'classical' assumptions have insinuated themselves into the
body of the *Critique* itself. For instance, it may be that the concept of
'state' which Kant employs in the formulation of the Second Analogy
embodies Newtonian classical assumptions no longer acceptable today.
However, before we turn to such problems, it seems required that we
should first obtain a clearer view of the whole structure of the Kantian
argument, and the connections which it spins between the different parts
of the edifice of science.

University of Cambridge

NOTES

[1] See for instance my *Metaphysics and the Philosophy of Science: Descartes to Kant*,
Oxford and Cambridge, Mass. 1969 [referred to as MPS]; Ch. VIII, especially sections
8(d) to 8(e); 'The Kantian "Dynamic of Reason" with special reference to the place of
causality in Kant's system', in *Kant Studies Today* (ed. by L. W. Beck), LaSalle, Ill.
1969, pp. 341–74; 'Causality, Causal Laws and Scientific Theory in the Philosophy of
Kant', *British J. Phil. Sci.*, XVI (1965) 187–208; 'The Relation between "Understanding" and "Reason" in the Architectonic of Kant's Philosophy', *Proc. Arist. Soc.* 67
(1967), 209–26.
[2] Cf. *Prolegomena*, paras. 14, 16–17; *Kant's gesammelte Schriften*, Berlin 1910, Akademie ed. Vol. 4, 1947, 295.27, 296.8–9; (transl. by P. G. Lucas), Manchester 1953,
52–54. [Referred to as P.; e.g. P.294.7/52. 294.7 means p. 294, line 7.]
[3] *Metaphysical Foundations of Natural Science*, Preface; *Schriften*, vol. 4, 170.2–5,
427.8; (transl. by E. B. Bax), *Kant's Prolegomena and Metaphysical Foundations of
Natural Science*, London 1883, 140, 142, [Referred to as M, e.g. M.170.2–5/140.]
[4] For the 'transcendental' case of lawlikeness, cf. Reference 1; also B 164–5. For the
contract with the 'empirical' case, cf. the *First Introduction to the Critique of Judgment*,
Schriften, Vol. 20, 203.3–21, 204.1–11; (transl. by J. Haden), Libr. of Lib. Arts,
Indianapolis, 1965, 9–10. [Referred to as IJ; e.g. 203.3/9.]
[5] Cf. B165; A792/B820; *Critique of Judgment, Schriften*, Vol. 5, 180.1, 184.31–2;
(transl. by J. H. Barnard), New York 1951, 16, 21. [Referred to as J; e.g. J.180.1/16.]
[6] Reflexion 5414; *Schriften*, Vol. **18**, 176.27–8. Since the whole Reflexion is important,
I here quote it in full:

"It may be possible empirically to discover rules, but not laws; for instance Kepler as
contrasted with Newton. For laws involve necessity, hence that they can be grasped
a priori. However, as regards the rules of nature we do always assume that – qua nature
– they are necessary, and that they can be grasped *a priori*, for which reason we speak
of them as being posited *anticipando*. The understanding is the ground of empirical
laws, and hence of an empirical necessity where, although the ground of the lawlikeness
can be grasped *a priori* – e.g. the law of causality – it is not possible to grasp the ground

of the particular determinate law. All metaphysical principles of nature are only grounds of lawlikeness' (*loc. cit.*, 176.19–28).

7 Cf. M.470.19/140; 494.16–28/166; 508.12/182; 510.29/186; 521.14/196; 524.25/200; 550.8/229.

8 Cf. A647/B675; A790/B818; A770/B798; cf. A222–3/B269; *Logic, Schriften*, Vol. 9, 85.17–19; (transl. by T. K. Abbott), *Kant's Introduction to Logic*, New York 1964, 76.

9 E. F. Apelt, *Die Theorie der Induction*, Leipzig 1854, 163; my italics.

10 Martin Heidegger, *Die Frage nach dem Ding*, Tübingen 1962, 98; (transl. by Barton and Deutsch), *What is a Thing?*, New York, 1965, 126.

11 M.473.7/143. The translation unaccountably omits the words 'metaphysical and', where Kant's text has 'where metaphysical and mathematical constructions traverse one another'.

12 Peter Strawson, *The Bounds of Sense*, London 1966, 137. For a criticism of this, cf. my MPS, 661–65.

13 Jonathan Bennett, *Kant's Analytic*, Cambridge 1966, 229.

14 For a more detailed discussion, cf. my MPS, 648ff; also *Kant Studies Today, loc. cit.*, 346ff.

15 A199/B245. For 'accidental', cf. my MPS, 628–41.

16 Cf. J.179.31–180.30/15–16; 182.37–185.22/19–22. Many Kant commentators seem to overlook these pages and thus fail to recognize that Kant interpolates an additional step between transcendental lawlikeness and the 'resort to experience' (B165), required in order to obtain 'empirical laws'; the step in question being the provision of a ground for 'empirical lawlikeness'.

17 Cf. A671/B699; A681/B709; also my MPS, 523–30.

18 M.472.5/142; 473.7/143; 476.7–9/146.

19 For this 'balance', cf. MPS, 619, 638–9.

20 Matter is defined as 'the movable in space', qua object of 'outer sense'; and this is *a priori* in so far as motion is conceived by Kant as a 'combination' (cf. A41/B58) of spatial and temporal determinations. On the other hand, as B155a tells us, 'that something is movable cannot be known *a priori*, but only through experience'. In an interesting comment, Peter Plaass, in *Kant's Theorie der Naturwissenschaft* (Göttingen 1965), argues that 'it is not the content of the concept [of matter] that is empirical, but only the fact of its objective reality' (loc. cit. p. 88) – the latter, for the reason given at B155n. However, the 'content' of the concept of matter is not exhausted by its 'explanation' as 'the movable in space', but by those further explanations given at the start of the sections on 'dynamics' and 'mechanics'. Plaass says that Kant 'develops' the additional specifications required 'under the four category-headings', 'out of the content of the concept of motion', and that 'what matters here is... what one has to add in thought [dazudenken muss]' (*loc. cit.*, 102). But what has to be 'added in thought' borrows heavily from contemporary science, whether Kant realizes it or not. There is however a hint of the way in which Kant conceived all this to be quite explicitly an empirical matter. For although Plaass says that there is in Kant's writings no reference to what he can have meant by an 'empirical' analysis, and that it would be 'desirable to obtain some verbatim references' (*loc. cit.*, 87), we do have a primary locus of such a reference in the pre-critical *Clarity of Principles*.

21 *Enquiry concerning the Clarity of the Principles of Natural Theology and Ethics, Schriften*, Vol. 2, 289.4–5; (transl. by G. B. Kerferd and D. E. Walford), *Kant: Selected Pre-Critical Writings*, Manchester 1968, 21. For 'confused', cf. CP.283.32/15. [Referred to as CP; e.g. CP.289.4–5/21.]

[22] CP.287.7–15/20. This recurs later at M.513.1–514.10/187–8.

[23] See for instance John Keill, *An Introduction to Natural Philosophy* (London, 1920), 7–8, 12.

[24] M.498.9/171; cf. also 525.11/201.

[25] Cf. M.525.14–15/201, where Kant remarks that the Newtonian conceptual scheme, contrary to his own, is forced to operate with the 'empty concept' of 'absolute impenetrability', and to give up all notion of 'forces inherent [eigene] in matter itself'.

[26] M.468.26/138; 470.36–471.10/141; 468.35/138; 469.1–3/139.

[27] A211/B256ff. Cf. my MPS, 665–71; and for its application to the Third Law, *loc. cit.*, 678–81.

[28] *On the Form and Principles of the Sensible and Intelligible World* (Inaugural Dissertation); *Schriften*, Vol. 2, 406.27; (transl. by Kerferd and Walford), *op. cit.*, 74. [Referred to as ID; e.g. ID.406.27/74.]

[29] ID.407.4–5/74. For 'formal intuition', cf. B160a. For my interpretation and defence of this concept, cf. MPS, index under 'space, formal intuition (determinate space)'.

[30] *Principiorum Cognitionis Metaphysicae Nova Dilucidatio*, *Schriften*, Vol. 1, 415.5–8. German transl. in W. Weischedel. *Werke*, Wiesbaden 1960, Vol. 1, 505. [Referred to as ND; e.g. ND.415.5–8/505.]

[31] ND.415.23–4/505; ID.407.23/75; 409.16/78.

[32] ND.412–14/497–501; ID.409–10/77–8; 406–7/74–5. For Newton's physicotheological approach towards the question of the 'cause of gravity', cf. my 'History of Science and Criteria of Choice', section II, in *Minnesota Studies in the Philosophy of Science*, Vol. V (ed. W.-R. Steuwer), Minneapolis 1971. For Kant's doctrine that space presupposes interaction, cf. my MPS, 580–87.

[33] M.536.6–7/214. For the distinction between construction regarded 'implicitly' *vs.* 'explicitly', cf. MPS, 561–2. The distinction (though not in these terms) seems also to be recognized in Plaass, *op. cit.*, 74, and in Hansgeorg Hoppe, *Kants Theorie der Physik*, Frankfurt 1969, 50.

[34] Cf. for instance, Brian Ellis, 'The Origin and Nature of Newton's Laws of Motion', in *Beyond the Edge of Certainty* (ed. by R. G. Colodny), Englewood Cliffs, 1965), 29–68; Dudley Shapere, 'The Philosophical Significance of Newton's Science', *Texas Quarterly* **10** (1967) 102–15.

RALPH C. S. WALKER

THE STATUS OF KANT'S THEORY OF MATTER

The four sections of the *Metaphysische Anfangsgründe der Naturwissenschaft*[1] are each introduced by a new definition of matter. For the Phoronomy it is defined as the movable in space (Ak. IV, 480); the other definitions presuppose this one. What is the status of the propositions ascribing existence to matter in these senses? Are the metaphysical principles of natural science as pure as the principles of pure understanding, or are they only required for experience which happens, in fact, to contain matter as defined at the beginnings of the sections?

Adickes adopts the latter alternative[2]; more recently, Vuillemin and Plaass have argued in favour of the former.[3] Kant says, in several places[4], that the argumentation here involves an empirical element: at Ak. IV: 470 he says this is the empirical concept of matter. But according to Plaass (pp. 84ff, 98f), though he means by this that to know that matter exists we must appeal to experience, this is only because there might be no matter and so no outer experience. Plaass thinks it necessarily true that there could be no spatial experience without movable matter, but he does not think this constitutes an *a priori* proof of the objective validity of the concept of matter. For he thinks such a proof must apply to *all* experience, not just experience of a special kind (like spatio-temporal experience) (pp. 58, 86): and Kant did not think it can be shown that the concept of matter must apply even in non-spatio-temporal experience. – But Kant allows that to show that a particular concept must have application if *spatio-temporal* experience is to prove *a priori* the objective validity to that concept, for otherwise the conclusions of the Analytic of Principles would not be fully *a priori*. So presumably Kant would think that to show that there could be no spatial experience unless the concept of matter had application just would be to give an *a priori* proof of the objective validity of that concept.

Vuillemin suggests that the principles of MAdN are like the dynamical, and unlike the mathematical, principles of KdrV in that to establish them one has to presuppose that there *is* sensible experience – 'un *minimum sensibile* donné' (p. 24). Granting that Kant made this distinction between mathematical and dynamical principles in KdrV[5], this does not give us that *extra* element of the empirical which Kant thinks characterizes MAdN. Vuillemin agrees there is a difference between the use made of the given empirical element in the dynamical principles and in MAdN: the notion has to be made more precise in the latter (pp. 24, 39). But he thinks this difference does not affect the status of the arguments, because like Plaass he considers it to be Kant's view that if there is to be spatio-temporal experience at all there must be experience of movable matter. So neither Plaass nor Vuillemin gives an adequate account of what Kant means by saying that MAdN involves a special empirical element, the concept of matter.

Had Kant held that any spatio-temporal experience must contain movable matter, he would surely have argued for this. Two arguments have been cited to show that he did. The first has been extracted from what he says in the Refutation of Idealism. The other is more explicit, but turns on what Kant says in the *Opus Postumum*, and from the fact that Kant held a view there one cannot infer that he held it in the Critical period.

If the argument of the Refutation were valid, it would show that one must be aware of some permanent, objective item in space. Let us grant that it is. The argument which some commentators extract from Kant goes on: if one were aware of nothing in space that was *not* permanent one could still not have the idea of an objective time-series.[6] If the external world were changeless, how could one place one's experiences in an objective time-order? – But not all change is local change. We are trying to show that spatial objects must be the sort of things that *move*, but this argument only supports the conclusion that they must be the sort of things that *change*. One can imagine a world in which there are coloured objects in space, including the bodies of various percipients; these objects change in colour, but never move. Perhaps the percipients even communicate by using subtle and complex colour changes. They may be able to act on one another and on things, though this action will not involve physical contact but causal correlations between colour-changes in the agent and colour-changes in that which is acted upon; so they can apply the concepts of action and change, but not that of motion. This may ultimately turn out to be incoherent, but I do not think the incoherence is immediately obvious.

There is no evidence that Kant wanted to use the above invalid argument.[7] But in the *Opus Postumum* he tries to give a transcendental deduction of the concept of aether. He argues that there must be moving forces everywhere in space, since otherwise we could never have unified experience of things in space; for my experience of such a thing must be caused (in virtue of the second Analogy), and it can be caused only by the action on me of some moving force.[8]

It is true that given the organs we in fact possess we could not perceive objects in space unless things moved, but it is not clear that there could not be a percipient whose sense-organs could be acted upon by something analogous to colour-changes, without this action being effected by particles in motion. Causal generalisations could be established by observing correlations between the behaviour of certain items and that of certain other items (sense-organs).[9] Kant's argument will only do if we suppose that the only way in which events can be caused is by the motion, or moving force, exerted by things.

It may be said that Kant also used this invalid argument in MAdN. For in the preface to that work he says,

Die Grundbestimmung eines Etwas, das ein Gegenstand äußerer Sinne sein soll, mußte Bewegung sein; denn dadurch allein können diese Sinne affiziert werden.[10]

But it is quite reasonable to read this as saying only what must be so for *us*, because of the way our sense-organs are constituted.[11] And unless we read it this way Kant is contradicting what he has just said about the empirical status of the concept of matter as the movable in space.

Probably the main reason people think Kant held, in MAdN, that to have the idea of an object in space one must think of it as movable, is that they regard this proposition as obviously true. But though it *may* be true, it is not easy to prove. Not that it is easy to prove its falsity: that would be to show that a picture like the one I have given, of a world in which there is only qualitative and not local change, contains no latent inconsistency.

I have already considered and rejected two arguments, ascribed to Kant, for the proposition. Another argument worth considering may be extracted from Strawson's *Bounds of Sense*, p. 128. Strawson says that any self-conscious being must experience things in a spatial order (or in an order importantly analogous to a spatial order), because to have the idea

of something which can exist unperceived is to think of it as capable of
being somewhere else than in one's perceptual field. We might apply this
here by saying that a world lacking motion would have nowhere that objects could *go* to when existent but not being perceived by me, and nowhere that I could go to to avoid perceiving static objects.

But we can introduce into the picture of a static spatial world another
feature: intensity. Items can now alter not only in (something like) colour
but also in (something like) brightness. At one time there is visible a round
yellow light-source with a black dot in the middle; gradually the yellow
circle grows brighter, but the dot does not, and before long the yellow has
become so bright that the dot is no longer visible. Then the yellow becomes
less bright again, and once more the dot is visible.[12] One can imagine, also,
that at a certain stage some percipients can see the dot, others not. If this
sort of phenomenon occurred pretty regularly, would it not be reasonable
to think of the dot as continuing to exist all the time, even when it was not
perceived? The grounds for saying this are apparently of the same sort as
the grounds we in fact have for speaking of unperceived existents.

One might, however, object that the imagined world was not *spatial*;
and so that it is, after all, true that a spatial world must contain movable
matter. Not only would the imagined percipients think quite differently
from us about distance, lacking operational definitions; they would not
make the same use of position in reidentifying objects as we do. What is
necessary for an arrangement of coexistents to count as spatial? Any
parameter could be accounted a dimension: change on it could be called
motion. And *any* change, apart from creation and annihilation, could be
represented as change of position on *some* parameter. So we could then
say that in any world of which self-conscious beings could be aware there
must be room for motion, since there must be room for change (if only
in one's mental states). If this conclusion is to be resisted, a difference
must be found between spatial dimensions and other parameters.[13]

I think there might be a being who perceived a world as so arranged
that we, if we could see it as well, should describe it as spatial, yet who
lacked any idea of motion. This suggestion unpacks into two. In one case,
the world can be our own familiar spatial world, except that all motion
has stopped. We should then be dead, but is it logically impossible that
there should be some other percipient who was not? He would be aware
of a number of coexistent items which we, if we were still alive, would

recognize to be spatially related; he will not think of space quite as we do, but there is a sense in which he can be said to perceive things as spatially related. In the other case, which would be more congenial to Kant, the percipient not only receives similar data to us, he also orders them similarly: he uses an order which has a great many of the properties of space – and not just abstract mathematical ones, but phenomenological ones. I do not want to press this second version of the suggestion: there are notorious difficulties about the intelligibility of phenomenological comparisons.[14] If the first version makes sense, that will do: we can distinguish the thesis that items must be subject to change (and so to 'motion' in some parameter) from the thesis that spatial objects must be movable in space. And it has not been shown that we cannot assert the former while refusing to assert the latter. If this is right, Kant should not be presumed to have held that one must think of spatial things as movable just because one obviously must.

I suggest then that there is no reason at all, either in Kant's works or outside them, to suppose that when Kant called the concept of matter empirical he did not mean at least to exclude the possibility of proving that any self-conscious being with spatio-temporal experience must have the idea of movable matter.

Merton College, Oxford

NOTES

[1] Henceforth abbreviated 'MAdN'.

[2] Erich Adickes, *Kant als Naturforscher*, Berlin 1924, I 247–71.

[3] Jules Vuillemin, *Physique et Métaphysique Kantiennes*, Paris 1955, ch. 1. Peter Plaass, *Kants Theorie der Naturwissenschaft*, Göttingen 1960, esp. ch. 4 and 5.

[4] Thus in MAdN, Ak. IV: 469f. and 482; in KdrV, A 845/B873, A 847f./B 875f.; and elsewhere, Ak. IV: 295, V: 181, XX: 285. What is important about matter in MAdN is that it is movable: and in KdrV we find Kant saying that the movable in space is found only through experience (A 41/B 58, B 155n.) and that *motus* is an empirical concept. (A 81/B 107.) Cf. also Ak. IV: 482, XX: 272.

[5] He does seem to be making some such distinction at A 160/B 199, though A 221f/B 268f apparently goes against it.

[6] E.g. K. Hübner, *Das transzendentale Subjekt als Teil der Natur* (Diss. Kiel, 1951), p. 33.

[7] It is true that Kant uses the term 'matter' as the generic term for objects of outer sense at B 278, for example; but given his distrust of technical terms there is no reason to suppose he conflates this usage with that of MAdN.

8 The argument appears in various forms. Cf. for example Ak. XXI: 216, XXI: 572ff, XXII: 535, XXII: 609–15.

9 This would involve action at a distance, but one would not expect the author of the *Monadologia Physica* and MAdN to cast doubts on the intelligibility of that. Adickes (*Kants Opus Postumum*, Berlin, 1920, pp. 415ff) claims that he does in the XIth Konvolut, at Ak. XXII: 425–38 and XXII: 514–38, but I think here Kant is only ruling out attraction over empty space because he thinks empty space can never be perceived – the argument is just the MAdN argument for a plenum (Ak. IV: 523–35).

10 Ak. IV: 476. Cf. also B 291f, and no doubt other passages in KdrV in which it seems to be assumed that we have to think of things in space as movable. But Kant often also speaks as though all intuition must be spatio-temporal, though this is certainly not his considered opinion. It is tempting and convenient to make a point by considering only the familiar case of the sort of knowledge we have, even though the point itself may be more general. Thus in B 291f his real point is that if we are to see what an alteration is we must appeal to outer intuition. He says indeed that we must take movement in space as our example; but in default of any argument there is no reason to suppose he means more than that it is the example we human beings rely upon, and not that there could not be beings, with spatial intuition and no idea of motion, for whom some other sort of alteration in spatial objects would fulfil the same purpose.

11 In support of this reading one can point out that Kant does not actually say an object of outer *sense* must be movable, but that an object of outer *senses* must, which would suggest he is thinking of sense-organs.

12 This experiment may of course be carried out in our world, by looking at a lightbulb end on and using a dimmer.

13 I am indebted to Mr W. Newton-Smith for this elaboration of the objection.

14 Though these would not have worried Kant – cf. A 353f – and it is the second version rather than the first that would have seemed to him to provide the counterexample to the thesis that all spatial experience must be of movable items.

It is arguable that in either version the static spatial world would have to be thought of as only two-dimensional, since we could not distinguish small objects from distant objects unless we could move. This may be true of us as our senses are at present constituted, but it is not obvious that a different sort of percipient might not be directly able to make the distinction. The exigency of space prevents me discussing this here; but even if the imagined percipient has to think of his world as two-dimensional there may still be point in calling it spatial if the dimensions are both spatial ones.

PART VI

THE THING IN ITSELF

PETER KRAUSSER

KANT'S THEORY OF THE STRUCTURE OF EMPIRICAL SCIENTIFIC INQUIRY AND TWO IMPLIED POSTULATES REGARDING THINGS IN THEMSELVES

I

What this paper is going to present is not – strictly speaking – my work alone, but rather the outcome of the cooperation of all the participants in a series of seminar courses that is still running at the Free University of Berlin and started 1967–68 at the University of Pennsylvania, Philadelphia.

We restricted our undertaking at the outset to be strictly a systematic analysis of the text of the *Critique*, not an analysis of Kant and not a historical analysis. This soon led us into selecting a somewhat unusual but to us especially interesting point of view from which to look at the theories propounded in the *Critique*. When we came to the *Preface* of the second edition it struck us that Kant there, in explaining what he calls the 'Copernican Revolution' made by his *Critique* with respect to Philosophy of Science and epistemology in general, argues in a curiously pragmatistic way. (I am alluding here to the pragmatism of Charles S. Peirce or Wilhelm Dilthey, not to that of William James.)

There are two traits which later have become centrally associated with what Peirce called Pragmatism right in the first sentence of the second *Preface* which says: "Whether the treatment of such knowledge as lies within the province of reason does or does not follow the secure path of a science, is easily to be determined from the outcome" (B VII).

In the context 'outcome' does not refer to a final or static product like a certain theory but to the character of systematic progress which the development of the science in question takes on. The two pragmatistic traits are (1) that science here is not taken as an aggregate or system of sentences believed to be true but as a *process*; and (2) that this process is characterized as scientific by exhibiting a certain peculiar kind of systematic controlled *progress*.

II

The question then is: what is the structure that gives the process that peculiar dynamic property of being a systematic progress? The answer to this question is given by a rough sketch of the structure in B XII–XIV. The text there says:

> ... reason *gains* insight only into that which it *produces* after *a plan* of its own, ... it must proceed with *principles for its judgments*, according to unchanging *laws*, forcing *nature* to answer reasons' own *questions*...; because otherwise, without a previously designed plan, mere accidental *observations* can not be connected in a necessary law, which alone is what reason *needs* and is *searching for*. Reason, with its principles, according to which alone *concordant appearances* can be validly connected by laws, in one hand, and with the *experiment*, which it devised in conformity with (the principles and laws) in the other, must confront nature *to be taught by it*, not as a pupil listening to whatever the teacher says, but like an appointed judge who compels the witnesses to answer the questions which he puts to them (B XIII).

It is possible to aid a little more detail to this summary description of the structure of inquiry by looking into the text of *The Doctrine of Method*.

There we are told with respect to hypotheses and proofs that an opinion as to the actuality of some object or event not given can be entitled an hypothesis only if it brings the alleged object or event as an explanatory cause or reason in connection with something actually given (B 798; see also 803). "In the explanation of given appearances, no things or grounds of explanation may be adduced other than those which have been connected with given appearances in accordance with already known laws of the appearances (B 800; see also 803). Such hypotheses must be 'physical' and not 'hyperphysical' (B 800–1). A "requirement for the admissibility of an hypothesis is its sufficiency for an a priori derivation from it of consequences which are given (B 802, see also 803). " ... various sciences ... when the grounds from which some knowledge is to be derived are too numerous or too deeply concealed try to arrive at the knowledge in question through its consequences. But the *modus ponens*, inferring the truth of an assertion from the truth of its consequences presupposes that all possible consequences are (known to be) true ... But ... to discover all possible consequences of any given proposition exceeds our powers". Thus the use of this mode of reasoning can at best serve us to make something plausible as an hypothesis "on the ground that if all examined consequences agree with an assumed ground, all other possible consequences will do so too". On the other hand "the *modus tollens* of arguments proceeding from consequences to their gronds is not only a quite rigorous but also an extremely easy mode of proof. For if even a single false consequence can be drawn from a proposition, the proposition is itself false (B 818–819).

Now a merely verbal interpretation of this passage in the context of the *Critique* would have to be rather lengthy. Nevertheless, on account of the linear structure of our language it could never directly exhibit the nonlinear structure implied in the text. Therefore I will give in as much detail as possible an integrating interpretation in the form of a directed graph. Such interpreting graphs should exhibit all and only those factors and their relations which are explicitly or implicitly to be found in the text, and they should do this under the general rule for fair controlled interpretations: to make sense and not nonsense out of the text as long and as far as this is possible.

Proceeding thus, we arrive, as it seems, at the graphical interpretation of the outlined structure given in Figure 1.

Now one sees immediately:

(1) The upper part, which in itself does not interest us here, roughly takes the connection of the theory in question with the whole context of the *Critique* into consideration. Agreement on the details given in this part is not presupposed here.

(2) The lower parts, enclosed and connected by thicker lines are the focus of interest in this paper. They form what we nowadays call a 'system with feedback'. It is the dynamic, proceeding subsystem of the whole system.

(3) As the *Critique* in B 818–819 stresses that the testing of hypotheses basically, though not only, works by way of employing the *modus tollens*, we may safely say that the dynamic subsystem is more especially a system controlling itself by negative feedback.

(4) There is no feedback to the 'principles of reason', the 'needs and aims of reason' and the 'a priori laws of nature', which, according to Kant, a so-called 'pure part of natural science' or 'metaphysics of nature' can derive from the principles. In other words: the blocks of the principles and of the purely apriori laws are *not* blocks of subsystems of *variables* but blocks of absolutely constant factors governing everything going on in the variable subsystems, without being affected in any way by the what, why or how of what is going on there.

Many more highly interesting features of Kant's theory could be pointed out here as being exhibited by the graph. Even more could be brought

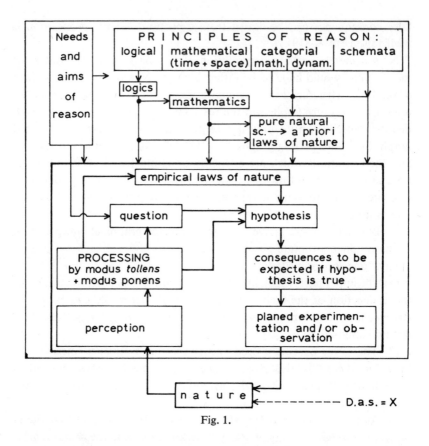

Fig. 1.

out by making the graph more detailed without changing the basic structure. I must leave all this aside for now and focus attention on only one point of special interest for this paper.

III

This point concerns the block 'nature' and the arrows coming to and from it. The graph shows that, according to Kant's theory 'nature' is experienced nature, and that this experienced nature as a lawful, consistent, intersubjective system of objects of possible experience can not be 'constituted' without the principles of reason, the pure a priori laws deducible from them and the hypothetical empirical laws and hypotheses thought up by reason in accordance with those principles and a priori laws. At the same time the graph also shows that reason must go to nature 'to be taught by it' something 'which reason could not possibly know by itself alone' (B XIV).

Thus, experienced nature in Kants theory can not be solely and completely a product of reason. If it were, reason would not have to learn anything from nature, and experienced nature could not contradict or disappoint logically expected consequences of laws and hypotheses thought up according to the principles of reason. But that just this happens is implied when Kant insists that empirical laws always remain hypothetical and must have testable consequences through the experimental test of which reason may be forced to eliminate them and/or hypotheses under them and to replace them by new and better ones.

To speak in modern terms: the block 'nature' must be a genuine source of information. But that, in terms of our graph, means it must be a block with a second and *independent* input besides the input coming from reason via planned experimentation and observation. Thus we come to see that the structure of empirical inquiry as Kant conceived it implies the necessity or *unavoidability of postulating* an independent input into 'nature' and thus into experience from the 'things in themselves'. This is *not* to be taken as saying that we *know* about the existence of the *Ding an sich*. What we come to know is only that in order to be able to explain the kind of progress Kant's theory envisions for science, namely by sophisticated trial and error for the elimination of wrong hypotheses, we have to postulate an independent input of which, precisely because of its necessary independence, we can *not know* anything.

In this way the necessity of postulating unknowable things in themselves can be shown to be implied in Kants theory. Kant's own way of trying the same thing seems not acceptable. He argued that

though we cannot have knowledge of any object *as* thing in itself, but only in so far *as* it is an object of sensible perception, that is, as an appearance ... we must yet be in position at least to *think* them as things in themselves; otherwise there would follow the absurd conclusion that there are appearances without anything that appears (B XXVI–XXVII, see also A 251/252).

This is open to the simple but strong objection that it may be merely falling into the trap of the accidental historical structure of Indoeuropean languages.

IV

Up to now I have departed in my arguments but not in my conclusion from the text of the *Critique*. From here on I am concerned with a different conclusion too. Because there seems to me to be at least one further postulate concerning the things in themselves implied in Kant's theory of the structure of empirical scientific inquiry. And this postulate is not recognized in the text in any way at all.

The argument for this second postulate and its unavoidability in *any* theory that conceives the structure of controlled scientific inquiry and/or of learning processes in general as basically the same as that represented by the lower parts of the graphical interpretation of Kant's theory, runs just like the first, it only is more specific. What it more specifically attends to are the 'empirical laws of nature' in Kant's theory.

Kant's whole *Critique* qua philosophy of science and experience turns on the point that the a priori principles or forms of reason are *necessary but not sufficient* conditions of possible experience and experimental science. Consequently and rightly he repeatedly insists that, though all acceptable empirical laws must always be in accord with the principles and a priori laws of reason, empirical laws as such can never be derived (from them, i.e.) from pure understanding as their origin (A 127, see also B 165, 508), "we learn (them) through experience" (A 126; see also B 213), they are products of empirical syntheses "which cannot be given a priori" (B 750; see also 748–751, 794).

Now let us put this into the structure of inquiry according to Kant's theory as interpreted by the graph. Then we must say: according to the structure reason connects regular experiences in accordance with its principles via *modus ponens* hypothetically by empirical laws, and then checks these laws as to their truth by applying them in planned experimentation and observation to further experiences. If these experiences disappoint the expectations that were logically based on the provisional assumption of the truth of the applied empirical laws, then reason will eliminate these hypothetically entertained laws and replace them by newly constructed ones until it has come up with better ones.

The critical point for our argument is again that the working of the structure in this way indispensably hinges on the possibility that the outcome of planned experience does contradict or disappoint those logical expectations (B 190) and thus can force reason to think up other new empirical laws. This centrally important fact of empirically controlled inquiry, without which there obviously would be no right even to speak of empirical science at all, can not be explained unless the independent input codetermining nature as experienced does not only provide for a formless and in itself connection-free mere manifold of material (B 145) but provides an already in *some* way *ordered* material of experience. (This was explicitly recognized by Kant at A 100–101).

Obviously, no absolutely unordered, purely hyletical material could give resistance to any way in which it might be connected and thus ordered by reason through empirical syntheses according to a priori principles and laws. But just such resistance is what we are speaking about when we say that actual experience, in spite of not being possible without syntheses having their principles and laws in reason, can and often does disappoint expectations logically following from the product of those syntheses. Therefore, if we accept the basic structure of empirical inquiry as described in Kants theory and graphically analysed in our diagram, then we are implicitly forced to say also that the already postulated independent input from the things qua things in themselves concerns some unknown and unknowable but nevertheless indispensable *order* of their own that we must postulate the things to have *qua* things in themselves.

Free University of Berlin

RALF MEERBOTE

THE UNKNOWABILITY OF THINGS IN THEMSELVES

The notions of things in themselves and of the unknowability of things in themselves have proved a persistent problem for commentators of Kant's. Little agreement about either the meaning or the truth of Kant's claims concerning these matters has ever been reached. Whatever disagreements there are can be explained in part by the fact that more than one of Kant's philosophical motives come into play in his repeated discussions of these problems.

In particular, in several of his writings[1] Kant is concerned to introduce an *ontological distinction* between various *types* of entity. Entities of one particular type he calls *noumena* or *things in themselves*, and he characterizes such entities by saying that they are not subsumable under any conditions of empirical knowledge. At the same time, he also assigns a certain explanatory role to such entities, *e.g.*, they are to play a role in the explanation of the possibility of empirical knowledge.

I shall call this use of the term 'thing in itself' its ontological use, and I shall distinguish from it a related but importantly different use which I shall call the *epistemological use* (of the term 'thing in itself' and consequently also of 'appearance'). If there is indeed such a use to be found in Kant's writings, there arises the not inconsiderable problem of how to identify and how to separate it from the ontological use. I shall adopt the following maxim: when the term 'thing in itself' is used to formulate specific existential hypotheses about objects which are not subject to conditions of empirical knowledge, or when it is used to formulate specific causal hypotheses about, for example, the origin or existence of the totality of appearances, then its use is ontological; if the term occurs in the context of a discussion concerning the conditions of empirical knowledge (and in the absence of any of the above causal models or existential hypotheses), as, for example, in the Transcendental Deduction in the second edition of KdrV, its use is epistemological.

Let me elaborate the notion of an epistemological use by briefly examining Norman Kemp Smith's attempt to explain the unknowability of things in themselves. Early in his *Commentary to Kant's 'Critique of Pure Reason'* (pp. 18–20 and also pp. 404–24), he discusses KdrV B XIX which is a good statement of the epistemological use of the terms 'appearance' and 'thing in itself'. Kant is here raising the question how a priori judgments can be justified. His answer is that they can be shown to be a priori conditions of the objects of our empirical knowledge. Such a priori conditions play a role analogous to that played by certain a priori constructions and principles introduced by scientists like Torricelli and Galileo in their construction of theories which are to explain certain sorts of natural phenomena (KdrV B XIII–XXIII). Statements of such conditions presumably cannot be shown to be true by reference to the very same subject matter which presupposes them unless a description of the subject matter and of the relation of the subject matter to those a priori conditions, that is independent of those same a priori conditions, is also available. But in the case of the conditions which make *all* of our empirical knowledge possible, we seem to be in the curious position of not being able to furnish such an independent description. *Transcendental idealism* is supposed to be the way out of this dilemma (KdrV B XIX-XXI and letter 362, Ak. XI). According to Kemp Smith,

Objects must be viewed as conforming to human thought, not human thought to the independently real (*op. cit.*, p. 18).

But if the objects of our knowledge require to be subject to particular a priori conditions, the following problem arises.

...objects are regarded as conforming to our forms of intuition and to our modes of conception [and hence] they can be anticipated by a priori reasoning... [but] if the a priori concepts have a mental origin, they can have no validity for the independently real. If we can know only what we ourselves originate, things in themselves must remain unknown... (*ibid.*, p. 19).

Unfortunately, Kemp Smith is rather unclear about the crucial phrase " . . . we can know only what [*i.e.*, that which] we ourselves originate". Since earlier in the quoted passage a priori concepts are said to be those which have a mental origin (and since Kemp Smith presumably takes "has a mental origin" to be the same as "is originated by us"), it looks as if he is saying that our own a priori concepts are all we can know. But of course he does not wish to conclude this. So what he may mean is that all we know are objects *which in order to be known*[2] must be subject to certain conditions which "we ourselves originate". Since objects which meet such conditions are what Kant calls 'appearances,' and since "things in themselves must be unknown" is to provide the contrast to "appearances are (what is) known", the force of 'things in themselves' at the end of the passage quoted above can only be *"objects apart from conditions originated by us"*.

If this is right, the terms 'appearance' and 'thing in itself' are used epistemologically, and not ontologically, at B XIX. They are not used ontologically because merely to distinguish between objects' being subject to conditions of knowledge and their not being subject to such conditions is not to distinguish between different types of object and it certainly is not to say that unknowable objects furnish an explanation of conditions of knowability. To say that things in themselves are unknowable is then merely to say that things are in and by themselves unknowable, *i.e.*, that objects in order to be known must satisfy particular conditions of knowledge. An appearance *is* an object of knowledge and *anything* that satisfies some such conditions is an appearance.

The most that can be concluded from the fact that conditions of knowledge are required is that it is *possible* that there be objects which as a matter of fact are not subsumable under a particular set of conditions and which therefore are unknowable on the strength of that set. By contrast, the ontological use of the term 'thing in itself' is specifically designed to *assert* the existence of unknowable entities. According to the ontological use, to say that objects must be subject to conditions of knowledge in order to be knowable is *ipso facto* to distinguish between two types of entity and to conclude that, since objects must meet such conditions in order to be knowable, it *follows* that there *are un*knowable entities.

But Kemp Smith in the end identifies Kant's distinction in B XIX with an ontological distinction between two types of object. Indeed, he identifies that distinction with that between 'appearance and reality' (*op. cit.*, pp. 416–17). Things in themselves make up 'reality' and hence we *can never* have any knowledge of 'reality.'[3] Such a conclusion is however exactly the sort of *dogmatic skepticism* with regard to empirical knowledge *against* which Kant argues repeatedly (*e.g.*, in *Logik*, Ak. IX, 84; Reflections 2638–70, Ak. XVI; *Logik Blomberg*, Ak. XXIV. I, 81, 201–14), and it is surprising that Kemp Smith and other commentators have found it so easy to commit Kant to this variety of skepticism.

Fortunately, Kant himself goes to some length to clarify the meaning of his doctrine of the unknowability of things in themselves, and his clarification generally proceeds along the lines sketched in my discussion of Kemp Smith above. The following two passages provide a sufficient indication.

...that which is itself initially only appearance, for example a rose, is a thing in itself for the empirical understanding and can appear differently to each observer with respect to its color. The transcendental concept of appearances...on the other hand is a critical reminder that...things in themselves are not at all known by us...[and in regard to which] no questions are ever asked in the course of experience (KdrV B 45).[4]

Hence when we say that the senses represent objects *as they appear* but that the understanding represents them *as they are*, the latter statement is to be taken merely in its empirical and not in its transcendental meaning, *i.e.*, it must be taken to mean that objects, as objects of experience, must be represented in the thoroughgoing inter-connection of appearances and not how they might be apart from their relation to possible experience...as objects of pure understanding (KdrV B 313-14).

In these passages, Kant clearly is distinguishing between an *empirical* and a *transcendental* use of the terms 'appearance' and 'thing in itself'. In the empirical use of these terms, a rose, which is an appearance in the transcendental use of the term, is a thing in itself and can appear different-ly to different observers. To call a rose an appearance is then not to deny that one can ever know what the rose is like, *e.g.*, that it is red (if it is red), and in particular it is not to assert that *all* one can *know* is that the rose *appears* to be red, since the understanding, in its empirical employment, can indeed succeed in representing the rose the way it is.

Consequently, the doctrine of the unknowability of things in themselves cannot be equated with the claim that we can never know things as they really are. Instead, these passages support my initial suggestion that the claim that things in themselves are unknowable, in the epistemological use of the term 'thing in itself', means no more and no less than that objects, in order to be knowable, must be subsumable under particular a priori conditions which make knowledge of such objects possible. Apart from such conditions, no knowledge can be had of such objects, but to say only this much is not to advocate any kind of skepticism.[5]

On the strength of the passages just quoted and others as well,[6] Kant's characterization of the uses of the terms 'thing in itself' and 'appearance' can be summarized in the following way.

In the empirical use of these terms, a thing in itself appears in a particular way to some person on some particular occasion (and the way it appears typically provides some evidence for or against some judgment about that thing in itself).

In the transcendental use of these terms, appearances *are* objects of empirical knowledge, and things in themselves are objects considered apart from the conditions of such knowledge (and, in particular, it can be shown that it is *possible* that there *be* objects which do *not* fall under a particular set of such conditions).

I now want to examine and to justify this dual use of these two terms in somewhat more detail.

Intuitively, the empirical use of these terms is their use by the understanding in its empirical employment. *I.e.,* when a person enters, challenges, or justifies a particular empirical judgment, the understanding is used empirically, the entering, challenging, or justifying of such claims is an empirical activity, and the terms 'thing in itself' and 'appearance' play their proper role, as stated above.

In the context of such activities we make an ordinary, common-sense distinction between what the objects of our claims really are like and what they appear to be to some person on some particular occasion. In such contexts, the use of our concepts is subject to particular a priori conditions, and such conditions are explanatory of the aforementioned features of such judgmental situations, including the above distinction between truth and appearance.

Such conditions can themselves become the subject matter of an inquiry. Such an inquiry is a *transcendental* inquiry in the sense that it is a second-order inquiry about the conditions which underlie some other, first-order activity. Human reason is capable of such transcendental inquiry since it is capable of *reflecting about* the empirical use of concepts rather than *just* of using concepts empirically. That is, a person can both make empirical judgments and investigate the conditions in accordance with which he makes such claims. In the course of such investigations, he is no longer making first-order judgments. Rather, he is making second-order judgments about his or other persons' first-order judgments, and the use of whatever concepts he employs in such transcendental inquiries is no longer that of the understanding in its empirical employment, that is, the use of concepts no longer occurs in the context of first-order empirical knowledge-claim situations (cf. KdrV B XIX (footnote) and *Logik Blomberg*, Ak. XXIV, 20–25).

So when we are using the terms 'appearance' and 'thing in itself' in the context of a transcendental inquiry, we are using them transcendentally. Moreover, it is only in the contexts of such inquiries that we say that all objects of our empirical knowledge are appearances and that things in themselves are unknowable. But if the understanding in its empirical employment can succeed in making correct empirical judgments, and if, as I have tried to show elsewhere,[7] a transcendental inquiry is not so much concerned with *disputing* the truth value of judgments entered by the empirical understanding, or with *disputing* the ordinary distinction between truth and appearance, but with discovering and *explaining how* the entering, challenging, and justifying of such judgments proceed, we arrive once again at the conclusion that to say that only appearances (in the transcendental use of the term) are knowable cannot be to deny that the understanding can have empirical knowledge.

Short of a thorough examination of Kant's conception and conduct of transcendental inquiries, we can now explain his dual use of 'appearance' and of 'thing in itself' in the following manner.

The understanding in its empirical employment can know things in themselves (such as tables, chairs, and roses), and it can legitimately distinguish between the way an object is and the way it appears on some particular occasion since even in a situation where some person makes an unsuccessful claim, he or some other person rightly will enter, challenge, and justify claims in accordance with some set of conditions making such claims possible. On the strength of some such conditions, he or some other person will introduce some special reason, or a bit of evidence, for or against a particular claim even in a situation where his claim as a matter of fact is unsuccessful. *E.g.*, even though on some particular occasion a particular table may look grey to some person and he judges that the table is grey whereas it is as a matter of fact brown, that person nevertheless knows what it would be like for the table (which he takes to be grey) to be brown and he knows how to tell and recognize tables (including brown ones) in other situations. Indeed, he may be in a position where he will say, correctly and with justification, that the table is brown (despite the fact that it looks grey to him), provided he can explain how it is that under the particular circumstances a table which *is brown* can or does *look grey* to him.

In short, the understanding, in its empirical employment, can both imagine and claim that an object X has property Y even in situations where it may not be in a position to know that the object X does have the property Y. At the same time, the special reasons or evidence on the strength of which some claim is justified may also vary from case to case: it is not a requirement that the same fact or type of fact be invariably introduced as evidence for a claim, and the understanding can imagine and claim that X has Y even in the absence on some particular occasion of some fact which in some other situation does function as evidence. It can know both how an object appears and what it is really like independent of any particular way in which it appears.

By contrast, the conditions *in accordance with which* empirical claims are entered, challenged, and justified, and which Kant derives by means of transcendental arguments are *standing conditions* and do not ordinarily vary from case to case. Moreover, although it may certainly seem possible and imaginable that there be alternative sets of such standing conditions, a person committed to a particular set is not in a position to claim that a particular knowledge-claim falls under any such set other than the one to which he is committed. That is, he is in no position to know any objects other than those which are in accordance with his conditions of knowledge. The point of describing this by saying that he knows only appearances and that he cannot know the things in themselves is simply that, in contrast to the earlier situation, he is no longer in a position to contrast and compare that which he can claim in accordance with his conditions of knowledge with that which is as a matter of fact true about the subject matter about which he is making a claim, and he is no longer in a position to vary, or to allow to have vary, the standing conditions to which he is committed in order to determine, as he could determine in the earlier situation, the truth of his claim independent of any particular condition on the strength of which he enters the claim. Hence, in the transcendental use of the term, things in themselves are unknowable.

So the transcendental distinction between appearances and things in themselves grows out of the corresponding empirical distinction in a rather natural way (and can now be seen not to commit Kant to dogmatic skepticism).

This interpretation also explains the dilemma concerning the justification of a priori conditions, which I mentioned at the beginning of this paper. Transcendental idealism is supposed to provide the way out, and such an idealism can now be seen to be, minimally, no more than the doctrine that, in the transcendental use of the term, things in themselves are unknowable. Hence the justification of such a priori conditions cannot and does not make any reference to things in themselves.

It has been my concern here to sketch an explanation, and to give the beginning of a justification, of Kant's doctrine that things in themselves are unknowable. The interpretation of transcendental idealism which I have given can be shown to have the consequence that Kant is committed after all to a variety of skepticism,[8] but it turns out to be skepticism importantly different from dogmatic skepticism. However, to establish this consequence would require a close look at Kant's derivation of individual a priori conditions which make our empirical knowledge possible, and such a task is beyond the scope of the present paper.[9]

University of Illinois at Chicago Circle

NOTES

[1] *E.g.*, in letter 751, Ak. XII; 'Morgenstunden', Ak. VIII, 151-54; 'Dreams of a Ghostseer', Ak. II, 348-52; *Dispute of the Faculties*, Ak. VII, 71-72. 'Ak.' refers to the standard edition of Kant's works by the Berlin Academy. The *Critique of Pure Reason* will be abbreviated as KdrV, followed by the standard pagination of either the first or the second edition.

[2] This would be closer to Kant's text. Kant – without being completely consistent – talks about objects *of*, or *in* experience. See KdrV B XVII-XVIII, B XXVI, and *Prolegomena*, Ak. IV, 351.

[3] Kemp Smith is by no means alone in this conclusion. Cf. H. J. Paton, *Kant's Metaphysic of Experience*, II, 458 (footnote 1); P. F. Strawson, *The Bounds of Sense*, pp. 38, 250.

[4] This, as well as the next quoted passage, is my translation. The present passage is still what Kemp Smith calls 'transcendentally subjectivist' and contains an analysis of, specifically, *color predicates*, which is of no inherent interest to the distinction between an empirical and a transcendental use, which I am ascribing to Kant.

[5] So the *transcendental* use turns out to be identical with what I earlier called the *epistemological* use. By contrast, the *ontological* use turns out to be a *transcendent* use, but I cannot pursue these matters here any further.

[6] For the empirical use of 'thing in itself', see KdrV B 70, A 45-46, A 258, A 393; *Progress*, vol. IV of *Kant's Kleinere Schriften zur Logik und Metaphysik*, ed. by J. H. von Kirchmann, pp. 108–9. For the empirical use of 'appearance', see KdrV A 45–46, B

44-45, B 70 (footnote); *Prolegomena*, Ak. IV, § 13; 'Entdeckung', Ak. VIII, 207–9.
More often than not, Kant wants do *deny* that cases of *mistaken* judgment (typically
due to some sense illusion) are cases of the empirical use of 'appearance', and he tends
to reserve the term 'Schein' for them. But, as Kemp Smith, *op. cit.*, pp. 148-154, has
argued convincingly, he is not consistent, and even illusory appearances may be called
appearances in the empirical use of that term. More importantly, that use covers the
cases where an object appears to a person in the way it really is. Lastly, for the transcendental use of 'thing in itself' and of 'appearance', see KdrV B 237–38, B 248–49;
Prolegomena, Ak. IV, §§ 19–20; *Opus Postumum*, Ak. XXII, 26, 29, 36, 92, 341, 393,
412; *Vorlesungen über die Metaphysik*, ed. by K. H. Schmidt, pp. 88–89.

⁷ In a Ph.D. dissertation at Harvard University, January, 1970.

⁸ This claim turns on my previous observation that, given an analysis of the notion of
(synthetic a priori) conditions of the possibility of empirical knowledge, one can then
show that it is *possible* that there be objects which do not fall under the particular set of
such conditions to which one is committed.

⁹ I pursue these matters further in my dissertation.

NICHOLAS RESCHER

NOUMENAL CAUSALITY

1. THE PROBLEM OF NOUMENAL CAUSALITY

In the *Critique of Pure Reason*, Kant repeatedly characterized the thing in itself (*Ding an sich* or noumenon) in such terms as "the non-sensible cause" of representations or as "the purely intelligible cause" of appearances (A 494 = B 522). Again and again he employs the language of causal efficacy with regard to things in themselves. Thus he speaks of "the representations through which they [things in themselves] affect us" (A 190 = B 235) and elsewhere says that things in themselves are in principle unknowable: "they can never be known by us except as they affect us" (*Foundations of the Metaphysic of Morals*, Ak. 452) because the thing itself is a "transcendental object, which is the cause of appearance and therefore not itself appearance" (A 288 = B 344). The thing in itself is described as "the true correlate of sensibility which is not known, and cannot be known" through its representations (A 30 = B 45).

But on the other hand, Kant is repeatedly and emphatically insistent upon the categorial fact that the linkage of cause and effect can only obtain as a relationship between phenomena and that any applicability of the principle of causality is to be strictly confined to the phenomenal sphere. The categories and all that depends upon them just cannot apply to the thing in itself at all (*Prol.*, §§ 26, 28).

From the very outset, perceptive students of the Kantian philosophy such as J. S. Beck have been troubled by the question of how these two seemingly conflicting positions are to be reconciled. And critics down to the present day continue to charge Kant with outright inconsistency on this head. Strawson, for example, objects as follows in *The Bounds of Sense*:

For the resultant transposition of the terminology of objects 'affecting' the constitution of subjects takes that terminology altogether out of the range of its intelligible employment, viz., the spatio-temporal range... the original model, the governing analogy is perverted or transposed into a form which violates any acceptable requirement of intelligibility, including Kant's own principle of significance (pp. 41–42).

The issue of noumenal causality obviously poses a basic and important problem for any cohesive interpretation of Kant's philosophy.

2. SUFFICIENT REASON

I shall attempt to establish that, on the most plausible construction of Kant's view, two quite different sorts of 'causality' are at issue here, viz., (1) *authentic causality* which is genuinely experientiable and is governed by the experientially *constitutive* Principle of Causality, and (2) a not properly causal *generic grounding* which is merely intelligible (i.e., can be *thought* but not *known*) and is governed by a *regulative* Principle of Sufficient Reason. The kinship between the two sorts of 'causality' is sufficiently remote that the employment of the same terms – such as 'affecting' – in both cases must be regarded as merely analogical (in the manner in which Kant speaks at A 206 = B 251-2).

The key to a proper understanding the role that Kant maintains for the thing in itself is his insistence that reason itself *compels* this:

For what necessarily forces us to transcend the limits of experience and of all appearances is the *unconditioned*, which reason, by necessity and by right, demands in things in themselves, as required to complete the series of conditions (B xx).

This passage not only says *that* reason demands the thing in itself, but also hints *why*. For Kant, the conception of à perceived object freed of the conditions of perception is every bit as senseless as would be that of a view-of-an-object that is freed from any and every *point of view*, and so regarded in separation from one of the essential conditions of viewability. But correlative with the conception of the conditioned object of perception goes that of an unconditioned noumenon. This conception is warranted and justified because it answers to the inexorable demands of a Principle of Sufficient Reason ("the unconditioned, which reason, by necessity and by right, demands... [something] to complete the series of conditions.")[1] As Kant puts the matter in one key passage:

The principle of [sufficient] reason is thus properly... a rule, prescribing a regress in the series of conditions of given appearances, and forbidding it [viz., reason] from bringing the regress to a close by treating anything at which it may arrive as absolutely unconditioned. (CPR, A 508 = B 536 – A 509 = B 537; tr. Kemp Smith)[2]

There is a significant parallel between this passage and cognate discussions in Leibniz. Thus in explaining the workings of the Principle of Sufficient Reason in his important essay 'On the Ultimate Origin of Things' Leibniz writes:

...the sufficient reason of existence can not be found either in any particular thing or in the whole aggregate or series... And even if you imagine the world eternal, nevertheless find a sufficient reason for them in none of them whatsoever, and as any number of them whatever does not aid you in giving a reason for them, it is evident that the reason must be sought elsewhere... From which it follows that... an ultimate extramundane reason of things... cannot be escaped.

The reasons of the world, therefore, lie hidden in something extramundane different from the chain of states or series of things, the aggregate of which constitutes the world.[3]

It is noteworthy – and characteristic of the writers involved – that whereas Leibniz here applies the Principle of Sufficient Reason *ontologically* to establish an extramundane source of existence (i.e., God), Kant applies it *epistemologically* to establish an extramundane source of perceptual experience (i.e., the noumenon).

Of course, for Kant any such application of the Principle of Sufficient Reason would not succeed in bringing the *Ding an sich* within the orbit of experience. It remains something outside experience – and so unknowable – which, by the very workings of reason we not only can but must *think*, that is to say must *postulate* (esp. B xxvi–xxvii).

It is crucially important to recognize that Kant's step from appearances to the thing in itself is accomplished through the Principle of Sufficient Reason and not through the Principle of Causality. For causality, according to Kant, is operative only between phenomena, so that causal relations only obtain within the phenomenal realm. Any recourse to causality could never point outside the area of the phenomenal: With the Principle of Causality, then, we must remain squarely inside the domain of experience.

But the operation of a Principle of Sufficient Reason can endow the phenomenal with an *intentional* character that points towards an external something outside the phenomenal domain. It does so by coming into play in a limited but very important way: by establishing the pivotal point that the phenomenal order must itself be grounded, and so producing the result *that* an underlying noumenal order must be accepted, without thereby going very far towards throwing light on the issue of *what* the nature of this noumenal order could be. Of course, such a principle cannot, on Kantian lines, be *known*, but it can, and indeed *must* be *thought*.

In the *Prolegomena*, Kant articulates the line of thought at issue in the following terms:

> Reason through all its concepts and laws of the understanding which are sufficient to it for empirical use, that is, within the sensible world, finds in it no satisfaction, because ever-recurring questions deprive us of all hope of their complete solution.... But it sees clearly that the sensuous world cannot contain this completion.... The sensuous world is nothing but a chain of appearances... it is not the thing in itself, and consequently must point to that which contains the basis of this appearance, to beings which cannot be known merely as appearances, but as things in themselves. In the knowledge of them alone can reason hope to satisfy its desire for completeness in proceeding from the conditioned to its conditions (Ak. 353–4).

A careful heed of this perspective – and so of the distinction between a generic Principle of Sufficient Reason and a specific Principle of Causality – enables us to see how Kant can be freed from the charge of inconsistency in regard to noumenal causality. The answer is simply that *the relationship of the thing in itself to the phenomenon is actually not to be construed in causal terms at all*. Kant's own occasional looseness of formulation notwithstanding, it is clear that while things in themselves somehow 'affect' the sensibility so as to bring representations of objects into being, the relationship here at issue is definitely not to be construed in properly causal terms. The linkage between phenomenon and thing in itself, rather than being actually causal in character, is not mediated by the Principle of Causality at all, but by a more basic and general Principle of Sufficient Reason. This principle is – I submit – the (essentially) non-causal principle of grounding to which Kant time and again makes appeal. And – use of activity-oriented language notwithstanding – an appeal to actual causality is just not at issue here, any more than when one says that 5 is 'produced' by the addition of 3 and 2. The relationships involved are essentially static linkages in a purely conceptual order. Even with Kant we still sail in the backwash of the linkage – inherent in the scholastic *causa* – between a generic *grounding* of reasons and a specifically efficient *causality* of natural process. The Principle of Sufficient Reason is as it were, a pre- or sub-categorial version of the Principle of Causality, even as an abstractly intelligible conception of *grounding* constitutes an unschematized counterpart to the conception of *cause*. The Principle of Sufficient Reason is a *generic framework* principle guaranteeing only *some* sort of grounding in general: the Principle of Causality is a *specific implementation* of this principle indicating that in one specific area (the domain of experience) a certain *specific* mode of grounding (viz., causal explanation) is always forthcoming.

3. THE IMPETUS TO ONTOLOGICAL AUTONOMY AND INSUPERABLE PROPENSITIES TO THINK

An object of experience – as it presents itself within the orbit of sensory experience – is inevitably subject to the conditions of experientiability. In the framework of Kant's philosophy, it makes no sense even to consider *this* object, the experienced object, as somehow self-subsistent in the full bloom of its mind-dependent qualifications. The object experienced is ineradicably heteronomous, it is inevitably qualified by the conditions of experience. But the mind leaps forward from the conditional object as given in experience to an unshakable belief in a reality somehow hidden away under the superficial appearances we men take hold of.

The Kantian doctrine of the noumenal object roots in the final analysis in the structure of a certain conceptual scheme woven around the very concept of knowledge. For *knowledge* of objects would not be knowledge *of objects* if the 'objects' at issue *did not have an ontological foothold outside the knowledge situation*. But Kant in effect makes a subtle but crucial shift from the ontological to the epistemological order; from "did not in fact have" to "were not warrantedly thought to have." And what provides the warrant for such a shift is a deployment of the Principle of Sufficient Reason.

Now if this leap toward the unconditioned behind conditioned objects as given in experience were not justified, then knowledge, objective knowledge, would collapse with it. For then we could not legitimately regard the experience of objects as a *transaction* – the upshot of a genuine encounter between mind and object – but it would be a mere *production* of the mind alone. (If there were no mind-independent basis, experience would lose all its claim to objectivity.) It is the fact that a justification *can* be given that shifts the Kantian position from a *subjective* to a *transcendental* idealism.

It is crucially important for Kant that the ontological leap from appearance to underlying reality is justified. Yet for him this justification proceeds not in terms of the ontology of nature, but rather in terms of the ontology of mind. (The 'Copernican Revolution' again.) The mind not only *can*, but it *must postulate* an experientially untouched reality to underly the experienced appearance by way of providing its grounding. Both the key terms here – 'must' and 'postulate' – require comment. But one central fact deserves restatement first: the mind engaged in the quest for knowledge approaches its experience with an insuperable impetus for ontological heteronomy, in virtue of which it insists upon (i.e., "necessarily postulates") the presence of an object that meets the demand for a realm of reality behind that of appearance.

Back now to the formula that the mind *must postulate* a 'causally' operative thing in itself as ground for the phenomenon. The 'must' is critical here – because what goes on here is no matter of choice, but represents an essential feature of human mind. In one key passage, Kant puts the matter as follows:

[The] unconditioned is not, indeed, given as being in itself real...; it is, however, what alone can complete the series of conditions when we proceed to trace these conditions to their grounds. This is the course which our human reason, by its very nature, leads all of us, even the least reflective, to adopt. (A 583 = B 611 – A 584 = B 612.)

And again, in the *Prolegomena* (§ 32) Kant puts the matter as follows:

And we indeed, rightly considering objects of sense as mere appearances, confess thereby that they are based upon a thing in itself.... The understanding, therefore, by assuming appearances, grants the existence of things in themselves also; and to this extent we may say that the representation of such things as are the basis of appearances, consequently of mere beings of the understanding, is not only admissible but unavoidable.

This unavoidability is centrally important. There would be a very sorry defense of objectivity where one could not even get intersubjective universality. On first thought this unavoidability seems not to be a matter of *logical* compulsion. For logical compulsion is hypothetical while this the presently operative compulsion seems not hypothetical but categorical. But this appearance is misleading. We have here the sort of compulsion through rational presuppositions that is operative at many places in Kant. The necessitation at issue is thus not absolute but relative: *If you are going to claim* genuinely objective knowledge, *then you must also be prepared to claim* a genuine object whose *existence* at any rate is something independent of the conditions of thought. That is, you 'must' do this if experience is to be thought of in a certain way – i.e., is to count as *knowledge*-producing. In a key passage, Kant puts the matter as follows:

In the first place, it is evident beyond all possibility of doubt, that if the conditioned is given, a regress in the series of all its conditions is *set* up *as a task*. For it is involved in the very concept of the conditioned that something is referred to a condition, and if this condition is again itself conditioned, to a more remote condition, and so through all the members of the series. The above proposition is thus analytic, and has nothing to fear from a transcendental criticism. It is a logical postulate of reason, that through the understanding we follow up and extend as far as possible that connection of a concept with its conditions which directly results from the concept itself. (A 497 = B 526 – A 498 = B 526.)

So much for the 'must'. Next we must consider 'postulate' – for it is this, I submit, that Kant essentially means by 'think' in the present context. Kant describes the postulation at issue in the following terms:

Appearances, so far as they are thought as objects according to the unity of the categories, are called *phaenomena*. But *if I postulate* things which are mere objects of understanding, and which, nevertheless, can be given as such to an intuition, although not to one that is sensible... such things would be entitled *noumena* (*intelligibilia*). How we must bear in mind that the concept of appearances, as limited by the Transcendental Aesthetic, already of itself establishes the objective reality of *noumena* and justifies the division of objects into *phaenomena* and *noumena*, and so of the world into a world of the senses and a world of the understanding (*mundus sensibilis et intelligibilis*). ...For if the senses represent to us something merely *as it appears*, this something must also in itself be a thing, and an object of a non-sensible intuition, that is, of the understanding.... All our representations are, it is true, referred by the understanding to some object; and since appearances are nothing but representations, the understanding refers them to a *something*, as the object of sensible intuition. But this something, thus conceived, is only the transcendental object; and by that is meant a something = *X*, of which we know, and with the present constitution of our understanding can know, nothing whatsoever (A 250).

Clearly, when we postulate a thing, use of the very word 'postulate' concedes that (1) we certainly do not encounter this thing in experience, and in fact (2) we do not actually *know* that it exists. But, of course, postulation is a step not to be taken at haphazard: it must have some rational foundation, some *validation*. The operation of the Principle of Sufficient Reason in its regulative guise can provide the warrant for a necessary postulation because it carries essentially conceptual (i.e., logical) force.

The idea of an existential postulation may seem strange, so much so that the whole process may be thought illegitimate. I should like to show by means of an example that this is not the case. Consider the question of the *sum* of an infinite series such as

$$\tfrac{1}{2} + \tfrac{1}{4} + \tfrac{1}{8} + \cdots + \frac{1}{2^n} + \cdots$$

Clearly we can never sum the series up to show that the sum-total in question exists: we not only cannot produce the infinite sum, we cannot even demonstrate (and so know) its existence by the usual machinery of arithmetic. (All we can demonstrate is that *if* the sum exists, then it can neither be <1 nor >1 – we cannot demonstrate that is exists and equals 1.) But if we postulate the existence of infinite sums – whose existence we admittedly cannot *prove* in the usual way – then we are in a position to make claims regarding the sum-total of our series. This example, then, may serve to motivate by way of analogy the conception of an existential postulation.

The example has close kinship to Kant's line of thought. We can show that the sum

$$\tfrac{1}{2} + \tfrac{1}{4} + \cdots$$

is subject to a limit (i.e., cannot exceed 1). But the actuality of a limit to a series does not establish the existence of something *at* the limit, something that *does* the limiting as Kant clearly says in the *Prolegomena* § 45 (Ak. 332). Similarly, the limitation of a regressus of grounds does not establish the existence of an ultimate ground, knowable in the same manner as the grounds themselves. To say that such a limit can – and in certain cases *must* – be *thought* to exist, is not to say that its existence can be *known*. A *limit of known grounds* does not constitute a *known limit of grounds*.

4. CONCLUSION

The crux of our position, then, is that noumenal causality is not actual causality at all, in the strict sense in which causality is governed by a specific, experientially constitutive Principle of Causality. Rather it is only analogical causality, governed by a generic and regulative principle of grounding, a Principle of Sufficient Reason, a principle that controls what we must think to be the case, rather than what we can claim to know regarding nature. Hence this use of Principle of Sufficient Reason does not demonstrate the *existence* of noumenal grounding. Rather, it only affords rational basis for the *necessary postulation* of noumenal causaity in terms of Kant's know vs. think distinction. The Principle of Sulfficient Reason accordingly provides the basis of postulation that is both inevitable and rationally warranted.

This principle thus does a job that needs doing for Kant and that other items of his system are not prepared to do. The Principle of Sufficient Reason is for him regulative: It signalizes a divine discontent, the unwillingness – nay inability – of the mind seeking for objective knowledge to rest satisfied with conditions and to press for unconditioned. But it also marks a critical limit – that which sets knowledge off from thinking (sc. postulating). The fact that a principle with a systematically solid standing is involved is crucial here, for only through such a principle could we obtain a rational *warrant* for the postulation that calls noumenal causality into operation.

If I am right in my view that a Principle of Sufficient Reason is importantly at work in Kant's teaching, this opens up possibility of a comparative exploration in this regard between his approach and that of Leibniz and Wolff. But for the present it must suffice to state dogmatically that what Leibniz has in mind in elaborating his Principle of Sufficient Reason is something quite different. Here, as elsewhere, the vicissitudes of philosophical history were such that Kant was able to see the philosophy of Leibniz only through a glass, darkly. But the key fact, I think, remains that Kant's system of critical philosophy needs a Principle of Sufficient Reason every bit as much as that of his 'dogmatic' predecessors, Leibniz and Wolff.

University of Pittsburgh

NOTES

[1] Kant is not always careful to distinguish the generic Principle of Sufficient Reason for the specific Principle of Causality. For example, at A 201 = B 246 "Principle of sufficient reason" is said where "principle of causality" is obviously wanted. Note the explicit (and favorable) mention of the Principle of Sufficient Reason as an *a priori* synthetic principle in the *Prolegomena* (§ 3).

[2] The entire context of this passage is important. See also the key passage at A 305 = B 362 – A 307 = B 368.

[3] 'On the Ultimate Origin of Things' (1967) tr. by P. P. Wiener, *Leibniz: Selections* (New York, 1951), pp. 345–346.

PART VII

KANT AND SOME MODERN CRITICS

J. N. FINDLAY

KANT AND ANGLO-SAXON CRITICISM

My aim in this lecture is to show how certain Anglo-Saxon thinkers, in virtue of their very critical attitude towards certain central doctrines and assumptions of Kant, have in fact purged Kant's thought of much that is merely peripheral and overlaying, and have so released Hermes in the block, the philosopher in the picture-thinker and model-maker, to a much greater extent than would otherwise have been possible. I am not, of course, so ignorant and so arrogant as not to know that German thought has throughout its history only gone back to Kant in order to go beyond him, and that it has long been an axiom of Kant-study that no one who truly understands Kant can do other than this. Anyone who enters profoundly into the living web of contradiction in which the Kantian writings consist must necessarily follow the illumination shed by some of its glinting facets and ignore that which beams from others. Few can hold in suspense, and in inconsistent unity, the many distinct approaches and interests that nestle together in the thought of Kant: everyone inevitably opts for some in preference to others.

My complaint, however, would not be that German philosophical criticism has failed to go beyond Kant, but that it has only too often gone beyond him in what seem to me wrong directions, and that the fascination of his myths and models, and the revolutionary light they at first seem to shed upon experience, has far outweighed the influence of his profound, permanent, interlocking insights into experience, knowledge and being.

The mythical Manifold that he inherited from Locke, the Understanding with its spontaneous acts of relational synthesis, the Forms of Intuition lying ready to hand in the soul, and mysteriously accommodating a material that does not intrinsically fit them, the professionally obscure Thing-in-itself, the Categories whose necessity is only alleged to stem from the empty focus of an unintelligible unity: all these are doctrines which involve so much strange, external encounter, and so many incredible workings of agencies not otherwise met with, as to be wholly destructive of intellectual light if not drastically reinterpreted, yet there

are still many who see in them the core of Transcendental Idealism. It is
not to me remarkable that Heidegger, who more than anyone has brought
Primal Night back into philosophy – a night perhaps welcome after the
too varied splendours of a brilliant day – should have seen in the doctrine
of the Productive Imagination the central contribution of Kant. It is
because I believe everything that has to do with the Productive Imagination, unless drastically reinterpreted and resited, represents all that is
most confused and also most irrelevant in Kant, that I wish to deal with
the criticisms, constructive or destructive, of certain Anglo-Saxon thinkers, who have done all that they could to do the Productive Imagination
to death. Kant in his moments of higher insightfulness simply soars beyond
all thinkers, and certainly beyond all Anglo-Saxon thinkers, in his ability
to see the complex gearing of apparently disparate factors in a quite
necessary unity. But such higher insightfulness, maintained with strain
and often with inadequate verbal and conceptual aids, necessarily falls
apart, at lower levels of concentration, into the holding of many crabbed,
obscure, mutually conflicting positions, and it is here that the clarity,
the consequence, the piecemeal care of the analytic, Anglo-Saxon intelligence comes into its own, and in fact provides the necessary complement
to Kant's soaring vision. It is in this humble role that I would cast the
Anglo-Saxon critics that I wish to talk about.

I am not confining myself to the narrowly present and there are a great
number of people who might be mentioned on this occasion. I could
speak of Edward Caird, the author of the truly remarkable *Critical
Philosophy of Kant*, first published in 1877, which astonished the German
as much as the British world, and which also showed a depth of compre-
hension of Hegel, and of Hegelian criticisms of Kant, which was at that
time unsurpassed. It was the true core of integrated sense that Caird dug
out in Kant, rather than his mythic surface-machinery, and Caird's
Scottish background, commonsensical yet profound, was doubtless
responsible for his achievement. I shall not, however, speak of Caird, since
his inspiration, though vast, is too much tied the controversies of the time,
to quarrels with superficial enlightenment or evolutionary optimism, to
benefit us now. Nor shall I speak of the two great British commentators
Norman Kemp-Smith and Herbert James Paton, the former of whom
brought the scholarship and views of Vaihinger into the British orbit,
and the latter of whom, in season and out of season, defended what he

thought was the pure milk of the Kantian gospel with unwavering, simple piety. Kemp-Smith brought out the baroque oddity of many Kantian doctrines, but failed to penetrate to their not so baroque kernel, while of Paton it may be said that he wholly failed to cast light on the many difficulties raised by the Kantian text because he was wholly unaware of them. No one who finds Kant difficult should go to Paton for guidance: he should only consult him if he desires to strengthen or simplify his faith. For a variety of reasons I shall say nothing of Ewing's painstaking, excellently reasoned treatments of Kant, nor shall I mention the many young writers, such as Bird and Bennett, whose works reveal a Kantian ferment in the currents of our own time. And I am not mentioning American interpreters of Kant, not because I scorn them, but because I know them less well than the British.

In the time at my disposal only two Anglo-Saxon commentators will be mentioned, both hailing from Oxford, England: one, fairly recent, is the present Waynflete Professor of Metaphysics at Oxford, P. F. Strawson, the author of *Bounds of Sense*, while the other, less recent, was a Whyte's Professor of Moral Philosophy in a previous decade, H. A. Prichard, whose book entitled *Kant's Theory of Knowledge* was published in 1909. The latter work is almost entirely unknown to present-day British thinkers, and, if unknown to them, more totally unknown to their German confrères. Even when Prichard wrote, it was said in Oxford that all he had succeeded in proving, at great length and with much documentation, was how little he understood of Kant. Yet Prichard's book reflects not only his own wisdom, but that of his greater teacher, J. Cook Wilson, who, in an environment full of countless well-smoothed, over-complacent versions of idealism, managed to fight his way clear to a realism that at least conforms to the meaning of the word 'knowledge'. If I were only performing an exercise of piety, I should mention H. A. Prichard on the present occasion, for it was he who opened my eyes to the simple incoherence of the alleged processes through which the phenomenal world on Kantian theory was constructed, and so turned my gaze, at a second remove, to what was truly majestic and enduring in Kant.

I proceed, therefore, to recall Prichard's mainly destructive criticisms, and then to go on to the views of Strawson, who has performed an operation on Kant that I shall call the Transcendental Excision, an operation which cuts out and relegates to an appendix the whole content of what he calls the Metaphysic of Transcendental Idealism, while expounding the improved remainder of Kant's doctrine, with a few additions to its unscathed integrity, in the first three parts of his book. If Kant wrote a great deal of myth-obsessed nonsense, it is nonsense that can without ceremony be dropped from his work, leaving the rest fundamentally intact, a thing that is, of course, not possible in the case of inferior thinkers, where the savour of nonsense pervades and corrupts the whole. After dealing with Prichard and Strawson, I shall perform my own version of the Transcendental Excision, making my cut at a slightly different place, and so saving a little more of the original philosopher. And I shall then join with complete sincerity in the paeans appropriate to the present occasion.

Prichard's book on Kant, in its earlier chapters, shows how the problems which trigger off Kant's researches all involve presuppositions which the further development of the theory serves only to nullify. Kant, we may say in modern phrase, does not solve, but dissolves his problems. But the dissolution is not recognized for the thoroughgoing dissolution that it is, nor as perhaps involving greater problems than those it dissolves, nor is the possibility canvassed of remaining, with some modification, within the original framework of one's problems, and of so genuinely solving them. Kant starts by treating it as a sheer mystery that we should have knowledge, not merely empty and analytic, regarding individuals that we have never encountered in experience, and that such knowledge should be of *all* possible individuals we may or may not encounter in the future. By implication, this wonderment suggests that there is *no* problem regarding knowledge based on empirical encounter: in empirical encounter we have the individuals themselves before us, and can check our judgments of them by simply looking at them and seeing what they are. The statement of Kant's problem is therefore naively realistic and naively empiricistic: in experience, it implies, we have real individuals before us and can find out what they are, whereas it is not at all clear how we can know what things are when we do not thus have them before us. Yet the whole course of the theory is such as to undermine its own problem, for it denies that in experience we have individuals before us as they themselves are, and so abolishes any special prerogative which empirical encounter might have over non-empirical general knowledge. It in fact comes to be held that non-empirical knowledge, so far from being a mysterious extension of empirical knowledge, is the necessary background and pre-supposition of the latter. If this is what we are coming to, why see a special mystery in such non-empirical knowledge, and devise special theories to account for it?

The same self-liquidation of a problem occurs in Kant's treatment of the contrast between Sensibility and Understanding. Sensibility is at first held to be the faculty through which objects are *given* to us, such givenness being passive and receptive, whereas Understanding is the faculty through which objects thus given are *thought* by us, such thought being necessarily spontaneous and active. A problem then arises as to how two such different faculties can be geared together: why should the one find fit application for its concepts in the data offered by the other, or why should the other's data fit the moulds imposed on them by the one? Obviously again, Prichard points out, the whole setting of the problem presupposes a direct access to things themselves in Sensibility, and a not so direct access to them through the Understanding, and the problem of gearing would perhaps be better solved by giving the Understanding an equally direct, if general, access to the things themselves, than by attempting a total transformation of the problem, in which Sensibility no longer gives us objects in any sense of the word, but is the mere living through of blind sensations, whereas it is the Understanding functioning as the Imagination which alone sets objects before us.

In his treatment of the Aesthetic Prichard similarly shows how Kant's conclusions as to the ideality of Space and Time destroy the arguments on which they themselves have been based. For these arguments stress the strangeness of our boundlessly ranging geometrical and chronometrical knowledge, and of our 'seeing', in one sense of 'seeing', whatever we 'see', in two boundless media which we do not 'see' in the sense in which we 'see' objects in them. This strangeness is only a strangeness if we might expect to gain our knowledge of Space and Time by extrapolation from perceptual fragments, and this expectation in its turn presupposes a commonsense contact with the Real in perception, and with Space and Time as part of that Real, which the whole of Kant's Theory of Knowledge is at such pains to deny.

Plainly it would be simpler to accept a boundlessly ranging, non-empirical geometrical and chronometrical knowledge, however odd its character, on the same basis as the perceptual knowledge which fills it out, than to transform both the problem and the things it concerns out of all recognition. Prichard's arguments, which I may not have restated perfectly, might seem confused to many. For is it not precisely Kant's merit that he dissolved rather than solved the problems of knowledge? The Prichardian answer here would be, as we shall see later, that one cannot throw light on concepts so fundamental as those of Knowledge and Reality by transforming them into something quite different.

Prichard goes on to show, in ensuing chapters, that the whole distinction between objective and subjective features, between things as they *appear* to us and things as they in themselves *are*, is always bound up with the possibility that there should be a *coincident* use of the two concepts, that while they may diverge in some cases they as plainly come together in others. "While there is no transition in principle from knowledge of what things look to knowledge of what things are, there is", Prichard tells us, "continuously such a transition in respect of details.... From the very beginning our knowledge of what a thing appears in respect of spatial characteristics implies the consciousness of it as spatial and therefore also as in particular three-dimensional. If we suppose the latter consciousness absent any assertion as to what a thing appears in respect of spatial characteristics loses significance" (*op. cit.*, p. 92).

This conclusion holds even when science banishes a quality so intimately conjoined with objects as colour into the realm of appearance: we may only be able to say what colour an object *appears* to have, but we can still contrast this appearance with its not merely apparent three-dimensional being in space. The argument here developed by Prichard is of course one that has since become classic among British analysts. It puts a stop, as not clearly significant, to that *total* withdrawal of faith from the empirical world in Space and Time which has in different ways been recommended and practised by Descartes, Kant, and in later times Husserl. Prichard does not say that we cannot make use of the distinction beyond empirical limits, but he does suggest that we must learn its use within the limits of experience, and that we have no good reason to regard that empirical use as being in any sense of a limited or qualified validity.

Before he passes on to the Analytic Prichard has a general chapter which grows out of the arguments that have been studied in the Aesthetic and looks forward to those that will be studied in the Analytic. It is entitled 'Knowledge and Reality', and in it Prichard deals with the idealistic contention that mind really can only come into the relation that we call knowledge, if reality stands in an essential relation to, and is inseparable from the knowledge which is of it, and that even if the mind gains access to an independent reality, it must modify the latter in the process, so that it is only known in relation to knowledge and not as it is in itself. The fundamental objection, Prichard says, to this line of thought is that it "contradicts the very nature of knowledge. Knowledge unconditionally presupposes that the reality known exists independently of the knowledge of it, and that we know it as it exists in this independence.... If a reality could only be or come to be in virtue of some activity or process on the part of the mind, that activity would not be 'knowing' but 'making' or 'creating', and to make and to know must in the end be admitted to be mutually exclusive. The presupposition that what is known exists independently of being known is quite general, and applies to feeling and sensation just as much as parts of the physical world. It must in the end be conceded of a toothache as much as a stone that it exists independently of the knowledge of it.... Hence if 'things in themselves' means 'things existing independently of our knowledge of them', knowledge is essentially of things in themselves" (*op. cit.*, pp. 118–119).

Prichard points out that this self-transcendence of knowledge is not incompatible with various forms of subjectivism, only that, if we embrace these, we must identify things-in-themselves with acts of consciousness or with the appearances that occur in them. Also that there is as great a problem in the knowledge of these as in the ordinarily accepted knowledge of the physical world. Subjectivism, however, loses its appeal when these points are noted, and when the facile confusion of the activities involved in knowing and perceiving with the realities known in such activities has been carefully avoided. Prichard's assertions are here axiomatic: there can be an idealistic or spiritualistic metaphysic, but not an idealistic epistemology. Even in the case of the self-positing Ego of Fichte – suppose this defensible – we must distinguish between the self-positing reality as such, and the knowledge that it can then have of itself as thus self-positing. We can study the manner in which objects come to be set up as objects *for us*, and how we gain assurance as to their reality, and Kant has of course contributed vastly to these enquiries, but if such assurance is to count as knowledge, the constitution of objects for us cannot count as the constitution of such objects.

In his treatment of the Analytic Prichard of course shatters the Meta-physical Deduction with arguments too familiar to be rehearsed here. But, as we move from the Metaphysical to the Transcendental Deduction, Prichard tells us that we also move to a totally new concept of Judgment. Hitherto Judgment has been either a union of conceptions or of a group of particulars with a common universal: now it is the union of an empirical or *a priori* manifold through a conception superinduced by thought and not capable of being extracted from the manifold by analysis. This superimposition is the work of the Imagination, a faculty introduced without notice, which is not less bizarre for being described as the Understanding working unreflectively. The Imagination must run through sensory items and unify them, it must unify them according to fixed rules which smooth the path from one item to another, and which make them cohere in the unity of an object, and which enable the mind to refer them to a transcendent source beyond itself: it must also generate, or be able to generate, an accompanying consciousness of its own procedures in unifying such items, and of something in or behind itself that does the unifying. Kant, as Prichard points out, argues from the possiblity of self-consciousness to the possibility of objective interconnection *and vice versa*, but, most curiously, he *identifies* the two lines of argument: the same procedure that constitutes objects for us must also constitute our thinking selves and their activities for those thinking selves and thinking activities themselves. Prichard, however, holds that there are logical priorities here: Kant has not clearly seen or said that even if the possibility of self-consciousness is necessary for a unified objective consciousness, it is so only because a unified objective consciousness is a *prior* condition for a possible self-conscious unity: we must have a prior objective unity of consciousness if we are to be conscious of such a unity and of its source.

And if I may here myself briefly interject, neither Kant nor Prichard has seen or said that the Unity of Consciousness is not merely a necessary condition for a synthesis according to rule, but also for a contingent subjective synthesis which does not follow rules at all, and which may be based on personal association or interest or on arbitrary choice. And yet nothing can in fact be clearer than that I can put items together arbitrarily, as I do in setting up many sets or collections, and that, even when I know items *have* an objective arrangement, I can ignore this and range capriciously over them. Nothing is clearer than that I can unite Queen Elizabeth with Virtue and the Number Ten and reckon them to be a well-formed triad, just as I can run over the parts of a well put-together house in an order that bears no relation to that house's construction.

And it is highly arguable that my consciousness of Self is at its *highest* when I thus put items together arbitrarily, and *not* when their synthesis seems compelled by an objective rule. These points are in fact conceded by Kant, and are central to his argument in the Analogies of Experience, where all turns on the *distinction* between an objective and a subjective synthesis. But in the Transcendental Deduction, and particularly in that of the Second Edition, all contrives to insinuate that Self-consciousness, or its possibility, is in *all cases inseparable* from Rule-governed Synthesis, which entails, if it entails anything, that no *non*-ruleful putting together of objects in thought is *possible at all*. As they stand, the two Transcendental Deductions prove altogether too much, and make no plain sense unless interpreted in the light of the Analogies of Experience, together with which they are in fact always discussed by Anglo-Saxon commentators. Taken in isolation, the hastily written Second Edition Transcendental Deduction proves so much too much, and is so grossly lacking in consequence or relevance, as only to be describable as a disgrace to human reason. I trust I shall be pardoned for uttering so impious a sentiment at an International Kant Conference.

That the Transcendental Deduction violates reason is, however, argued by Prichard in another way. He points out that Kant's conception of objective synthesis as instanced by the examples he uses, e.g. a triangle, is not capable of explanation in terms of wholly general notional forms like the Categories (on the one hand) and a disordered Manifold (on the other). Even if we schematize our Categories, the difficulty remains. Objective synthesis requires *particular* principles of union which differ from object to object: the synthesis which yields a triangle cannot be the synthesis which yields a sky-scraper or a butterfly. The Manifold, however, provides no guideline as to such particular principles, nor do the schematized Categories: the Imagination, therefore, will have to improvise, it will have *carte blanche* for its synthetic activities. What it imagines must conform to the Categories, but infinite schemes so conform, and we can imagine different minds, like children playing with blocks, building countless different, well-ordered, categorial worlds. If, however, we conceive the materials used in such building as somehow dictating its structure, we shall not have the pure Manifold as Kant conceives it, and we shall not have the certainty that the materials will be capable of being arranged in a categorial manner. Kant, Prichard points out, recognizes all this in his account of the necessary Affinity of phenomena, but points out that neither the Thing-in-itself nor the Manifold nor the Imagination can guarantee such an Affinity. The only way such an Affinity can be guaranteed is if the Imagination actually produces it, conjures it up, and this means, if it means anything, that the Imagination must conjure up its *materials* as much as their arrangement.

Prichard goes on to draw the moral which his criticism of Kant's Deductions entails. Kant, in his account of the synthetic activities in which objects are constituted for the mind, has described something which is not and cannot be knowledge. The syntheses through which perceptual objects are constituted by the mind are literally acts of making or construction. Knowing is for Kant manufacture, and Kant emphasizes this point when he says that "the order and conformity to law in the phenomena which we call *Nature* we ourselves introduce, and we could not find it there if we or the nature of the mind had not originally placed it there". Kant only conceals the totally creative character of his epistemology by letting the Understanding's right hand, as it were, fail to know what its left hand has been doing. As Understanding it recognizes a synthesis which as Imagination it has been half-consciously producing: it has salted the mine somnambulistically (metaphor not Prichard's) in order to find diamonds in it next day. But, says Prichard, "the fundamental objection to this account of knowledge seems so obvious as to be hardly worth stating: it is of course that knowing and making are not the same.... Even if the reality happens to be something that we make, e.g. a house, the knowing it is distinct from making it" (*op. cit.*, p. 235).

We may go further than Prichard: any picture of the mind in knowledge as introducing order into a disordered manifold is not merely baseless: it is also pernicious. It is the source of all the ὕβρις, of which Kant was of course wholly free, which led straight through Nietzsche and others to the Propaganda Ministerium of Dr. Goebbels. It is a falsehood of which Hegel, so often seen as the supreme source of German reaction, was likewise wholly free. For in Hegel it is the Eternal Idea, not any actual Self-consciousness, human or superhuman, that has externalized itself in Nature in order to become conscious of itself in Spirit.

From Prichard's painfully ruinous onslaught, we pass to the restorative reinterpretation of P. F. Strawson. Here in the Fourth Section of *Bounds of Sense* we have a treatment entitled 'The Metaphysics of Transcendental Idealism', in which are arranged, as in the glass bottles of a medical museum, all the excised organs of Transcendentalism, the precious models so dear to the picture-thinker, and so unhelpful from the point of view of a thought that seeks to penetrate and to shed light. And Strawson has provided these excised organs with new names so as to remove confusions regarding them, and has divided them or otherwise modified them so as to make them more remotely like viable concepts. He has obligingly posited an *A*-relation, which is an analogue of 'causally affecting' or 'being causally affected': this *A*-relation holds among items known as Things-in-themselves without prejudice to the partial or complete identity of its terms, or the partial or complete reflexivity of the *A*-relation. One term that is *A*-related is peculiar inasmuch as it is both *A*-affecting and *A*-affected. In the former capacity it is said to display Understanding, a 'form-producing' character, in the latter capacity it displays Sensibility, a 'form-yielding' character. There are other terms which enter into *A*-relations which may be said to be 'matter-producing' elements. Something called 'Experience' is now held to be the outcome of this complex, quasi-causal transaction among *A*-terms, and such Experience consists of 'Intuitions' all of which have an order called 'Temporality' derived from one form-yielding element, whereas some also have a second order called 'Spatiality' derived from another form-yielding element. Intuitions further possess the character of being Perceptions of a Law-governed World of Objects, due to the quasi-action of the form-producing element called Understanding on the other form-yielding or matter-producing factors, and this Law-governed World of Objects is nothing apart from the Perceptions in which it is constituted.

The contents of Experience consist of two different sorts of 'Appearances' which are also 'Appearances' in totally different senses – here Kant is greatly improved upon – the first, the Appearances of the common *A*-term which exercises Sensibility and Understanding, are truly existent but wholly attributive elements, whereas the second, the Appearances of Physical Nature, only *appear* to exist in these truly existent but wholly attributive Appearances just mentioned. Empirical Knowledge is the outcome of all these factors, including those which are matter-producing,

but there is also a Knowledge of Appearances which is independent of
the matter-producing factors, and which is therefore said to be Non-empirical or A Priori, such Non-empirical Knowledge being restricted to
Appearances.

This remarkable sketch thus set forth, and involving interpretable as
well as only semi-interpretable elements, is then put to the test, and
Strawson decides, after long consideration, that the semi-interpretable
elements in the model do little or no significant work, and that Kant fails
to provide a fully significant and even fully coherent account of the inter-
play of the various *A*-factors in the model with various empirical characters. We may add that Kant *did* try to work out a coherent but similar
scheme in the well-known *Dissertation* of 1770, concerning the Form and
Principles of the Sensible and Intelligible Worlds. There are difficulties in
this work, but it is at least not obviously self-destroying, it makes possible
a knowledge of phenomena and a knowledge that transcends phenomena, and it is very fit that we should remember this *Dissertation*, with
its roots in Kant's unique sense of the antinomic difficulties of Space and
Time, just two hundred years after it was shatteringly delivered in
Königsberg.

After the careful excision of all these transcendental organs, it might be
thought that Kant's Critical Philosophy would languish and die. The
reverse is the case: the patient bounds from the operating table in an
access of renewed vitality. The investigation of the limiting framework
of ideas and principles, the use and application of which are essential to
empirical knowledge, and we may add to any kind of being of which
truly significant thought is possible at all, remains a supremely important
task, to which Kant made the fundamental contributions, and to whose
carrying forward the various theses of metaphysical transcendentalism
have absolutely no relevance. Kant's contribution lay in saying and showing that the view of the logical held by the formal logicians, and the view
of experience and learning from experience held by the empiricists were
alike null and void *unless set in a wider framework*, necessary yet not merely
trivial, which rendered learning from experience and the limiting trivialities
of formal logic alike 'possible'.

Strawson (who is not responsible for my last sentence) sees the contribution of Kant as embracing the following 'theses', all of which he
finds acceptable: that experience is essentially temporal, that there must

be such unity among a temporally extended set of experiences as to make 'self-ascription' on the part of a subject of experiences 'possible', that experience must include an awareness of objects that can be judged about irrespective of the actual occurrence of particular experiences of them, that the objects thus judged about must be spatial, that there must be one unified spatio-temporal framework of empirical reality embracing all experience and its objects, and that certain principles of permanence and causality must be satisfied in the physical or objective world of things in space (*op. cit.*, p. 24). Strawson further points out that Kant rightly holds that all the other theses stand in the most intimate logical relation to the thesis of the necessary unity of consciousness. Without objects, without things in space, without the principles of permanence and causality, there could be no such necessary unity. No one, he argues, could be conscious of a temporally extended series of experiences as his own, unless he could be aware of them as yielding knowledge of a unified objective world through which the series of experiences forms just one subjective or experiential route. (It will be noted how Strawson qualifies and improves the bald exaggerations of the Transcendental Deduction.) Kant's genius, he says, and I agree with him, is nowhere more clearly shown than in his connection of the possibility of experience with the possibility of distinguishing a temporal order of perceptions from an order which the objects of those perceptions independently possess, and in his recognition that this distinction must be revealed in the *contents* of experience since there is no question of perceiving the pure framework itself. Strawson points out that it is not in the Transcendental Deduction taken alone, but only in its connection with the Aesthetic, and in its connection with the Refutation of Idealism, that a coherent body of Kantian principles can be worked out and justified.

As regards the rest of Kant's system, the Transcendental Dialectic, Strawson is content to see in it the application of a principle of which he approves and which he calls the Principle of Significance. This is the principle that there can be no legitimate or even meaningful employment of ideas and concepts which does not relate them to empirical or experiential conditions of their application. The connection of this interpretation of Kant's criticism of Transcendent Metaphysic with modern Positivism and Verificationism will be evident. Strawson considers that the main defect of the Metaphysic of Transcendental Idealism is that in it Kant

violated his own Principle of Significance: he tried to think both sides of
the limit of possible experience, instead of merely trying to think up to it.
I agree with Strawson that Kant violated his own Principle of Significance
in talking about the Productive Imagination and its marvellous feats: I
also think that he violated it unprofitably. But I do not myself accept the
Principle of Significance and am glad Kant violated it in other contexts.
For I think with the 1770 *Dissertation* that there are both meaningful
concepts and even meaningful possibilities of knowledge that go beyond
the limits of possible experience. Cantor's transfinite aggregates and the
full realities of social encounter are for me cases in point.

Some points in Strawson's treatment of the Kantian Analytic are
particularly noteworthy. He points out that Kant did not simply write
a reference to law-governed objectivity into his notion of experience, so
that a phantasmagoria of impressions, if such existed, would simply count
as a non-experience. It would be a very uninteresting proceeding simply
to legislate in this manner, and would, moreover, leave us open to the
unremoved possibility of encountering disorderly non-experiences at any
moment or for any length of time. It is as if one arbitrarily made an in-
capacity to fly part of one's definition of man, and then had to cope with
a situation in which all one's friends, now merely non-men, simply took
wing and flew out of the window. Kant, Strawson points out, bases his
declaration of necessary objectivity on *another* tautology, that experiences
belonging to a single consciousness must satisfy the conditions of belonging to a single consciousness, and this in its turn is made to entail
that such experiences should possess the rule-governed connectedness
which is also required for them to constitute a temporally extended
experience of a single objective world. Strawson therefore accepts the
Second Edition view that the Trancendental Unity of Self-Consciousness
is the supreme principle in the realm of the *A Priori*, but he makes of it
a somewhat different use from Kant. For he does not allow that the mere
activity of synthesis, or the mere possibility of this activity, is sufficient
to give rise to self-consciousness: to be self-conscious, it is not enough
to be an intelligence conscious of its power of combination, or of the
mere fact of its being.

Strawson first takes very seriously the suggestion that there might have
been a consciousness which put items together, assembled them in a
single thought-picture, without there being a vestige of 'fixed rule' in

their synthesis. Would a unified consciousness, capable of ascribing its presentations to itself, be possible on such a basis? Strawson points out that Kant at times seems willing to entertain such a suggestion: he says that if appearances were not such as to allow of knowledge expressible in objective judgements, they would be 'for us as good as nothing', 'a blind play of representations, less even than a dream'. Strawson finds it basically difficult that in such a situation it would be impossible to attach a sense to the notion of a single consciousness to which the successive experiences are supposed to belong: we seem, he says, to add nothing but a form of words to the hypothesis of an essentially disconnected set of impressions by stipulating that they all belong to an identical consciousness.

I am not myself disposed to accept this criticism of Strawson's, because I do not think that the unity and continuity of experience depends on our being able to *attach a sense* to any notion whatever, or to be conscious of that unity and continuity in any form or guise. I am one of those people who believe that experiences may be said to be experiences of this or of that in a far deeper sense that that they involve a consciousness of this or of that, in the sense, namely, that what they are said to be *of* is *itself* experienced, itself lived through. I believe myself that we live through both the continuity and successiveness of our own experiences, and both in close fusion, and that these traits, and their fusion, are simply descriptive characters of our experiences, which have nothing to do with any conscious reference to ourselves or to our own experiences which in fact presuppose such a continuity-in-succession. We do not require any act or process of self-ascription to hold us together, or make us continuous-in-flux: we simply *are* continuous-in-flux, and it is only to the Humean imagination that anything else is, or could be, the case.

But Strawson and Kant are still back at the stage where it seems that something is needed to save one from being a mere flux of impressions, and that an act of self-ascription will do the trick. But such self-ascription, Strawson rightly points out, involves a contrast: self-ascription is not possible when one's inner life is simply a rush of experiences, there must be something in one's experiences which enables one to distinguish an objective sequence revealed in those experiences, from the purely subjective sequence of the experiences themselves. This ground of distinction need not always be in evidence. There may be phantasmagoric 'trips' of great length. But not *all* experience can be of this phantasmagoric character if there is to be self-ascription: there can be meaningful reference to a subject only if there is also a contrasting reference to an object.

I am entirely at one with Strawson on this point, though I believe in arbitrary as well as phantasmagoric sequences, and ascribe great importance to the former. I also believe that it is possible to reach the point reached by Strawson in his argument without the false move involved in ascribing the unity of consciousness to an act of self-ascription. I should myself argue that, while the unity and continuity of experience is something we simply live through, and which requires no act of self-scription to render it 'possible', yet it does involve a contrast, a reference to another, not indeed for its consciousness of self, which need not exist, but for its very *being*. One can, I believe, only *be* the sort of continuity-in-flux that, as an experient, one is, if there are items, not parts of one's experienced being, but *given* in that being, which by their contrast make that being itself possible, items which can only contrast with one's experienced life if they have a rhythm distinct from and at times opposed to that life, and if we can for this reason be conscious of them as *objects*. Consciousness of self only arises at a third remove from the continuity-in-flux of experience: that continuity-in-flux requires a reference away from self in order to be itself, and this reference away from self in its turn makes possible a contrasting reference to self. We are because objects are given to us, and because objects are given to us, we ourselves can be given to ourselves. You will see that I am siding with Prichard in his belief in logical priorities in this difficult region. But as I reach the same conclusion as Strawson by a somewhat longer route, I shall cease to lay stress upon our differences.

Strawson, however, feels that one must go further than Kant in developing the implications of self-ascription. He thinks that it is not enough to be able to ascribe all our experiences to an 'abiding self', if this self remains merely vacuous and transcendental. He thinks that we can only give a full sense to self-ascription if there are empirically applicable criteria of identity by means of which a given self can be pinned down, and given a firm place among other selves and among other realities in the space-time world. The subjective unity of self-consciousness can only make full sense if it can be regarded as *one* experiential route through the complexities of the objective world, beside which *other* experiential routes are likewise possible. This means, though Strawson only spells it out fully elsewhere, that self-ascription always involves the possibility of other-ascription, that a social milieu, at least in possibility, is part and parcel of the possibility of experience. Strawson therefore provides a Transcendental Deduction of what Heidegger has called *Mitsein*. And he holds further, though again he only spells it out fully elsewhere, that self-ascription is only possible if there are *objective* criteria which enable one to pin this or that subject down, and oppose him to others, and these will, of course, have to be intersubjective, bodily criteria, and not merely subjective ones. We do not indeed identify our own subjective route of experience and ascribe it to ourselves by making use of any criteria whatever, but we can only give full meaning to such an ascription if our self is also given a definite bodily location in the world, if its states are given a definite bodily documentation, which makes it possible for both self and states to be given in other experiential routes, and for such other routes to appear in the route which is oneself. In some sense, then, a plurality of minds, and a plurality of embodied minds, able to identify one another in the world, are part and parcel of the necessary framework of experience.

Strawson has here extended Kant's transcendentalism in a manner that is at once deeply Kantian and also true and necessary. Kant's constant use of the pronoun 'we' instead of 'I' shows how for him sociality is built into the *a priori* structure of the world, and his criticisms of the conception of a world of pure spirits as it occurs in the early *Träume eines Geister-sehers* and in a passage in the Postulates of Empirical Knowledge, shows him to be well on the way to agreeing with Strawson. I myself believe profoundly that the notion of a possible plurality of selves is in the deepest sense *a priori*, a part of the possibility of there being any consciousness of knowledge or being whatsoever, and that all the modern difficulties regarding our knowledge of other minds rest on the simple ignoring or this fact. I also agree with Strawson that embodiment and bodily identifiability are part of the developed notion of a system of selves, though I also believe that the bodies by which selves are mutally identifiable may come to be the spiritual bodies of St. Paul rather than the natural bodies of ordinary experience.

I have now said all that can with comfort be said on the present occasion regarding the contributions to Kant-criticism of my two chosen exponents of Anglo-Saxon thought, H. A. Prichard and P. F. Strawson. I shall now wind up by saying a little on my own behalf, and in admiring assessment of Kant. The greatness of Kant, as I see it, lies in the fact that he erected a permanent thought-bastion against two deeply linked errors: the error that I shall call Logico-Mathematicism, on the one hand, and the error that I shall call Radical Empiricism, on the other. These two errors play into each other's hands, and together constitute a single 'monstrous regiment' under which all understanding of nature, knowledge and our selves, not to speak of morality and the ultimate forms of religion, necessarily melts away.

Both errors are very strong in Hume, and in his present-day logico-empiricistic admirers, and they are also very strong in Kant, leading to his whole naive wonderment when he considers that we know things about the world and ourselves, and must in fact know such things about the world and ourselves, things neither trivial nor yet derived from experience, if we are to utter significant judgments about anything at all and if we are to be able to learn anything from experience. The wonderment with which he regards what he calls the Synthetic *A Priori*, his own discovery and named by himself, is a wonderment derived in part from a superstitious reverence for a supposedly complete Formal Logic and in part from what one may call a deep-seated crypto-empiricism. It is the latter which leads Kant to resort to the most fantastic hypotheses, themselves cryptically empiricistic and psychologistic, as to the hidden mental mechanisms which have made it seem that we can understand and know things not trivial and not resting on piecemeal experience. All the worst things in Kant spring from the errors which he himself utterly repudiates and refutes. For what Kant shows is that Formal Logic is only possible if behind it lies a Transcendental Logic which drastically limits the objects and situations to which Formal Logic can have significant application, and that there is not, and cannot be, that boundless realm of logical and mathematical possibilities in which philosophical formalists have always believed, and with which many modern philosophers and also modern physicists have had such boundless fun. And what Kant also shows is that learning from experience is only possible if that learning proceeds within a framework of limiting conditions which we in a sense know in advance, in that our learning procedures conform to them, and that would get us nowhere, if such limiting conditions did not obtain.

And what he further shows, with some measure of success, is that these limiting conditions are involved in our being conscious of things or talking about things or entertaining hypotheses regarding things, and in the very existence or truth of anything of which we can be conscious or can talk about. So that there is absolutely no place for naive wonderment as to the fact that we have non-trivial, structural knowledge that goes beyond experience: without it we should not be able to learn from experience or even have trivial non-empirical knowledge. There is therefore absolutely no need to construct fantastic psychological hypotheses as to how we seem to possess this non-trivial non-empirical knowledge in which only an absurd theory finds a problem: it would only be a problem if we had, or could have, purely empirical knowledge or purely analytic knowledge *without* this transcendental background. This does not, of course, mean that there may not be a legitimate psychological enquiry as to how different kinds of objects come to be objects for us, or how we come to have assured knowledge regarding them, only such an enquiry will be an investigation into genuine, not seeming knowledge, and will be concerned with 'phenomena' only as they tend towards a limiting, necessary coincidence with things as they are in themselves.

I myself therefore accept devoutly what I take to be the Kantian view that our approach to anything always involves an absolute 'know-how' which governs our investigative procedures, and which can on reflection be teased out into a body of principles which can be shown to be necessary to the existence of conscious experience and of the world as we know it. I agree, further, with Strawson and others, that this *a priori* framework is much more extensive than Kant imagines. It includes not only the acceptance of our own stream of experience in time, and of objects out there in space which contrast with our experiential stream, and have a constancy and regularity of their own: it also includes the acceptance of many such streams of experience attached to suitable bodies scattered here and there in a common space, and joining with us in comment on the objects in that space. I believe that the *a priori*, if one so likes to describe it, goes very much further, and that there is not in fact a single region of experience not covered by what Husserl has called its regional *a priori*.

Husserl, we may here say in parenthesis, is the philosopher who, more than any other, has carried on the grand design of the Critical Philosophy, and who, in such works as his *Vorlesungen zur Phänomenologie des inneren Zeitbewusstseins* and his *Cartesian Meditations*, has really worked out further, and more organically, the inspiration lying behind the *A*

Priori of Kant. His careful analyses of Syntheses of Identification, and of the constitution of various types of objects, carry out coherently and concretely what Kant was only trying to do in certain darkly brilliant passages. But Husserl unfortunately took over from Kant no small share of his crypto-empiricism. The various noetic-noematic structures that he distinguishes are often merely described, not deduced: they may be denominated 'necessary', but methodologically they do not differ from empirical findings, and are in fact often mixed up with the latter. And Husserl, of course, took over from Kant that baneful psychologism which, whether styled 'transcendental' or 'phenomenological', really makes nonsense of his own recommended ἐποχή, and which is likewise untrue to the inner claims of our experience in dealing with the transcendently real. All this does not remove Husserl from the high place on which he stands with Kant, and, I should also hold, with Hegel, as a philosopher comparable in stature with the two greatest among the Greeks.

I shall conclude by saying that I would wish the last trace of constructive subjectivism to be excised from Kant: we must altogether reverse the Copernican revolution, and hold him not merely to have shown what sort of a world can be given in experience and handled in thought, but what sort of a world there can in any sense *be*. For neither the boundless 'possibilities' envisaged by logico-mathematical thought, nor the 'possibilities' envisaged by the empirical imagination, are in any sense really possible. On deep reflection we may argue that to be *capable* of being gathered together in unity and understanding by a conscious mind is a readily ignored but necessary side to any real system of things, and that in discoursing of the limits of experience and intelligibility we are in fact only discoursing about the limits of what can be, though in a somewhat more perspicuous and easy way. For it is only a false and absurd view that regards intelligence as an external accident imposed upon the world, rather than as the supreme expression of that defined, articulate, dynamic togetherness which is necessary to the being of anything whatever. The possible, or even supposedly actual worlds in which there is no such thing as becoming in time, nothing having the separative continuity of space, no such limit to undisciplined variety as established the natural kinds, and no tendency to blossom in conscious creatures in whom the world becomes lucid to itself: all these are not really possible worlds at all. They are, in a true and proper sense, products of the Productive Imagination, obedient only to a logic which imposes no restrictions whatsoever.

I would add, finally, in disagreement with Strawson, that I think that Kant's persistent use of the Categories beyond experience, with what may be called a mystico-moral intent, is very far from being the absurd proceeding that a superficial Kantianism would hold it to be. For it is not un-Kantian nor unintelligible to hold that the world of articulate experience and real being necessarily terminates in certain 'objects of the horizon', whose obscurity is as necessary to the whole ordered structure of things as are the middle-distance objects which they explain and order, and which we can talk of intelligibly only in a different, properly obscurer sense than the sense in which we can talk intelligibly of such middle-distance objects. This at least I believe, and I believe that my belief is in harmony with the deeper thought of Kant.

Yale University

MARGARET D. WILSON

ON KANT AND THE REFUTATION OF
SUBJECTIVISM

I

In the *Critique of Pure Reason* Kant claims that he provided refutations of the subjectivist, "idealist," or skeptical positions developed by such predecessors as Descartes, Berkeley, and Hume. Despite Kant's efforts, however, these positions have remained quite influential into the present century. Recently some valuable new commentaries on the first *Critique* have encouraged reconsideration of Kant's defense of realism.[1] Typically, the authors of these commentaries attempt to derive from the text of the Transcendental Analytic a system of argumentation that genuinely reflects Kant's procedure, and at the same time can claim the attention (perhaps the conviction) of contemporary epistemologists. Different writers, of course, show different degrees of concern with the historical soundness of their interpretations or 'reconstructions'.

In this paper I will consider one of these versions of the anti-subjectivist arguments of the *Critique*: that expounded by P. F. Strawson in *The Bounds of Sense*. I shall not be concerned to assess the historical validity of Strawson's conception, either absolutely or relative to other comparable efforts at philosophical reconstruction. Nor shall I be *primarily* concerned with establishing the philosophical limitations or weaknesses of the anti-subjectivist line of argument that Strawson attributes to Kant.[2] Rather I am interested in showing that, contrary to what Strawson himself assumes, his version of Kant's argument bears with very unequal weight on Humean and Cartesian skepticism. Failure to distinguish adequately the different types of subjectivist arguments is not, I think, a problem peculiar to Strawson's approach. Such imprecision is a fairly common source of confusion or over-simplification in discussions of subjectivist positions, and of Kant's replies to them. In Strawson's case, the assimilation of the Cartesian and Humean positions results in the error of ascribing *general* effectiveness to a defense of realism which is at best effective against the rather peculiar doctrine of Hume.

II

Towards the beginning of *The Bounds of Sense*, Strawson remarks that in some respects Kant is "close to the tradition of classical empiricism, the tradition of Berkeley and Hume, which has probably ... received its clearest modern expression in the writings of A. J. Ayer" (p. 18). But, he continues, Kant departs sharply from that tradition in his rejection of the classical empiricist view that experience "really offers us nothing but separate and fleeting sense-impressions" – a view which set for the empiricist the "central problem" of showing how, "on this exiguous basis, we could supply a rational justification of our ordinary picture of the world as containing continuously and independently existing and interacting material things and persons" (*Ibid.*). As Strawson puts it, Kant's rejection

took the form ... of a proof that the minimal empiricist conception of experience was incoherent in isolation, that it made sense only within a larger framework which necessarily included the use and application in experience of concepts of an objective world (p. 19).

Strawson's paragraph continues (and concludes) as follows:

Thus the execution of Kant's programme for a positive metaphysics is held to entail the rejection of what he calls "problematic" idealism, even if such idealism is only the methodological starting-point ... of philosophical reflection. Any philosopher who invites, or challenges, us to justify our belief in the objective world by working outwards, as it were, from the private data of individual consciousness thereby demonstrates his failure to have grasped the conditions of the possibility of experience in general. Philosophers as unlike in other respects as Descartes and Hume are held to be alike ... guilty of this failure (*Ibid.*).

According to Strawson, then, Kant is able to refute both Cartesian and Humean subjectivism by establishing that "a purely sense-datum experience" (*Ibid.*, p. 100) is impossible. All self-conscious experience, so far as we can conceive it, necessarily involves on a bed-rock level 'experience of objects'. Thus it is incoherent to suppose that our judgments about outer objects must be conceived as 'derived' (with more or less warrant) from strictly subjective, sensory elements of experience. The subjectivist is wrong to attribute such priority to sense-data judgments.

Superficially, at least, it may well seem surprising that *Descartes*, of all philosophers, could be refuted by a proof "that the minimal empiricist conception of experience [is] incoherent is isolation." And to understand that there is a really significant objection to assimilating Cartesian and Humean types of subjectivism in this way, we need only consider with more precision the logic of their respective positions. The truth is that Hume's position does seem straight-forwardly to depend on a sensationalist conception of the nature of experience, while Descartes' definitely does not. This is not to deny that the Cartesian does, in a sense, challenge us "to justify our belief in the objective world by working outwards ... from the private data of individual consciousness." It is only to deny that such a challenge presupposes the sensationalist conception of experience as "offering us nothing but separate and fleeting sense-impressions."

III

The skeptical or subjectivist strain in Hume's position[3] as developed especially in Book I of the *Treatise of Human Nature*,[4] rests on two fundamental assumptions. The first is the view that every meaningful concept is directly correlatable, as copy to original, with a previously discriminated sensory datum (or set of such data). This may be characterized as the thesis that meaning is sensory content. The second assumption is the doctrine that "nothing is ever present to the mind but its own perceptions."[5] This is the thesis that the *objects* of our thought are sensory contents. These two theses yield the view that the 'real content' of our beliefs must be reducible without remainder to the sensory elements. Hume conceives of the beliefs or judgments themselves as directly generated out of the antecedently given sensory stream by rather rigid mechanisms of association, inertial continuation, and so forth. These sensationalist premises then lead him to conclude that our beliefs in enduring outer objects as well as in 'objective connection', are so to speak only pseudo-beliefs, in so far as they cannot be reduced to judgments about sense impressions.

Thus, with respect to the issue of necessary connections between outer objects or events, Hume does not simply conclude that, our experience being what it is, we cannot really know whether there are any. He concludes (paradoxically) that we cannot meaningfully assert that there are, in the sense that we seem to intend. (Hume himself stresses that repeated conjunction of events, together with spatial and temporal contiguity, would not strike many people as exhausting the meaning of "causal connection.")[6] For instance, when we ask whether virus infections are the cause of cancer, we may well think of ourselves as asking whether there is a necessary connection between the two physical events or types of events. We thus seem to assume that it is at least possible meaningfully to speak of necessary connections between outer things. But Hume holds that the meaning of a concept can only derive from a corresponding sense impression, and there can be no outer impression corresponding to the 'idea of necessary connection'. While '*A* causes *B*' can be salvaged as a meaningful utterance distinct from '*A* is constantly conjoined with *B*', this can be done only at the cost of introducing reference to a subjective disposition to form expectations;[7] only by such reference is any possible content provided for the concept of necessary connection. With respect to the supposition of an enduring world of 'outer' objects, the situation is somewhat analogous. If the meaningful content of our beliefs is essentially restricted to fleeting sensations (plus copies, combinations, etc. of fleeting sensations), there is no way to accept as coherent or intelligible a belief in entities distinguished precisely by the contrast between their properties (e.g. endurance) and the properties of fleeting sensations. Thus Hume is led to produce his tortured account of the fictions and contradictions inherent in our beliefs about "outer objects"[8] – beliefs which on his premises can be interpreted on no other basis than our attribution to *sense impressions* of properties which they could not conceivably possess.

Even if one wants partly to forgive Hume his theory of meaning, his position can still be expressed in quite strong terms. The problem is not that our experience provides insufficient evidence or warrant for believing in an outer world of causally inter-connected, enduring objects; the problem is that experience, by its very nature, can provide *no reason at all* for such beliefs.

Now the alleged impossibility of a 'purely sense-datum experience' may actually constitute a relevant objection to such a position as this. For if we cannot be conceptually conscious of sensory states, except in so far as we 'apply in experience the concepts of an objective world', then it is surely incoherent to construe our beliefs about physical objects as genetically derived from beliefs about the content of our sensory experience. Once this point is admitted, it becomes very difficult to draw the line between 'what is given in experience' and 'our thought about what is given' in such a way as to secure the credibility of Hume's premiss that 'perceptions are our only objects'. For perceptions can no longer be conceived as 'given' to us independently of our physical-object judgments.

In a similar manner the 'Kantian' view undermines the contention that only concepts directly matchable with discriminable sensory qualities or relations are meaningful. If thought about, say, tables and chairs were *really nothing but* thought about sense-data, a proof that a purely sense-datum experience is impossible would entail that a 'physical world experience' is impossible too. Such a proof would then constitute a *reductio ad absurdum* of the sensationalist position. But if thought about tables and chairs is *not really just* thought about sense-data, then presumably the meaning of 'table' and 'chair' cannot be adequately explicated through a sense-datum language alone.[9] But if conceptual operations that are not fully analyzable in a sense datum language are among the conditions of the possibility of experience, and to this extent no less basic than sense-data concepts, the Humean type of severe meaning-criterion can hardly claim to derive its legitimacy from 'experience'.

In these ways Hume's position, that experience provides meaning and justification for sense-data propositions only, may be held to rest on the assumption that a pure sense-datum experience is not only possible but (at least at some stages of our cognitive development) actual.

IV

So let it be granted, in accordance with the above considerations, that belief in an enduring world of interrelated objects and events is coherent and meaningful; that a self-conscious experience in which perceptions are not often 'related to objects' is impossible; that, indeed, belief in 'the external world' is not wholly unjustified. All of these conclusions are consistent with the claim that our beliefs in real outer objects are always *incompletely* justified by experience; and this is the only claim essential to the *Cartesian* skeptic's position.

One might suppose that once a sensationalist account of meaning and experience is denied, there can remain no rational basis at all for claiming a gap between 'judgments of experience' and 'unimpugnable objective judgments.' But here is where the characteristic Cartesian arguments may be introduced – the arguments from illusion, dreaming, and the possibility of systematic hallucination. For the point of such arguments is just that *the presence or existence of an outer object is not a necessary condition of 'experience of objects'*, nor of the sincere belief that there is an object present. Thus it may be the case that in order to 'have experience' we must make objective judgments: the argument from hallucination suggests that it is still consistent with our experience that all our objective judgments could be false.

I would like to develop this point with reference to Kant's famous treatment of the distinction between subjective and objective time orders (A 189ff = B 232). Kant maintains that the notion of an objective time order, in contrast to the notion of a subjective time order, involves the concept of necessary, non-accidental, or rule-governed succession. Now let us suppose that the possibility of self-conscious experience does in some manner entail a distinction between objective and subjective orders. From this it will follow that perceptions are not 'given' in subjective order independently of the employment of non-sensory concepts; and that belief in a lawful world cannot be construed as an imaginative superstructure on a directly experienced bed-rock reality of sensory impressions. But do such considerations lead ineluctably to the conclusion that the existence of a 'real world in space' is as immediately and unproblematically *known* to me as the existence of myself and my perceptual experience?

Consider, the Cartesian may say, the case of a man approaching an oasis across the desert. First he perceives only the tops of the palm trees. After a while he perceives the trunks. Although his perceptions of the trunks occur after his perceptions of the leafy tops, he will naturally take both to be perceptions of one set of stable objects, not of temporally successive sets of objects. As he gets nearer, he sees a bird in one of the trees. He sees the bird stretch open its beak, then close it, then fly off. Then he hears a shrill note. While he perceives the bird-flight before the bird-cry, he takes it to have occurred afterwards. In other words, he implicitly makes all the usual distinctions between subjective and objective time order, in complete conformity with the examples of the Second Analogy. Now let us suppose (1) that the oasis was a mirage; or (2) that the man was not awake; or (3) that he was in the clutches of a deceitful demon or super-scientist, who was in some manner providing him with a fantastic series of perceptual experiences. Certainly, the Cartesian will continue, there is a sense in which this man was not deceived about the character of his own perceptual experiences. Yet he certainly was deceived in taking them directly to represent an outer reality. Now, how can we *ever* be sure that our 'outer experience' is not deceptive in precisely this manner, etc. ...?

It certainly seems that this argument does not in anyway presuppose a sensationalist conception of experience. To make his point, the Cartesian does not need to hold that the man 'approaching the oasis' should be able to isolate from the original account of what he believes himself to see, a more limited, true account of what he *really* sees (fleeting sense impressions). Nor need he hold that the man's judgments about physical objects and their intrinsic time-relations are incoherent or unwarranted. And certainly he need not claim that these objective judgments are inferred psychologically from a genetically more basic 'given' of experience. His only essential contentions are that (1) our most confident ordinary employment of physical object concepts is in a significant sense compatible with the non-existence of physical objects, and (2) judgments which purport only to describe our experience, without claiming the actual existence of entities other than ourselves, are not similarly challengeable. While there may well be good – even conclusive – arguments against this conception of the epistemological priority of subjective judgments, the Strawsonian version of Kant's realism does not seem to advance the case against it.

V

There is, to be sure, a way of interpreting Kant's central defense of realism which does not result in such manifest question-begging against Cartesian arguments. Kant must be represented as arguing, not that 'self-consciousness' requires the use and application of objective concepts, but rather something like the following: one cannot be said to *know the truth* of subjective judgments unless one can *also* be said to *know the truth* of some objective judgments. I would like briefly to illustrate this contrast of strategies, with reference to the so-called Refutation of Idealism, inserted into the Postulates section of the second edition of the *Critique*. (This illustration may also help to indicate how Kant's wording can support the Strawsonian interpretation of his intentions.)

In the introduction to this famous Refutation Kant remarks that an adequate answer to Descartes must establish that we have "experience, and not merely imagination of outer things" (B 275). This, he claims, is possible only if it can be shown that "even our inner experience, which for Descartes is indubitable, is possible only on the assumption of outer experience." Kant goes on to argue that since "all determination of time presupposes something *permanent* in perception," so "consciousness of" oneself as a being enduring through time requires "consciousness of" a permanent entity. Since nothing but changing representations are encountered in inner experience, "the perception of this permanent is possible only through a *thing* outside me." Hence, he concludes, "the determination of my existence in time is possible only through the existence of actual things which I perceive outside me" (B 275–6).

Now, in this passage Kant does not provide the slightest support for the proposition that 'time-determination' presupposes 'consciousness of a permanent', nor the slightest indication of what sort of 'presupposition' might be in question. His position here evidently rests on the argument of the First Analogy – but unfortunately the latter passage is, by fairly wide agreement, one of the most obscure sections of the *Critique*. It seems sufficiently clear, however, that the conclusion of the Refutation might naturally be construed in either of two ways: one Strawsonian, and one counter-Strawsonian. The two possibilities I have in mind are (respectively) the following.

(1) "It would not be possible for me to have and apply the conception of my own existence through time, unless I also had and applied the conception of a permanent entity outside me."

(2) "There is some connection between the concept of a permanent entity and the concept of a time-order, or between the concepts of an outer 'permanent' and of truth, such that 'I know I exist in time' can be true only if 'I perceive a permanent (in space)' is true."

The first interpretation seems to me at *least* as plausible a reading of the text as the second: the repeated expression "conciousness of" fits the Strawsonian framework all too well. On this interpretation, Kant's conclusion is indeed incompatible with the contention that my judgments about outer things may perhaps be non-rationally *derived from* my direct experience of my own successive representations. In this respect it *is* incompatible with the view that I have experience of my own inner states, and have only 'imagination' of outer things. However, on the basis of the previous discussion, I would suppose that even the most convincing demonstration of this proposition would leave a Cartesian unmoved. He will simply reiterate the claim that judgments about outer things (based on experience) are not as certain as judgments about the character of his own perceptual experience.

The second construal of Kant's conclusion is, in a sense, more hopeful. According to this proposition, to doubt that one either has or has had veridical perceptions of an outer entity, while affirming the certainty of one's own existence as a temporal being, is to maintain a position which is incoherent – though not necessarily so *obviously* incoherent as to be psychologically impossible. On this interpretation, Kant's conclusion could be rephrased as follows: "I know I exist in time" *entails* (in conjunction with other knowable premisses) that I have or have had veridical perceptions of a permanent entity in space. Such a conclusion could be said to 'answer' the Cartesian by establishing that, contrary to what the arguments from hallucination, etc. seem to suggest, there is actually an inconsistency in maintaining the Cartesian assumptions about self-knowledge in conjunction with the view that all one's 'outer' perceptions might be non-veridical.

On the other hand, it is not quite clear that to accept even *this* conclusion is to reject problematic idealism as 'the methodological starting-point of philosophical reflection'. After all the 'starting-point' of the argument is still the premiss that "I am conscious of my own existence as determined in time." And the aim of the argument is just to show that my outer perceptions are to some extent veridical. Is this not, in a way, to "justify our belief in the objective world by working outwards ... from the private data of individual consciousness?" If so, even on this most favorable construal of Kant's Refutation of (Cartesian) Idealism, it cannot strictly be held that Kant 'rejects' the Cartesian challenge as thoroughly misconceived.[10]

The Rockefeller University

NOTES

[1] Among those which include substantial discussion of this issue are: P. F. Strawson, *The Bounds of Sense* (London: Methuen, 1966); R. P. Wolff, *Kant's Theory of Mental Activity* (Cambridge, Mass., Harvard University Press, 1963); J. Bennett, *Kant's Analytic* (Cambridge, Cambridge University Press, 1966). See also W. Sellars, 'Some

Remarks on Kant's Theory of Experience', *The Journal of Philosophy*, LXIV (1967), pp. 633–647.

[2] Philosophically, the points I will make in criticism of this line of argument are similar to the sort of objection that has been developed by some others against anti-skeptical arguments in Strawson's earlier book, *Individuals*. See particularly the title essay of A. J. Ayer's *The Concept of a Person* (London: Macmillan, 1963), and Barry Stroud, 'Transcendental Arguments', *The Journal of Philosophy*, LXV (1968), pp. 241–256.

[3] Hume's philosophical system is, of course, subject to various interpretations, not all of which represent him as fundamentally a subjectivist or skeptic. Here, however, I am interested in just that side of Hume's thought that most strongly resists rehabilitation into common sense realism, and that accounts for his reputation as a skeptic in so far as he does have such a reputation. In other words, I shall not be concerned with either balanced or complete interpretation of his remarks.

[4] Hume discusses the problem of "external existence" in the *Treatise* at much greater length than in the *Inquiry Concerning Human Understanding*. His discussion in the latter work seems to me to have a less distinctive, more Cartesian character than the earlier treatment. I am aware that Kant had probably only a very slight knowledge of the text of the *Treatise*, but this fact seems immaterial to present purposes.

[5] David Hume, *A Treatise of Human Nature* (ed. by L. A. Selby-Bigge) Oxford, Clarendon Press, 1888, Book I, part II, section vi, p. 67. Cf. *ibid.*, part IV, sec. ii, *passim*.

[6] Cf. *Treatise*, Book I, part III, sec. xiv, esp. pp. 161–168. For instance, with reference of the idea of power or causal efficacy, Hume comments: "... it follows that we deceive ourselves, when we imagine we are possest of any idea of this kind, after the manner we commonly understand it" (*ibid.*, p. 161). Surely Hume is deceived.

[7] *Ibid.*, pp. 165ff. However, I do not wish to claim that Hume's use of the notion of disposition is itself strictly defensible within the terms of his own theory.

[8] *Ibid.*, part IV, sec. ii ("Of scepticism with regard to the senses.")

[9] This is not intended to represent a rigorous argument, but merely to indicate a likely path towards one.

[10] I would like to thank Michael Slote for helpful comments on an earlier version of this paper.